Student Companion to

F. Scott
FITZGERALD

Recent Titles in
Student Companions to Classic Writers

Jane Austen *by Debra Teachman*

Charles Dickens *by Ruth Glancy*

Nathaniel Hawthorne *by Melissa McFarland Pennell*

Arthur Miller *by Susan C. W. Abbotson*

George Orwell *by Mitzi M. Brunsdale*

Richard Wright *by Robert Felgar*

Student Companion to
F. Scott
FITZGERALD

Linda C. Pelzer

Student Companions to Classic Writers

Greenwood Press
Westport, Connecticut • London

Library of Congress Cataloging-in-Publication Data

Pelzer, Linda Claycomb.
    Student companion to F. Scott Fitzgerald / Linda C. Pelzer.
        p.   cm.—(Student companions to classic writers, ISSN 1522–7979)
    Includes bibliographical references and index.
    ISBN 0–313–30594–3 (alk. paper)
        1. Fitzgerald, F. Scott (Francis Scott), 1896–1940—Criticism and interpretation.   2.
    Fitzgerald, F. Scott (Francis Scott), 1896–1940—Outlines, syllabi, etc.   I. Title
    II. Series.
    PS3511.I9 Z812   2000
    813'.52—dc21   99–462058

British Library Cataloguing in Publication Data is available.

Library of Congress Catalog Card Number: 99–462058
ISBN: 0–313–30594–3
ISSN: 1522–7979

First published in 2000

Greenwood Press, 88 Post Road West, Westport, CT 06881
An imprint of Greenwood Publishing Group, Inc.
www.greenwood.com

Printed in the United States of America

∞™

The paper used in this book complies with the
Permanent Paper Standard issued by the National
Information Standards Organization (Z39.48–1984).

10 9 8 7 6 5 4 3 2

In memory, always,
John

Contents

Series Foreword

This series has been designed to meet the needs of students and general readers for accessible literary criticism on the American and world writers most frequently studied and read in the secondary school, community college, and four-year college classrooms. Unlike other works of literary criticism that are written for the specialist and graduate student, or that feature a variety of reprinted scholarly essays on sometimes obscure aspects of the writer's work, the Student Companions to Classic Writers series is carefully crafted to examine each writer's major works fully and in a systematic way, at the level of the non-specialist and general reader. The objective is to enable the reader to gain a deeper understanding of the work and to apply critical thinking skills to the act of reading. The proven format for the volumes in this series was developed by an advisory board of teachers and librarians for a successful series published by Greenwood Press, Critical Companions to Popular Contemporary Writers. Responding to their request for easy-to-use and yet challenging literary criticism for students and adult library patrons, Greenwood Press developed a systematic format that is not intimidating but helps the reader to develop the ability to analyze literature.

How does this work? Each volume in the Student Companions to Classic Writers series is written by a subject specialist, an academic who understands students' needs for basic and yet challenging examination of the writer's canon. Each volume begins with a biographical chapter, drawn from published sources, biographies, and autobiographies, that relates the writer's life to his or her work. The next chapter examines the writer's literary heritage, tracing the literary influences of other writers on that writer and explaining and discussing the literary genres into which the writer's work falls. Each of the following chapters examines a major work by the writer, those works most frequently read and studied by high school and college students. Depending on the writer's canon, generally between four and eight major works are examined, each in an individual chapter. The discussion of each work is organized into separate sections on plot development, character development, and major themes. Literary devices and style, narrative point of view, and historical setting are also discussed in turn if pertinent to the work. Each chapter concludes with an alternate critical perspective from which to read the work, such as a psychological or feminist criticism. The critical theory is defined briefly in easy, comprehensible language for the student. Looking at the literature from the point of view of a particular critical approach will help the reader to understand and apply critical theory to the act of reading and analyzing literature.

Of particular value in each volume is the bibliography, which includes a complete bibliography of the writer's major works, a selected bibliography of biographical and critical works suitable for students, and lists of reviews of each work examined in the companion, all of which will be helpful to readers, teachers, and librarians who would like to consult additional sources.

As a source of literary criticism for the student or for the general reader, this series will help the reader to gain understanding of the writer's work and skill in critical reading.

Acknowledgments

Without the steadfast support of family, friends, and colleagues, I could not have written this book, but I take pleasure in acknowledging the special efforts of Betsy and Mike Nielsen, Debbie and Tom Rickard, and Marie and Jerry Cusick, all of whom have erased the boundaries between friend and family during the past two years. To my friends in England, James Hobbs and Carrie Sandercock, I am grateful for providing a summer's respite. The effort of my secretary, Susan Bentley, was also indispensible because it went far beyond the scope of clerical duties. What great fortune to have them in my life.

1

"Too Many People": The Life of F. Scott Fitzgerald

> "There never was a good biography of a good novelist. There couldn't be. He is too many people, if he's any good."
>
> "Notebooks," in *The Crack-Up* 177

Life and art converged in the fiction of F. Scott Fitzgerald. The yearning boy from provincial St. Paul, Minnesota, grew into a man whose life epitomized the gay and carefree excesses of the period, that "roaring" time between World War I and the stock market crash of 1929 that he christened the Jazz Age. He never lost his awe of wealth and power or his desire to attain their tangible rewards. What he did develop, however, was double vision, the ability not only to document the manners and mores, the fashions and fads of his times, but also to evaluate them—and himself—objectively. Fitzgerald thus created art from the life he lived, and his stories and novels, among the most important in twentieth-century American literature, reveal all the contradictions of both the age and their author.

Fitzgerald's "fictional themes," as biographer Jeffrey Meyers aptly notes, "evolve from his origins in St. Paul" (1). There, on September 24, 1896, Francis Scott Key Fitzgerald was born to Edward Fitzgerald and Mollie McQuillan Fitzgerald, the product of two vastly different Celtic strains. Edward, who came from tired, old Maryland stock and claimed distant kinship with the composer of "The Star Spangled Banner," instilled in his son the old-fashioned virtues of honor and courage and taught by example the beauty of genteel manners. Years later, in a moving essay entitled "The Death of My Father," Fitzgerald acknowledged, "I loved my father—always deep in my subconscious I have referred judgments back to him, to what he would have thought or done" (Meyers 8). Such virtues and manners did not, however, guarantee financial success, and Fitzgerald found it difficult to respect a father who could not support a family by his own efforts.

Equally complicated were his feelings about his mother. Mollie McQuillan, whose family was "straight potato-famine Irish," as Fitzgerald once called them (Eble, *Fitzgerald* 20), brought to her marriage a substantial fortune—the profits of a wholesale grocery business founded by her energetic grandfather—but none of the aristocratic pretensions of the Fitzgeralds. In turn-of-the-century St. Paul, however, commercial wealth translated into social standing, and Mollie, who doted on her bright, handsome son, was ambitious for him socially. When company called, she dressed Scott in black velvet and lace collar like the hero of Frances Hodgson Burnett's children's novel *Little Lord Fauntleroy* (1886) to sing and recite for her guests. She also sent him to dancing school with the children of St. Paul's elite. Fitzgerald gave fictional treatment to his boyhood and early adolescent relationship with his mother in his first novel, *This Side of Paradise* (1920). Pampered and sheltered by a mother who invested her hopes and dreams in her son, Fitzgerald, like his fictional counterpart, Amory Blaine, found himself under Mollie's influence, and little in his life seemed permanent or stable. Years later, an abandoned novel, at one point titled "The Boy Who Killed His Mother," begun in 1925, was a story of matricide (Stern, *Moment* 293), a plot that suggests some ambivalence about mother-son relationships, perhaps including his own.

In St. Paul, as literary critic Kenneth Eble observes, Fitzgerald was, "as Midwestern urban society goes, 'somebody,' and he moved naturally into the country club set that defines society in the smaller American cities" (*Fitzgerald* 19). Yet his father's inability to support his family by his own efforts made economies necessary to preserve the McQuillan inheritance, and thus the Fitzgerald affluence was to some extent a matter of posturing. Scott may have been sent to Newman Academy, a Roman Catholic preparatory school in New Jersey, and later to Princeton University for his education, but these advantages could not have prevented his knowing that his family skirted the edges of "good society." If he needed a lesson to confirm this truth, his first serious infatuation, with Ginevra King, of Lake Forest, an exclusive Chicago suburb on the Lake Michigan shore, certainly provided it.

Fitzgerald was smitten by the sophisticated sixteen-year-old at a St. Paul Christmas dance in 1914 during his sophomore year at Princeton. For the next two years, he conducted a one-sided romance both in person and through ardent correspondence with a girl who embodied his ideal of wealth and social position. Ginevra, however, was more interested in adding to her collection of suitors than in restricting herself to one. Legend has it, moreover, that Fitzgerald overheard someone, perhaps Ginevra's father, remark that poor boys should never think of marrying rich girls. By 1916, the romance had ended, but its effect lingered long in Fitzgerald's psyche. In fact, the thwarted yearnings for position and privilege of a handsome and clever but insecure young man give shape to the plot of many of Fitzgerald's best stories and novels, and Ginevra King serves as the embodiment of those longings. Her image and this disappointment lie behind Isabelle Borgé and Rosalind Connage in *This Side of Paradise* (1920), Judy Jones in "Winter Dreams" (1922), *The Great Gatsby*'s Daisy Buchanan (1925), and Josephine of the Basil and Josephine stories (1930–1931).

If Fitzgerald's St. Paul boyhood and adolescence give shape to the emotional facts of both his life and his art, so, too, do his experiences at the Newman Academy and Princeton University. During his two years at Newman, from 1911 to 1913, Fitzgerald, an indifferent student, expended his efforts in pursuit of popularity and praise. His handsome face, social graces, and acute intelligence, he felt certain, would guarantee his success. But Fitzgerald had overestimated his talents and gifts. Shorter and slighter than his classmates, he lacked athletic prowess, and his conceit and good looks contributed to their view that he was a "sissy" (Meyers 15). Lonely and disappointed by his failure to attain the acceptance for which he longed, Fitzgerald took solace from the recognition of Father Cyril Sigourney Webster Fay, a charming and worldly Catholic convert and school trustee. Fay took a fatherly interest in the unhappy youth, engaging him in adult conversation, encouraging his literary efforts, and strengthening his religious conviction, just as Monsignor Darcy in *This Side of Paradise* champions Amory Blaine, Fitzgerald's fictional self. Until his death in 1919, Fay served as Fitzgerald's first and most important mentor, imbuing his young acolyte with some of his own romantic notions and literary taste, building his self-confidence, and strengthening his resolve to pursue his dreams.

In *This Side of Paradise*, Fitzgerald summarizes Amory's education at St. Regis', Newman's fictional counterpart, and his first two years at Princeton, writing that "for the next four years the best of Amory's intellect was concentrated on matters of popularity, the intricacies of a university social system and American Society as represented by Biltmore Teas and Hot Springs golflinks" (34). The same judgment might be passed on Fitzgerald's own academic experience. Princeton's "Spires and Gargoyles," as Fitzgerald denoted the distinguishing architectural features of his alma mater in Chapter Two of *This Side of Paradise*, provided the perfect backdrop to his romanticized notions of college life. Keenly interested in his study of English literature, Fitzgerald immersed himself in nineteenth-century British poetry and read appreciatively the work of modern British authors such as H. G. Wells and Compton Mackenzie. Bored by his professors' teaching, however, and deficient in academic preparation and self- discipline, he earned barely passing marks in his English courses, failed other subjects, and was never out of academic difficulties throughout his Princeton career. Instead, the earnest young man intent on success distinguished himself by his social and literary achievements.

Princeton's tradition of club life perfectly suited Fitzgerald, and he zealously embraced it. He joined the Triangle Club, which wrote and produced a lively musical comedy each fall and performed it during the Christmas holidays in major cities across the country, becoming one of its principal authors. He also published early stories such as "The Debutante" (1917), which was later incorporated into *This Side of Paradise*, in Princeton's *Nassau Literary Magazine* and *The Tiger*, its humor magazine. He also served on *The Tiger's* editorial board. During his sophomore year, Fitzgerald was elected to the Cottage Club, one of the four most important of Princeton's eighteen eating clubs, the primary function of which was to provide a system of distinguishing students' social standing.

Fitzgerald's desired social and literary success contributed to his academic failure. In fact, in 1924 Fitzgerald recalled, "I spent my entire freshman year writing an operetta for the Triangle Club. I failed in algebra, trigonometry, coordinate geometry and hygiene, but the Triangle Club accepted my show, and by tutoring all through a stuffy August I managed to come back a sophomore and act in it as a chorus girl" (*Fitzgerald In His Own Time* 269). The success that bred such failure also prevented Fitzgerald from assuming coveted leadership positions in these clubs and even deprived him of earning official recognition for his talents and efforts. As a student on academic probation, he was ineligible to act, even in his own compositions. As Fitzgerald recorded in his *Ledger*, a monthly account of his own life that he kept from 1919 to 1936, 1916 was "a year of terrible disappointments & the end of all college dreams" (Meyers 33). His spirit crushed by the knowledge that there would be no medals of honor or badges of distinction, Fitzgerald returned to Princeton in the fall of 1917 with little zeal for a life reduced to struggling through course work. During the summer of 1917, he sat for the exams required for an appointment as second lieutenant in the regular army, so his return to Princeton that fall was little more than a matter of passing the time until his twenty-first birthday, when he would be eligible to accept his commission. With orders to report to Fort Leavenworth, Kansas, in November 1917, Fitzgerald ended his Princeton career.

As disappointing as his academic career proved to be, it did provide Fitzgerald with friends and experiences central to his literary success. John Peale Bishop, for instance, who served as the model for Thomas Parke D'Invilliers in *This Side of Paradise*, and Edmund Wilson, who would become one of the most influential literary critics of the modern era, were among his friends at Princeton. Far more intellectual than Fitzgerald, they helped their friend refine his literary tastes and taught him more about poetry than any of his professors. They remained critics whose judgment Fitzgerald valued and sought throughout his life. Equally important to his career were the stories and plays that Fitzgerald wrote for Princeton's literary magazines. In fact, writing for these publications served as his literary apprenticeship. Thus he left Princeton with the rough manuscript of the novel that was to become *This Side of Paradise*, a novel based largely on his college experience, packed in his suitcase.

World War I may have been raging in Europe in 1917, but little patriotic fervor fueled Fitzgerald's military career. A self-absorbed young man, he was largely indifferent to the great historical event of his era and joined the army primarily for social reasons. It was, after all, the expected thing, and he would look smart in a military uniform. Like college, which interfered with his career as a club man, military service interrupted his efforts to become a novelist. When he should have been studying infantry tactics and preparing to assume responsibility on the battlefield, Fitzgerald was outlining his novel and drafting its first chapters, concealing his notebook behind the covers of a boring military manual. Fortunately for those he might have commanded, the war ended before Fitzgerald was posted to Europe. He did, however, submit the novel he called "The Romantic Egotist" to Charles Scribner's publishing house and meet the woman he would love for the remainder of his life, Zelda Sayre.

The pampered daughter of a prominent Montgomery, Alabama, family, Zelda represented, much to Scott's delight, the thoroughly modern new woman. He was entranced by her striking beauty and unconventional behavior from their first meeting at a country club dance in July 1918. Sensuous and impulsive, the eighteen-year-old Zelda was accustomed to the limelight and even courted center stage with antics such as pinning mistletoe to the back of her skirt as if to challenge men to an inappropriate kiss (Meyers 45). Convention mattered little to the unrestrained belle; the Sayre prestige and respectability protected her from the condemnation that her reputation for sexual promiscuity should have warranted. Fitzgerald was one of many army officers who pursued her that summer, but by the spring of 1919, he was the one engaged to this dream girl and working in a New York advertising agency to earn enough money to marry her.

Fitzgerald, however, was as unsuited to the business world as he was to academe and the military. Determined instead to make his fortune by his pen, and undaunted by the rejection slips he had collected from his literary efforts, he quit his boring job in advertising, retreated to the family home in St. Paul, and devoted his summer to the revision of his novel "The Romantic Egotist." On September 16, 1919, he received a letter from Maxwell Perkins, the Scribner's editor who had first recognized and encouraged his talent and would remain throughout his career his staunchest friend and supporter, informing him that his novel would be published as *This Side of Paradise* in the spring of 1920. Buoyed by his prospects, Fitzgerald returned triumphantly to New York to await success. He did not wait long.

In the process of revising his first novel during the summer of 1919, Fitzgerald clearly found a style, subject, and voice that appealed to the reading public. Suddenly editors were buying his cleverly plotted, witty stories of America's bright upper-class youth culture, and he found himself published in the pages of *The Smart Set*, *Scribner's Magazine*, and *Saturday Evening Post*. By the time *This Side of Paradise* was published on March 26, 1920, to both critical acclaim and popular success, Fitzgerald was indeed earning a living as a writer. His future seemingly secure, he could now marry Zelda, who, impatient with his failures, had previously broken their engagement. On April 3, 1920, eight days after his first novel's publication, Scott and Zelda were married in the rectory of St. Patrick's Cathedral in New York City.

In the flush of first success and the glow of early married life, the Fitzgeralds stormed New York. They earned a reputation for outrageous behavior and incessant partying that made them symbolic of the excesses of the 1920s, which Fitzgerald chronicled in his stories and novels. Their alcohol-fueled pranks made them notorious. Ejected from the Biltmore Hotel for disturbing the other guests, they announced their arrival at the Commodore Hotel by spinning through the revolving doors for a half hour. They jumped into the fountain in New York City's Union Square and the one near the Plaza Hotel and laughed from their front row theater seats at all the wrong places during a comedy. Once Zelda even paid a surcharge to ride down a New York street extended on the hood of a taxi like the figurehead on the prow of a ship. Settling nowhere and living everywhere, the Fitzgeralds gave as their address a series of hotel rooms and rented houses, establishing a nomadic pattern for their lives. When Zelda discovered that she was pregnant in February 1921, they set off for their first trip to Europe. Returning in July to settle near St. Paul, they awaited the birth on October 26, 1921, of their only child, a daughter, Frances Scott Fitzgerald, who was always called Scottie. Outrageous antics and unconventional behavior, however, exacted payment, and the price strained both their marriage and their financial resources.

As Fitzgerald had discovered while awaiting publication of his first novel, his stories were now a bankable commodity; popular magazines were offering princely sums for his efforts. In fact, at one stage the *Saturday Evening Post* would pay Fitzgerald $4,000 per story. Money flowed rapidly in but just as rapidly out, and the Fitzgeralds' conspicuous extravagance plunged them into debt. He might joke in a 1924 magazine piece entitled "How to Live on $36,000 a Year" (nearly twenty times the average American income) about the effort to live up to his newly-found wealth, but the crisis in his bank account was real. Eager to complete his second novel, begun in 1920, Fitzgerald found himself forced instead to expend time and energy composing the slick, formulaic stories that would pay his immediate expenses. He was pulled between the opposing forces of money and art.

Fitzgerald's best stories, such as "The Diamond as Big as the Ritz" (1922), were hard to write and to sell. His comic, mildly satirical portrayals of the sophisticated manners and mores of the country club set, as depicted in "The Popular Girl" (1922), one of his typical *Saturday Evening Post* stories, could be dashed off, however, with minimal effort and certain reward. In 1920, Scribner's capitalized on the success of *This Side of Paradise* and established a pattern of publishing a volume of stories after each novel by releasing Fitzgerald's first collection of stories, *Flappers and Philosophers*, which included one of his best efforts, "The Ice Palace." In all, Fitzgerald published four volumes of short fiction during his lifetime as well as several hundred stories, articles, and poems in magazines. All helped to pay his bills but interrupted what he saw as his real vocation as a serious novelist and thus exacted their own price. In fact, in his *Notebooks* of the 1930s, Fitzgerald acknowledged the emotional and artistic cost: "I have asked a lot of my emotions—one hundred and twenty stories," he wrote. "The price was high, right up with Kipling, because there was one little drop of something not blood, not a tear, not my seed, but me more intimately than these, in every story, it was the extra I had. Now it has gone" (*Notebooks* 131).

Scottie's birth coincided with the serial publication of *The Beautiful and Damned* (1922), a bleak tale of excess and dissipation. Like most of Fitzgerald's fiction, the novel was intensely autobiographical. The courtship and early married life of its central characters, Anthony and Gloria Patch, recapitulated aspects of Scott and Zelda's own: the drunken parties, the wild antics, the rootless search for stability, and always the specter of debt. Published by Scribner's in March 1922, the novel cemented Fitzgerald's critical reputation and, equally important, sold well. Fitzgerald capitalized on its success by releasing a second collection of stories, *Tales of the Jazz Age*, which included two of his best stories, "May Day" and "The Diamond as Big as the Ritz," in September 1922. He devoted much of his time in the period both before and after the novel's publication, however, to his play *The Vegetable*.

From his boyhood in St. Paul, where he had written and acted in several plays, to his Princeton years writing lyrics for Triangle Club musicals, Fitzgerald clearly had a penchant for self-dramatization and had always been attracted to the theater. Like all fashionable New Yorkers, the Fitzgeralds frequented the theater, and they included among their friends theater people. Perhaps not surprisingly, then, Fitzgerald began writing a political satire intended for the stage in 1921 and worked on it sporadically until 1923, when its publication finally attracted the financial backing needed to mount a production. Taking its title from a satiric essay in a contemporary magazine that attacked American conformity and referred to the American businessman as a "vegetable" (Bruccoli, *Grandeur* 168), the play was inspired by the scandal-ridden administration of President Warren G. Harding at the beginning of the decade. Subtitled *From President to Postman, The Vegetable* focuses on an unhappily married railroad clerk named Jerry Frost who aspires to be a postman but awakens one day from a drunken sleep to discover that he has become the Republican candidate for president. Transported in the second act to the White House, Frost experiences a series of political and personal disasters that prove in the final act to be nothing more than nightmare fantasies.

The Vegetable opened in tryout on November 10, 1923, in Atlantic City, New Jersey, and closed within a week, never reaching Broadway. Bored or offended by its bad puns, bad jokes, and patently absurd action, the audience shifted in their seats, rustled their programs, and loudly whispered. Some even walked out. Fitzgerald himself was so mortified by the hostile reception that he spent the second and third acts in a bar. The play's failure offered convincing evidence that Fitzgerald was neither a satirist nor a playwright. It also prompted him to realize that he was squandering his talent in drink and sheer laziness.

Fitzgerald had counted on a hit play that would make him a small fortune; in the aftermath of his first professional failure, however, he was forced once again to ply his trade for the popular magazines. By March 1924, he had written himself out of debt. By May he had sailed for France for the sake of both economy and art because it was there, he believed, on the Riviera, that he would find a place conducive to writing his next novel. There, in an alien culture for which he had no great love or deep understanding and about which he had no real interest in learning, Fitzgerald and his family would spend most of the remainder of the decade.

Upon their arrival in France, the Fitzgeralds traveled along the coast for several weeks until they found the Villa Marie, a charming house with terraced gardens and tiled balconies located on a hill above St. Raphaël and overlooking the Mediterranean Sea that they would call home. They soon were included within the social circle of Gerald and Sara Murphy, wealthy American expatriates who lived in hedonistic luxury in the south of France. Gracious and cultured, the Murphys, who served as models for *Tender is the Night*'s Dick and

Nicole Diver, were seriously interested in the arts, and at their Villa America they lavished their generous hospitality on many of the leading French and American artists of the 1920s, including writers such as John Dos Passos and Ernest Hemingway, the musician Cole Porter, the playwright Philip Barry, and artists such as Pablo Picasso and Joan Miro. Amid such heady companionship, Scott settled down to write the novel that would become his masterpiece, *The Great Gatsby* (1925). Bored and restless, Zelda, who had always found it difficult to be ignored, had a brief affair with a French aviator, straining the fiber of their already fragile marriage. In an effort to repair the damage, the Fitzgeralds abandoned the Riviera for Italy, where Scott continued to revise his novel.

On April 10, 1925, Fitzgerald's most perfectly realized work of art, *The Great Gatsby*, was published to almost universal critical acclaim. Jay Gatsby's attempt to reinvent himself, rise into the upper class, and recapture his lost love, Daisy Buchanan, expresses some of the dominant themes in American literature and explores some of the contradictions of American culture. It marked a significant advancement in Fitzgerald's artistic maturity. Yet sales of the novel met neither Fitzgerald's needs nor his expectations. In fact, its royalties barely covered his advance. A disappointed and disillusioned Fitzgerald turned again to his slick but lucrative stories, aware, as he confessed in a letter to H. L. Mencken, that "My trash for the Post grows worse and worse as there is less and less heart in it" (*Life in Letters* 111). Three of his best stories, "The Rich Boy," "Winter Dreams," and "Absolution," were reprinted in *All the Sad Young Men* (1926), the collection of stories that followed *The Great Gatsby's* publication. Other than that collection, however, Fitzgerald did not publish any books between 1925 and 1934. Although he made a number of false starts on another novel, he spent much of his energies playing on the Riviera and in Paris. In his *Ledger* Fitzgerald himself noted of the summer of 1925, "1000 parties and no work" (Eble, *Fitzgerald* 102). The observation could have been applied to subsequent seasons as well.

From May 1924 to December 1931, the Fitzgeralds spent more than five years living abroad. Unlike the exile of other expatriate writers, however, such as Dos Passos' and Hemingway's, Fitzgerald's was largely a matter of circumstance—the need to economize—rather than choice; neither he nor Zelda thrived on foreign shores. Drinking escalated the terrible rows that had long plagued their relationship. Zelda's infidelity heightened Scott's jealousy and insecurities; his success contributed to her frustrated desire for an artistic identity of her own. Their behavior became increasingly destructive and bizarre in response to their personal and professional disappointments. Scott steadily grew more dependent on alcohol. Zelda threw herself into dancing lessons, studying with the head of the Diaghilev ballet school, Madame Egorova, and, at the age of twenty-six, working twice as hard as the younger aspirants, became obsessed by her need to succeed in this demanding career. By 1930, Scott was struggling to complete yet another version of the novel that would eventually become *Tender is the Night* (1934). Zelda, disappointed by her failure to achieve artistic fame, had slipped into madness and was being treated for schizophrenia in a Swiss sanatorium. Their gay, gaudy spree was over.

In addition to the publication of *The Great Gatsby*, one other incident of literary consequence marked this period in Fitzgerald's life. In April 1925, just two weeks after his novel's publication, Fitzgerald met Ernest Hemingway at the Dingo bar in Paris. From the beginning of their ultimately sad friendship, Fitzgerald, the successful author, was in awe of the talented newcomer. Hemingway, after all, had a reputation for athletic prowess and a war record, and he exemplified rugged masculinity and brash self-sufficiency, all of which Fitzgerald lacked. In time Fitzgerald came to respect Hemingway's disciplined devotion to his craft and his sheer talent. In conversations and letters throughout the 1920s and 1930s, the two writers exchanged views about their craft and sought advice about their art. Eventually, Fitzgerald viewed Hemingway as his "artistic conscience" (*The Crack-Up* 79), the writer against whom he measured his literary successes and failures. For his part, Hemingway admired Fitzgerald's talent and welcomed his efforts to advance his career, but he was critical of his friend's inability to apply himself to his work. Fitzgerald's drunken excesses and self-destructive behavior were, to Hemingway at that time, symptoms of personal and moral weakness.

As his career rose and his friend's began to fall, Hemingway, who tended eventually to resent others' assistance, began to distance himself from Fitzgerald and to criticize him both privately and publicly. In fact, he satirized his friend as an alcoholic clown in his 1926 novel *The Torrents of Spring* and attacked him personally in the original version of "The Snows of Kilimanjaro" published in *Esquire* magazine in 1936. Deeply wounded by these and other betrayals, Fitzgerald wrote a brief note asking Hemingway to cut his name from the story when he included it in a book. "Please lay off me in print," Fitzgerald began. "If I choose to write *de profundis* sometimes it doesn't mean I want friends praying aloud over my corpse" (*Life in Letters* 302). Although he signed the note "Ever Your Friend," he never forgot Hemingway's cruelty. It was a "damned rotten thing to do" (*Life in Letters* 353), he confided to his editor, Maxwell Perkins. In his *Notebooks*, he also observed, "I talk with the authority of failure—Ernest with the authority of success. We could never sit across the same table again" (*The Crack-Up* 181).

In the fall of 1931, following Zelda's release from the sanatorium and one final European holiday, the Fitzgeralds sailed for America, permanently leaving behind the scene of so much contradictory living that Scott would eventually transmute into one of his best stories, "Babylon Revisited" (1931), and his fourth novel, *Tender is the Night* (1934). Upon their arrival, they settled for a time in Zelda's hometown, Montgomery, Alabama, and then Scott accepted an offer from Metro-Goldwyn-Mayer (MGM) to adapt a light sexual comedy, *Red-Headed Woman*, for the screen. Although Fitzgerald was eager to work on the project, the producer Irving Thalberg, whose genius for developing stars and scripts Fitzgerald much admired, ultimately rejected his screenplay. Shortly after he embarrassed himself at a Thalberg party, the humiliated author was dismissed from his job. The experience, which Fitzgerald fictionalized in one of his best stories, "Crazy Sunday" (1932), foreshadowed the tenor of his subsequent Hollywood years.

If the 1920s were a decade of gay abandon and the 1930s were the price of what Fitzgerald called "the most expensive orgy in history" ("Echoes of the Jazz Age," *The Crack-Up* 21), then Fitzgerald's literary career, which spanned that period, followed the same trajectory. Flush with success during the 1920s, Fitzgerald found it increasingly difficult during the 1930s to sustain his writing career in the face of personal collapse. The novel that he had begun in 1925, following the completion of *The Great Gatsby*, and on which he had worked during short, alcohol-fueled bursts of creativity for the remainder of the decade, was still nowhere near completion in 1932, and he wasted much of his time writing an ill-conceived and eventually abandoned medieval novel about a Dark Ages knight, "Phillipe, The Count of Darkness" (Mellow 429–430). Although he published forty-nine stories, some of which were among his best, during the eight years between 1926 and 1934, "the same number included in Ernest Hemingway's major collection" (Eble, *Fitzgerald* 114), and numerous magazine articles, his literary career seemed in decline. Increasingly beset by the pressures of Zelda's fragile mental health (she had suffered a second breakdown in 1932 and would spend the remainder of her life in and out of hospitals and clinics), the financial burden of her treatment, and the difficulty of being both father and mother to his daughter Scottie, Fitzgerald unsuccessfully battled his own alcoholism, guilt, doubt, and despair. What is perhaps most remarkable about this period of his life is that he managed to write at all, for as he recorded in his *Notebooks*, he had left his "capacity for hoping on the little roads that led to Zelda's sanitarium" (Meyers 193).

Write, however, Fitzgerald did, and on April 12, 1934, he finally published his fourth novel, *Tender is the Night*. An ambitious and complex study of a self-destructive relationship that mirrored his own with Zelda, the novel revealed Fitzgerald's advancement in narrative technique and psychological depth and his ability to link symbolically and thematically personal history and public events. Wrought from personal pain and disappointment, including a sense of betrayal when Zelda mined the same material in her own novel, *Save*

Me the Waltz (1932), Fitzgerald had high hopes for the novel's success. But its bleak tone and unfashionable subject—the privileged upper class—did not appeal to Depression-era readers. In fact, Fitzgerald did not even earn enough from the sale of the book to repay his debts to his publisher and his agent.

The generally unfavorable reviews of Fitzgerald's fourth collection of stories and the last book to appear in his lifetime, *Taps at Reveille*, on March 20, 1935, did nothing to redeem the disappointment of failure. By 1935, Fitzgerald had slipped inexorably into his own physical and emotional collapse, from which he never entirely recovered. Suffering from tuberculosis and battling alcoholism, he struggled with his demons: guilt over his role in Zelda's breakdowns, anxiety about his waning success, and, above all, regret for his squandered talent and damaged literary legacy. Twice during the period between Zelda's admission to the Highland Sanitorium near Asheville, North Carolina, in April 1936 and his departure for Hollywood in June 1937, Fitzgerald attempted suicide. Witness to his own collapse, Fitzgerald documented the disintegration of his personality in a series of "Crack-Up" essays published in *Esquire* magazine in 1935–1936. No longer was there any doubt. Fitzgerald had indeed touched bottom.

In the three "Crack-Up" essays, Fitzgerald dissected the cause of his creative sterility, locating its source in "the disintegration of [his] own personality" (*The Crack-Up* 76). He began with two statements of personal philosophy, one previously held but now rejected and one retained. Once, he confessed, experience (and his own early success) had convinced him that "Life was something you dominated if you were any good" (*The Crack-Up* 69). In truth, however, Fitzgerald now understood that "the test of a first-rate intelligence is the ability to hold two opposed ideas in the mind at the same time, and still retain the ability to function" (*The Crack-Up* 69) and that sometime during his thirty-ninth year he had "prematurely cracked" (*The Crack-Up* 70). "For two years," he acknowledged, "my life had been a drawing on resources that I did not possess"; he had been "mortgaging [himself] physically and spiritually up to the hilt" (*The Crack-Up* 72). For too long, he had entrusted to others his intellectual conscience, his moral conscience, his artistic conscience, indeed every aspect that constitutes the self, and "so there was not an 'I' any more" (*The Crack-Up* 79). Part confession, part apology, part self-justification, the "Crack-Up" essays are a remarkable exercise in self-dramatization. In them, Fitzgerald crafted a new public persona and retrieved a measure of dignity from his collapse by writing about the experience with candor and objectivity.

By July 1937, Fitzgerald, like Charlie Wales in his story "Babylon Revisited" (1931), had recovered enough of himself to move forward in life. Deeply in debt and faced with the expense of Zelda's extended hospitalization and Scottie's schooling, Fitzgerald sought to recoup his credit and restore his self-worth by returning to the only activity that he valued—his work. Although he had not, on two previous visits to Hollywood, had much success as a screenwriter, he now accepted a six-month contract from MGM for $1,000 a week, seizing the opportunity to redeem his career and his reputation and knowing that it might be his last. The revelations of the "Crack-Up" essays, in which he had announced his emotional bankruptcy, had been followed by a damaging piece about the supposedly ruined chronicler of the Jazz Age penned by Michel Mok, an ambitious journalist for the *New York Post,* and reprinted in part by *Time* magazine (Meyers 277–280). He could not afford to fail again.

The difficulty for writers in Hollywood is lack of control over their own work, and Fitzgerald, like established authors William Faulkner, Nathanael West, and Raymond Chandler who also endured stints as screenwriters, chafed under the restriction. He worked on several scripts, including *A Yank at Oxford, The Women,* and *Madame Curie,* and collaborated with as many as fifteen writers on the screenplay for *Gone With the Wind,* but he earned only one screen credit for his efforts, on the film *Three Comrades.* When his contract was not renewed after eighteen months, Fitzgerald struggled to earn a living as a free-lance scriptwriter and by churning out, for $250 each, seventeen Pat Hobby stories. These tales of a washed-up alcoholic Hollywood hack writer's desperate struggle to survive by his wits portrayed some of the worst aspects of Fitzgerald's own character. During this time, Fitzgerald also began work on his final novel, *The Last Tycoon,* which was unfinished at his death on December 21, 1940, at the age of forty-four. The novel, published posthumously in 1941, strips the facade from the Hollywood illusion and exposes the greed and corruption that destroy artistic integrity and moral identity in those, like Monroe Stahr, Fitzgerald's singular "tycoon," who strive to remain true to their ideals. Clearly, there was something of Fitzgerald in Stahr, too.

It seems somehow appropriate that Fitzgerald suffered his fatal heart attack in Hollywood, a city of false hopes and broken dreams to so many aspiring men and women. There, Fitzgerald had found a woman, gossip columnist Sheilah Graham, who cared enough to help him battle his alcoholism and thus to regain a measure of self-control. There, he had worked diligently to reclaim his reputation and to redeem his self-respect. But Hollywood had never been kind to Fitzgerald, and in the end his dismal record there had as much to do with a system as it did with his own flaws. In Hollywood, he simply could not be the kind of writer he aspired to be.

Denied a Catholic burial service in St. Mary's Church in Rockville, Maryland, or burial next to his parents in the ancestral cemetery because he was not practicing his faith, Fitzgerald was buried in Rockville Union Cemetery following an Episcopal service on December 27, 1940. Eight years later, Zelda was buried next to her husband following her death in a fire on March 10,

1948, that destroyed the Highland Hospital, where she had lived the major portion of the previous twelve years. In 1975, Catholic authorities finally gave permission for the bodies of Scott and Zelda to be disinterred and moved to St. Mary's Church. Cut into their gravestones was the final line of *The Great Gatsby*: "So we beat on, boats against the current, borne back ceaselessly into the past."

In death, Fitzgerald nearly fell victim to his Jazz Age image. Many of the brief obituaries marking his death tended to emphasize the life and not the work of a writer whose excesses still epitomized the gay, gaudy spree of the 1920s and suggested that he had squandered his talent and failed to achieve his potential. His Princeton friend, the writer and critic Edmund Wilson, rescued Fitzgerald's reputation, however, by editing *The Last Tycoon* (1941) and compiling *The Crack-Up* (1945), a collection of essays, letters, notebook entries, and critical appreciations of Fitzgerald's work by other well-respected writers. The reviews of *The Last Tycoon* also helped to confirm Fitzgerald's place among the major American writers of the twentieth century. In fact, poet Stephen Vincent Benét concluded his review of the novel by asserting, "This is not a legend, this is a reputation—and, seen in perspective, it may well be one of the most secure reputations of our time" (Bryer, *Reputation* 375–376). That judgment certainly persists today.

In the end, F. Scott Fitzgerald's life was as tragically romantic as the lives of his most memorable characters. A legend in his own time, he and his wife Zelda epitomized a generation—popularized in his own fiction—intent on risking all to live fully. He paid the price of such abandon, however, both personally and professionally. As Zelda descended into madness, he battled his own mental demons unsuccessfully, bolstering his spirits with an alcohol high. As his career waned, he struggled to restore his reputation by writing fiction that expressed his acute understanding of the contradictions inherent in American life, the contradictions that he had himself experienced and by which he was virtually destroyed. The record of that struggle exists in the pages of *The Great Gatsby* and *Tender is the Night*, "Babylon Revisited" and "Crazy Sunday," "The Crack-Up" essays and *The Last Tycoon*. In his fiction and essays Fitzgerald made of the personal something universal, and self-examination became a measure of both personal and artistic integrity and ultimately the measure of the man.

2

Greatness in the Conception: Fitzgerald's Literary Career

When F. Scott Fitzgerald died in December 1940, his reputation was that of a failed writer who had squandered his talent in drink and excess. He may have written the novel that defined a decade, *This Side of Paradise* (1920), and another that exposed the dreams and illusions of a nation, *The Great Gatsby* (1925), but his achievement had been overshadowed and largely blighted by his life. Writing to his wife Zelda in March 1940, Fitzgerald described himself as "a forgotten man" (*Life in Letters* 439), and his friend and fellow novelist John O'Hara recalled that at the end of his life Fitzgerald was "a prematurely little old man haunting bookshops unrecognized" (Bruccoli, *Grandeur* 489). His last royalty statement from Scribner's, in August 1940, listed sales of forty copies of his books earning the princely sum of $13.13. Yet a half century later, Fitzgerald's stature as a major twentieth-century American novelist rests secure, and *The Great Gatsby* is generally considered a quintessential American novel. From the vantage point of time, readers and critics now acknowledge what Fitzgerald rather wistfully said of himself in a letter to his editor, Maxwell Perkins, "in a *small* way I was an original" (*Dear Scott/Dear Max* 261). However flawed the life, however imperfect the novels, Fitzgerald's greatness lies as much in the conception as in the achievement. In this way Fitzgerald and his fiction capture some essential quality of the American myth and dream that were the focus his lifetime of personal and literary effort.

Without doubt, Fitzgerald's art was a response to his life. He immersed himself in his age and became its chief chronicler, bringing to his fiction a realism that gives it the quality of a photograph or, perhaps more appropriately, a documentary film. With the clothing, the music, the slang, the automobiles, the dances, the fads—in the specificity of its social milieu–Fitzgerald's fiction documents a moment in time in all its historical reality. Yet Fitzgerald captures more than just the physical evidence of that time. He conveys with equal clarity the psychology (the dreams and hopes, the anxieties and fears) reflected in that world because he lived the life he recorded. Autobiography thus forms the basis of the social realism that is a hallmark of Fitzgerald's fiction, but it is autobiography transmuted through the critical lens of both a personal and a cultural romantic sensibility, a second defining characteristic of his art. These two strands help to place Fitzgerald within American literary history.

FITZGERALD AND THE MODERN MOMENT

Fitzgerald came to prominence as a writer in the 1920s, a period dominated by the postwar novel, and thus his fiction reflects all the contradictions of his age. World War I was a defining event for Fitzgerald and the writers of his generation whether or not they saw action in the field. "I was certain that all the young people were going to be killed in the war," Fitzgerald recalled in describing the genesis of his first novel, *This Side of Paradise* (1920), "and I wanted to put on paper a record of the strange life they had lived in their time" (Bradbury 77). World War I had demolished fundamental truths (for instance, the ideal of heroism) and notions of culture as a body of established beliefs and values, leaving in its aftermath disillusionment and anxiety. The modern world had been severed from its past. Images of fragmentation, waste, sterility, and castration permeate the literature of the 1920s, from Ezra Pound's "Hugh Selwyn Mauberley" (1920) and T. S. Eliot's *The Wasteland* (1922) to Ernest Hemingway's *The Sun Also Rises* (1926) and Fitzgerald's own *The Great Gatsby* (1925). Hemingway's genitally wounded hero, Fitzgerald's Valley of Ashes, Eliot's Fisher King were all evidence of the modern moment and the existence of what Gertrude Stein would christen "a Lost Generation."

Postwar developments on the homefront contributed as well to the sense of purposelessness, decay, political failure, and cultural emptiness that pervades the literature of the 1920s. A new conservatism dominated America. Increasingly isolationist, the U.S. Senate failed to ratify support for the League of Nations. The "Red Scare" in 1920, during which thousands of suspected Communists and anarchists throughout the United States were arrested, ushered in a period of immigration restriction. Prohibition signalled the rise of a new Puritanism. Teapot Dome, a notorious government scandal over the leasing of government-owned oil reserves, and widespread speculation in the stock market announced a renewal of capitalism. A shift from idealism to materialism led to a boom in personal income and the development of new technologies that made possible the mass production of automobiles, radios, telephones, and refrigerators. Conservatism, however, sat uneasy in the modern moment, for it was being challenged by flappers, jazz music, films, the new science of psychology, and the teaching of evolution. In the midst of conservatism, in other words, the Jazz Age was evolving. Traditional views about proper behavior and styles of dress, as the title character in Fitzgerald's 1920 story "Bernice Bobs Her Hair" learns all too well, were giving way to public displays of affection and speakeasies, to short skirts and the Charleston dance, to whole new notions about manners and mores. As America modernized in the 1920s, its citizens clearly faced a new set of challenges to the meaning of their national life, and they struggled to reconcile often conflicting views of what had once seemed so certain, so clearly defined.

Fitzgerald's fiction of the 1920s reveals the tensions inherent in this mixture of anxious longing for the old certainties and heady excitement at the prospect of the new, just as his fiction of the 1930s captures the human cost—the wasted potential and psychic dislocation—of the gay, gaudy spree and its subsequent crash. His critics argue that he is no more than a stylish chronicler of his age, a mere recorder of the fashions and amusements, the manners and mores of his postwar generation, and he is certainly that. Yet verisimilitude, the truthful rendering of experience, is a distinguishing feature of realistic fiction, and particularly of the novel of manners, a literary form that examines a people and their culture in a specific time and place and a category into which much of Fitzgerald's fiction fits. Thus, Fitzgerald's ability to convey accurately his own generation is not necessarily a weakness. In fact, it helped to account for the tremendous success of his first novel, *This Side of Paradise*; readers were intrigued to see themselves and their world mirrored in its pages. When the best writers pen them, novels of manners both record and respond to the worlds they examine, as the fiction of Edith Wharton, for instance, clearly demonstrates.

Fitzgerald's fiction must be granted this same doubleness of recording and responding. His first novel may have been too enthusiastically a report from the trenches; it was so full of daring, excitement, and flamboyant excess that it became the text for the postwar generation. The title of his second novel, *The Beautiful and Damned* (1922), however, indicates that his youthful passion for his age was already being tempered by a knowledge of its contradictory realities. Already he was developing the double consciousness of which he would write in "The Crack-Up" essays more than a decade later, "the ability to hold two opposed ideas in the mind at the same time, and still retain the ability to function" (*The Crack-Up* 69). No mere recorder, then, of his time, Fitzgerald examined and measured its cost. He knew it, and lived it, but like Nick Carraway, the semi-detached narrator of *The Great Gatsby*, he did indeed develop a critical perspective on both himself and his age. In that way, he was also a product of the modern moment.

FITZGERALD AND THE SYMBOLIC IMAGINATION

Despite Fitzgerald's affinity for and understanding of the modern world, his fiction bears few of the characteristics of literary modernism, perhaps because his works are grounded in their social realism. As a literary movement, Modernism, which developed and reigned in the period between World Wars I and II, was itself a reaction to and an expression of the social, political, cultural, and technological changes that were transforming Fitzgerald's world. Such a world demanded a new mode of expression. New realities could not be dressed in outmoded fashions, and writers everywhere responded to Ezra Pound's cry of "Make it New." It was a period of experimentation in the arts, and novelists such as Gertrude Stein, John Dos Passos, Ernest Hemingway, and William Faulkner were challenging traditional forms of narrative structure and point-of-view. They were seeking, for instance, through montage and repetition and stream-of-consciousness, to get beneath the surface of life in order to render its moral, intellectual, and psychological realities.

Fitzgerald's fiction generally lacks this experimental quality. Granted, *This Side of Paradise* is a mix of literary styles, even containing a comedy of manners. The novel's stylistic features, however, seem to have less to do with purposeful literary experimentation than a sort of adolescent showmanship; the first novelist is announcing his ability to master the skills of established writers. Fitzgerald also uses a semi-detached first-person narrator in *The Great Gatsby* to achieve critical distance from his subject, but the technique is hardly innovative. In fact, he credited novelist Joseph Conrad for the strategy. What Fitzgerald brought to his fiction, however, was a poetic sensibility and a symbolic imagination that made him a remarkable prose stylist and invested his best writing with an evocative sense of felt experience. As novelist John O'Hara put it to his contemporary John Steinbeck, "Fitzgerald was a better just plain writer than all of us put together" (Bruccoli, *Grandeur* 478).

Fitzgerald's symbolic imagination achieves its most sustained and controlled expression in his masterwork, *The Great Gatsby*. The Valley of Ashes, the vacant eyes of Doctor T. J. Eckleburg, the green light at the end of Daisy's dock, the rainbow cascade of Gatsby's shirts—these and many other elements of the novel Fitzgerald invests with symbolic meaning far beyond their physical reality, and the poetic intensity of his prose even heightens his evocation of the mythic. In the novel's final backward look at the American Dream, the authorial voice makes clear that what in its achievement may have been diminished to the tawdry and vulgar by crass materialism is in its conception a grand and glorious affirmation of the human capacity for hope. The poetry in effect redeems the dream.

Such artistry, although less sustained, highlights other Fitzgerald novels as well; it is especially pronounced in his incomplete final novel, *The Last Tycoon* (1941). There Fitzgerald captures the otherworldliness of the Hollywood dream factory in the sharp images of a shawl-draped Abraham Lincoln nobly eating a slice of pie in the studio commissary (48–49) and a beautiful young woman sitting atop a studio prop—the severed head of the Indian goddess Siva as it floats down an "impromptu river" (26) following an earthquake. In the haunting image of a man and a woman perched on high stools at the counter of an American drugstore, eating tomato soup and sandwiches, he evokes as well the pathos of loneliness, the intimacy of anonymity in the modern American landscape as surely as Edward Hopper's 1942 painting "Nighthawks." Close examination of and personal experience with the largely urban landscape of the modern world helped Fitzgerald understand the significance of its bright surfaces, and his poetic sensibility gave symbolic expression to their meanings.

FITZGERALD AND THE ROMANTIC SENSIBILITY

Fitzgerald's lyricism and symbolist mode of writing reveal an essentially romantic sensibility that not only gives shape to his worldview, linking it to some traditional attitudes about the individual and human existence, but also supports his thematic preoccupations. That Fitzgerald felt deeply the poetry of the British Romantic John Keats, using a phrase from "Ode to a Nightingale," in fact, as the title of his fourth novel, *Tender is the Night*, is not insignificant. Like Keats and other Romantic philosophers and poets British and American, Fitzgerald held a firm belief in the primacy of the individual and his or her responses to life. For the Romantics, truth lay in felt experience and is thus to some extent an individual construct, a synthesis of each person's unique perceptions of and thoughts about the world. Others' experiences may be equally sincere, but are nevertheless open to question because they arise from their own unique sensibilities and perceptions. The Romantics also held a corollary conviction that the meaningful link between consciousness and the external world is the association of strong personal emotion with the particularities of object and place. In other words, the intensity of an individual's feelings endows the external world with significance and thus makes it real. Without the sensate and perceiving consciousness, the external world is mere dross, meaningless forms and shapes of existence.

The Romantic egotism that forms the basis of Fitzgerald's worldview arises from other influences as well, many of which are distinctly American. Puritanism, for instance, had provided Americans with a seminal myth about their nation and helped to shape beliefs about the relationship between the human and the divine that would form the backbone of nineteenth-century transcendentalism, a visionary idealism. From the time of its first settlement, America was conceived as a virgin land waiting for a people to realize opportunities denied them in Europe. Both the Pilgrims of Plymouth Colony and the Puritans who founded the Massachusetts Bay Colony sustained this view with religious conviction. Convinced that a providential act had brought them to the barren shores of a new world to fulfill a divine purpose, they established what Puritan John Winthrop called their "city on a hill" in the full belief that they were creating a "New Eden," a kingdom of heaven on earth where, uninhibited by the restraints of older societies, they would be free to control their individual and political destinies. In the fullness of time, they would thus redeem history by beginning it again.

The Puritan belief in the providential nature of their endeavor extended to their understanding of the relationship between the human and the divine, the real and the ideal. For the Puritans, the world was a shadowing forth of divine things, a revelation of God, and thus its interpretation could provide a coherent system of transcendent meanings, a way of understanding the ideal and the spiritual. In effect, the "real" world of daily experience offered up the signs and symbols of an ideal world of spirit, and these signs and symbols essentially connected humankind to divine truth. This aspect of Puritan thought anticipated many elements of Romanticism, especially the American expression of Romantic ideology known as transcendentalism.

For the transcendentalists, whose views were given most eloquent expression in the work of Ralph Waldo Emerson and Henry David Thoreau, God had made material nature not as a mere commodity but as a hieroglyph, or symbol, of the spiritual world. Like the Puritans, then, the transcendentalists reasserted a belief in the ideal, but that ideal was apprehended not through piety, as it had been for the Puritans, but through the imagination. Nature, they believed, spoke directly to the individual, and through this potent combination of self and universe, humankind knew and participated in the divine. Advocating an original relation with the universe, the transcendentalists celebrated individualism, self, and consciousness much as the Romantics did before them.

All of these beliefs and attitudes helped to establish the foundation of American national consciousness and shaped Fitzgerald's own romantic response to life. Certainly, romanticism is reflected in his tendency to view the world symbolically, to find in the "real" evidence of the ideal. It surfaces as well in his privileging of experience, in his conviction that individuals must experience life in order to understand its reality. Thus he and his fictional protagonists, especially those of his early novels, *This Side of Paradise*'s Amory Blaine and *The Beautiful and Damned*'s Anthony Patch, spend themselves in motion, sensation, and phenomena in a restless search for authenticity. Nobody else's experience will do. This romantic sensibility also gives Fitzgerald a heightened sensitivity to the possibilities of life that manifests itself as an aspiration to, and even a longing for, some sort of perfect moment that encapsulates the ideal. *The Great Gatsby*'s Daisy Buchanan, for instance, is as much, if not more, a projection of Gatsby's consciousness, of his desire to make real a dream of success, than a living being fraught with human imperfections. Fitzgerald also shares the romantic anxiety about time, the desire to preserve the ideal by clinging to the moment of perfection and thus redeeming history: "Can't repeat the past," Gatsby cries incredulously. "Why of course you can!" (*Gatsby* 116). Fitzgerald's romantic response to life also made him a perceptive interpreter of the ultimate myth of national longing, the American Dream.

FITZGERALD AND THE AMERICAN DREAM

In its very conception, the American Dream encapsulates a romantic ideal. With its emphasis on a kind of rugged individualism that is frequently associated with the frontier, that symbol of the new and the unsullied, the American Dream is a promise, a number of promises, to those who are willing to seize the opportunity and expend the effort to attain it. For many, one of the promises of the American Dream is material success of the sort that Jay Gatsby and his mentor Dan Cody epitomize. In *The Great Gatsby* the set of directions for self-improvement James Gatz sets down for himself on the last fly-leaf of a book called *Hopalong Cassidy* are the keys to that success. Through discipline and industry a poor boy from the Midwest could rise to fortune and fame. In a new world, he could reinvent himself, thus becoming his own ideal.

Jay Gatsby and *The Last Tycoon*'s Monroe Stahr testify to Fitzgerald's understanding of this aspect of the American Dream. Yet as the concluding paragraphs of *The Great Gatsby* make clear, Fitzgerald recognized something more than material success in the dream's promise. Because it encompasses the American myth of a New Eden, the dream also offers the hope of freedom and equality. In a world uncorrupted by political tyranny and social divisions, by the prejudices of privilege, in the promise of life, liberty, and the pursuit of happiness and the founding of a republic dedicated to these ideals, according to Fitzgerald, were "the history of all aspiration" (Bruccoli, *Grandeur* 493). It was the aspiration rather than the trivializing commercial element to which Fitzgerald, the romantic idealist, most responded.

Recognizing these two strands of the American Dream (in part because he was himself torn between them), Fitzgerald became one of its chief chroniclers. He admired his Jay Gatsbys and Monroe Stahrs not merely because they epitomized the rag-to-riches strand of the dream, but primarily because they desired so much more than money and position. They sought to make real an ideal with all the naive good faith of the original settlers, and that desire enobled them and their efforts. Thus, Nick Carraway can indeed tell Gatsby, who has earned his money from bootlegging and other illegal enterprises, "You're worth the whole damn bunch put together" (*Gatsby* 162). Yet Gatsby falls short of his dream, and so, too, does Monroe Stahr, not so much because they had the wrong dream but because the corollary dream of material success has corrupted and even overwhelmed the original. Humankind, in all its fallibility, simply lacks the ability to create a world "commensurate to [its] capacity for wonder" (*Gatsby* 189).

America for Fitzgerald is an idea. It stands in opposition to European civilizations, as he observed in his *Notebooks*: "France was a land, England was a people, but America, having about it still that quality of the idea, was harder to utter. . . . It was a willingness of the heart" (*The Crack-Up* 197). Yet for all its promise, it has somehow failed, so Fitzgerald's commentary on his nation and the idea of America that is the American Dream is ultimately a chronicle of failure.

THE OUTLINE OF A LITERARY CAREER

The mature novelist who would eventually bring to bear on his fiction all of these various influences and sensibilities is only just in evidence in F. Scott Fitzgerald's first novel, *This Side of Paradise* (1920). In the story of Amory Blaine, a "romantic egotist" (23), the largely autobiographical novel chronicles the efforts of one young man to realize his conception of himself in a world that is, like its central character, in process of enormous change. Written, Fitzgerald said, for "*my own personal public*, that is . . . the countless flappers and college kids who think I am a sort of oracle" (*Dear Scott/Dear Max* 59), *This Side of Paradise* captured the flamboyant style of a youth culture set free by war from the strictures of previous generations and virtually created the idea of the Jazz Age. The novel has all the naive exuberance, in both style and substance, of youth. It celebrates the bonds of friendship, the excitement of ideas, the appeal of beauty, and the exhilaration of life lived but also hints at the decade's dark contradictions and moral uncertainties. In Amory's quest to establish his essential self is a desperate knowledge of transience and flux, of the ways in which time and change erode the stability of self and society, that ever threatens his brash self-confidence by an over-expenditure of daring and bravado, a futile waste of passionate idealism. A huge popular success, the novel not only launched Fitzgerald's career but also created his public image, forever connecting his name to the 1920s decade in ways that both served and hampered his subsequent literary life.

Just two years after the publication of a novel celebrating the modern generation, Fitzgerald published *The Beautiful and Damned* (1922), a novel that, as its title suggests, makes clear the cost of a life lived on the promise of brilliance. Anthony Patch, the novel's central character, is a slightly older version of Amory Blaine, and like his predecessor, he, too, believes in the inevitability of a singular and exalted destiny. When he marries Gloria Gilbert, the ideal of youth and beauty, they vow to make their marriage a "live, lovely, glamourous [*sic*] performance" (147). Their pledge, however, soon falls victim to the vicious realities of time and change, the perverse necessities of wealth and style, and, above all, the sad degradations of moral carelessness. Like his stories, which now, Fitzgerald observed, had "a touch of disaster in them" ("Early Success," *The Crack-Up* 87), *The Beautiful and Damned* also reflects an increasingly pessimistic tone of postwar despair and conveys without doubt Fitzgerald's acute understanding of the inevitable price of the modern.

Critics who complain of Fitzgerald's inability to evaluate the world that he so brilliantly records (and the life that he so intensely lived) need look no further than his third novel, *The Great Gatsby* (1925), for proof of his double consciousness. Increasingly aware of the complex social, psychic, and economic forces that were driving his generation to excess and emptiness, Fitzgerald found the literary forms to give them expression in a novel that is now considered a modern masterpiece. Through his indirect, often ironic first-person narrative, Fitzgerald was able to give the story of Jay Gatsby, a man who reinvents himself to capture a dream, a sad nobility, and the novel's complex symbolic landscape reinforces this view. Gatsby may initially be just another corrupt product of his material world, but through the eyes of Nick Carraway, readers gradually come to see him as a romantic idealist who has somehow managed, despite his shadowy past and equally shady present, to remain uncorrupted. Fitzgerald's complex symbolic landscape also elevates Gatsby's quest to the realm of myth, the myth of the American Dream, and thus the novel offers a critical perspective on a nation and a people as well as on a generation.

Fitzgerald's most perfectly controlled novel, *The Great Gatsby*, rather ironically, marked the end of his popular success. The novel that followed it, *Tender is the Night* (1934), was on the surface a bleak postwar love story about the idle rich set amid expatriate life on the French Riviera and in Paris, hardly the sort of reading a Depression-wearied public desired. Yet it is also a perceptive analysis of the historical forces that gave shape to that violent, disordered, despairing postwar world, conflating personal and public histories to expose the consequences, both social and psychic, of such disintegration. Its central couple, Dick and Nicole Diver, typifies a generation at swim in the sea of historical change. Seduced by the lure of material wealth, Dick, trained as a Freudian psychoanalyst, sinks slowly but inexorably into obscurity when he abandons his good intentions and high ideals to minister to a mind diseased by marrying his beautiful patient Nicole. Cocooned by Nicole's money, they shuffle restlessly and aimlessly throughout a Europe no longer the bastion of culture, of shared beliefs grounded in tradition and order, but rather a Europe transformed into a vulgar carnival of chaos. Fitzgerald struggled to find an appropriate form for his tale, which took nearly a decade to write, and even at its publication he was dissatisfied with it. Indeed, the novel exists in two different versions because Fitzgerald began to revise it almost upon publication, and it lacks the lyricism and the symbolic framework of *The Great Gatsby*. Yet despite its imperfections, *Tender is the Night* is a major work of fiction, greater in some ways, especially its thematic reach, than his masterpiece, and it testifies to Fitzgerald's artistic seriousness and his ability to transmute autobiography into a universal.

Fitzgerald's final novel, *The Last Tycoon*, published posthumously in 1941, gives every indication of being another major work of fiction, and despite its incompleteness, it is certainly one of the best Hollywood novels. Monroe Stahr, the novel's central character, is one of the last great producers, a man of vision and industry who has virtually created the Hollywood dream factory. Yet all about him the world is in process of change as men with lesser vision and greater interest in profit seek to maximize their investments and writers and directors begin to demand more autonomy over their work. Stahr, the epitome of the self-made man, resists such efforts, and his struggle, complicated by his desire to find fulfillment in love, pushes him to ever greater, but ultimately futile, expenditures of self. In its narrative design and symbolic structure, *The Last Tycoon* challenges some of the central precepts of the American Dream by asking readers to admire the habits of mind and being that Stahr embodies but to recognize—and regret—that such men are a dying breed. The new America is simply inimical to them.

Taken together, the pattern of Fitzgerald's five novels reveals a certain symmetry of theme and composition of which the novelist himself was quite aware. The novels of his bright young men in pursuit of their singular and exalted destinies that characterize his early career—*This Side of Paradise* and *The Beautiful and Damned*—reach their culmination and achieve their most complex expression in his last completed novel, *Tender is the Night*. There, Fitzgerald places within the context of historical processes Dick Diver's own efforts to achieve greatness and thereby deepens the significance of his failure. It is a summing up of the boom of the 1920s from the perspective of the crash in the

1930s, a recognition and understanding of the inevitable price of splendor and excess. Similarly, Fitzgerald's masterpiece, *The Great Gatsby*, and his final (and incomplete) novel, *The Last Tycoon*, his tales of the west, offer poignant meditations on the national myth: its function, its veracity, its viability. They are tales of failure, and yet their heroes' valiant struggles and, most important, the greatness in the conception of their dreams and visions ultimately affirm their lives.

FITZGERALD AND THE SHORT STORY

Fitzgerald punctuated the publication of his four completed novels with the release of a collection of short stories: *Flappers and Philosophers* in 1920, following publication of *This Side of Paradise*; *Tales of the Jazz Age* following publication of *The Beautiful and Damned* in 1922; *All the Sad Young Men* in 1926, following publication of *The Great Gatsby*; and *Taps at Reveille* in 1935, following publication of *Tender is the Night*. While the tactic was obviously designed to capitalize on the success of the novels, the stories themselves attest to Fitzgerald's prolific career as a writer for popular magazines. In fact, he earned a substantial income, which he quickly spent, and frequently wrote himself out of debt by producing formulaic romances, primarily for the *Saturday Evening Post*. At the height of his popularity he earned as much as $4,000 for a story. Typical of these popular romances was "The Popular Girl," published in the *Saturday Evening Post* in February 1922 and never reprinted in his lifetime. In the story, two young men, a handsome and charming Yale undergraduate who represents Eastern values and a poor but worthy Midwesterner, pursue a seventeen-year-old beauty who uses all her wiles to capture the hero. The romance plot turns on a series of complications and reversals: Her drunken father dies, leaving her penniless. Yet inevitably, all is resolved, as it must be given the demands of the form, when the wealthy heir saves the popular girl from the circumstances that nearly bring her to ruin.

Fitzgerald was a master at writing such stories, but many of his friends feared that he expended too much energy and talent in their production. Novelist Charles Norris, for instance, warned Fitzgerald that he would ruin himself as a writer if he continued to satisfy the pedestrian tastes of the *Post's* readers. "You can re-christen that worthy periodical 'The Grave-Yard of the Genius of F. Scott Fitzgerald,'" he wrote to the author, "if you go on contributing to it until [editor George Horace] Lorimer sucks you dry and tosses you into the discard where nobody will care to find you" (Meyers 80). Fitzgerald justified his efforts with the argument that the money he earned from writing magazine stories would buy him the freedom to pursue his serious fiction, but eventually he found himself disgusted by his own trivialities and unable to produce them, despite his need for the income they would have provided. In May 1940, he confessed in a letter to Zelda that he could no longer write the commercial short story. "As soon as I feel I am writing to a cheap specification," he noted, "my pen freezes and my talent vanishes over the hill" (*Life in Letters* 444).

The majority of his 164 published short stories are indeed forgettable, written, as Fitzgerald eventually acknowledged, at great cost to both his emotional life and his professional career. "I have asked a lot of my emotions—one hundred and twenty stories," he wrote in his *Notebooks* of the 1930s. "The price was high, right up with [Joseph Rudyard] Kipling, because there was one little drop of something not blood, not a tear, not my seed, but me more intimately than these, in every story, it was the extra I had. Now it is gone" (131). Yet many of his stories are among the masterworks of the genre, tales that attest to his artistic control of both form and content. Perhaps the best of the lot is his 1931 story "Babylon Revisited." All of his best stories are connected thematically to his novels. In fact, several seem to anticipate or repeat not only thematic concerns, but also plot elements and figurative motifs that are integral to the novels. "Babylon Revisited," for instance, like *Tender is the Night*, explores the price of disorder and moral carelessness by tracing the efforts of Charlie Wales, a man who lost everything that mattered in the boom, to regain custody of his daughter Honoria. Similarly, "Winter Dreams" (1922), which focuses on Dexter Green's idealistic love of and subsequent disillusionment about the beautiful but shallow Judy Jones, anticipates some of the themes and motifs of *The Great Gatsby*. Because this study focuses on Fitzgerald's novels, his most significant literary contribution, the connections between representative major stories and the novels will be drawn in the appropriate chapters, not to diminish the stories' achievements but to emphasize the genesis and development of his art. It was, after all, as a serious novelist that Fitzgerald staked his reputation. Yet a brief analysis of several of his best stories gives some indication of both the range and depth of Fitzgerald's short fiction.

In "Bernice Bobs Her Hair" (1920), for instance, one of his most anthologized stories, Fitzgerald explores one of his characteristic subjects—the competitive nature of social success—in a witty tale of jealousy and revenge. Based on a detailed memo in which Fitzgerald advised his younger sister Annabel on strategies to achieve popularity with boys (*Correspondence* 15–18), "Bernice Bobs Her Hair" focuses on the unexpected rivalry between Marjorie Harvey, the self-absorbed representative of the new generation, and her cousin Bernice from Eau Claire. Bernice is the sort of "womanly woman" whose "whining cowardly mass of affectations" (*Short Stories* 34) Marjorie holds in contempt. During a month's visit with her cousin, Bernice, an attractive but dull young woman, enjoys anything but the social success that her wealth and status have granted her in her hometown, and a brutally honest Marjorie offers to transform her into a "gardenia girl" (*Short Stories* 31) like herself, the sort of woman who can glide no more than three or four feet on the dance floor before a new partner cuts in. Under Marjorie's tutelage, Bernice discovers the appeal of wit and verve and inadvertently steals her cousin's best beau, Warren McIntyre, a man for whom Marjorie has never really cared until he directs his attentions to another. Then, a jealous Marjorie, who has been feeding Bernice her lines, calls her cousin's bluff by challenging her to bob her hair, the chief source of her beauty, as she had promised to do. To refuse, Bernice realizes, will expose her to ridicule by revealing the superficiality of her new image. After submitting to the barber's shears, she realizes "that her chance at beauty had been sacrificed to the jealous whim of a selfish girl" (*Short Stories* 45) and exacts her own revenge. While Marjorie lies sleeping, Bernice takes the scissors to her cousin's blond plaits and tosses them on the front porch of the McIntyre house as she flees to Eau Claire in the middle of the night.

The clever twist of the story's ending certainly demonstrates the truth of Marjorie's assertion to her mother that "these days it's every girl for herself" (*Short Stories* 30) and underscores the competitiveness of social success. Yet the central conflict embodied by the two cousins also makes clear the changing manners and mores of Fitzgerald's social world. Bernice is the dutiful daughter of her mother's generation. Sweet and virtuous, she believes that women are "beloved because of certain mysterious womanly qualities, always mentioned but never displayed" (*Short Stories* 30). Marjorie, in contrast, understands that men find boring such a woman, who is little more than a "beautiful bundle of clothes" (*Short Stories* 34); they prefer her sort of toughness because it makes life anything but tiresome and colorless. This new woman, Fitzgerald's fiction makes clear, embodies the age, and she served as the model for all of his central women characters.

In 1926 Fitzgerald published his most important novelette, "The Rich Boy," which includes his famous and usually misquoted line about the rich: "They are different from you and me" (*Short Stories* 318). As the story's title suggests, Anson Hunter, the rich boy, is a singular example of a type. His money has made him hard and cynical; it has instilled in him a sense of superiority and selfishness. It is, in other words, the source of the emptiness and loneliness that are the consequences of such qualities. "The Rich Boy" is, then, a cautionary tale of the corruptive power of great wealth, one that in both its form and its theme is clearly connected to *The Great Gatsby*.

Told, like *The Great Gatsby*, from the perspective of an observer-narrator who occasionally participates in the action and whose judgments provide a moral frame for the story, "The Rich Boy" focuses on Anson Hunter, a man whose life begins rather than ends "a compromise" (*Short Stories* 320). The product of two conflicting generations, Anson is at once solid and conservative, extravagant and self-indulgent. The contradictions inherent in his personality eventually create a rift between him and Paula Legendre, the woman he loves but to whom he cannot commit. When Paula marries another man, Anson compensates for his own emotional emptiness by engaging in an empty affair with Dolly Karger, who he casually abandons. He then drives his aunt's lover to suicide by assuming the role of moral censor, even though he is "more concerned for the maintenance of outward forms" (*Short Stories* 328) than he is for the spirit of them. Some years later, Anson encounters Paula, who, following an unhappy first marriage, is happily pregnant by her second husband. When he learns of her death in childbirth, Anson is incapable of response. Grief and sympathy seem unable to penetrate the shell of his self-absorption, and the story ends not with a climax, but with a trailing off of interest. Because Anson is incapable of growth and change, his life, as the story's final paragraph makes clear, is doomed to vacuous repetition. After all, what he wants from life is nothing more than to attract and to be loved by a woman who will "nurse and protect that superiority he cherished in his heart" (*Short Stories* 349). What he wants from life is nothing more than what the Patches in *The Beautiful and Damned*, the Buchanans in *The Great Gatsby*, and the Warrens in *Tender is the Night* also want; their wealth ensures, Fitzgerald makes clear, that all are doomed to disappointment and disillusionment.

One of Fitzgerald's most poignant stories, "The Last of the Belles" (1929), examines one of his most pervasive themes—the losses that result from the inevitabilities of time. Andy, the story's retrospective narrator, regretfully recalls the loss of his youthful hopes and dreams as he tells the tale of his unrequited love for Ailie Calhoun, the object of so many men's desire during a long, hot summer of basic training in Tarleton, Georgia, in the waning days of World War I. Ailie, like Marjorie Harvey in "Bernice Bobs Her Hair," is as flirtatious as any modern young woman, but she is also a belle, redolent of magnolia flowers, her charm and grace linked in "a Northern man's dream of the South" (*Short Stories* 460) to its "heroic age" (*Short Stories* 450). Indeed, the poetry of the South that she embodies is a great part of her appeal.

During that summer of hopes and dreams, Andy finds himself Ailie's confidant rather than her beau. He watches as she becomes hopelessly smitten with an inappropriate suitor, Earl Schoen, a man whose uniform has admitted him into a world not his own. When Schoen returns to claim her following the war, Ailie quickly realizes her mistake. Without his uniform, Schoen is nothing more than a streetcar conductor, and Ailie, who has been deceived by her own desire to escape the South's provincialism and has thus misunderstood this Northerner, breaks their engagement.

Six years later, a Harvard-educated Andy returns to Tarleton himself, compelled by a glimpse of a girl dressed in pink organdy in a small Indiana town to recapture "the lost midsummer world of my early twenties" (*Short Stories* 460). Seeking out Ailie, he confesses his love for her, but she is not the same girl whose soft drawl once contained the "secrets of a brighter, finer ante-bellum day" (*Short Stories* 460). In fact, in her breathless banter Andy now hears the desperation of defeat. When she refuses his marriage proposal, Andy asks her for one favor—that she accompany him to the former site of the training camp. There, with the embodiment of one illusion, he searches for the remnants of others, "looking" especially, he confesses, "for my youth in a clapboard or a strip of roofing or a rusty tomato can" (*Short Stories* 462), but that youth, like the South of his dreams, is lost to him forever.

These representative stories, which are among his best, go far beyond the generic conventions of the popular romance that Fitzgerald ultimately came to despise and found unable to write. Superficial in neither form nor content, they bear the marks of Fitzgerald's distinctive style: the sophisticated wit, the poetic language, the ironic or elegiac tone. They also develop his distinctive subjects and explore his typical themes: the personal and moral consequences of great wealth; the sustaining illusions, perhaps the most important of which is love, that give meaning and significance to human life; the inevitable losses wrought by time. Fitzgerald's best stories are, then, like his novels, anything but forgettable.

THE ELEMENTS OF THE FITZGERALD NOVEL: CHARACTER, THEME, STYLE

The links between Fitzgerald's stories and novels and indeed between the novels themselves make clear some of the defining characteristics of his work. His central characters, for instance, generally represent a privileged class, both socially and economically. Insulated by their wealth from the brutal realities of hard physical labor, stultifying occupations, and the anxieties of want and need, they have the time and leisure to pursue, and even to be bored by, pleasure. Privilege has also made them selfish and morally careless. Someone, they know from experience, will step forward, as Nick Carraway says of Daisy and Tom Buchanan in *The Great Gatsby* (187–188), to clean up their messes, to assume responsibility for their benign neglect and calculated cruelties. Even Anthony and Gloria Patch, mere shadows of their former brilliant selves, believe themselves triumphantly validated by the legal victory that restores Anthony's long-anticipated inheritance at the end of *The Beautiful and Damned*. Their lives are golden, as they were meant to be.

From within this privileged class, Fitzgerald draws his central female characters: *This Side of Paradise*'s Rosalind Connage, *The Beautiful and Damned*'s *Gloria Patch*, *The Great Gatsby*'s Daisy Buchanan, *Tender is the Night*'s Nicole

Diver. Beautiful and self-absorbed, they move through the world with the ease and assurance of a lifetime of wealth and social position taken as a matter of course and full knowledge of their power to conquer all. Thoroughly modern and protected by their status, they flaunt convention and enjoy their pleasures, yet in spite of their experience of the world, they seem to have managed to retain their essential innocence. Their physical beauty in some way insulates them from corruption. It is just this innocent self-assurance that transforms them for Fitzgerald's male protagonists into ideals of truth and virtue. To possess them is to enter this world of the ideal, to know its secrets, and to share its brilliance. Fitzgerald's women are thus less fully realized characters than embodiments of desire. For the Fitzgerald male, even their self-absorption and aloofness are proof of their innate superiority and worth; they are a connection to some universal greatness.

Fitzgerald's male protagonists, as their idealization of his women suggests, tend to stand just on the periphery of the golden world of wealth and status that confer on their members' ease and happiness. Whether they are like *This Side of Paradise*'s Amory Blaine, whose fortune and credentials make him ever aware of his second-best status in the world's eyes, or *The Great Gatsby*'s James Gatz, who must earn a fortune and reinvent himself in order to be worthy of the woman he loves, Fitzgerald's male protagonists do not by right belong in the world of privilege. Yet they aspire to it, not for materialistic reasons but as confirmation of their self-conceived destiny and their sustaining visions. To a certain extent, they are all romantics, possessed of dreams and visions that they seek to make real. While Amory's dreams, as might be expected of an undergraduate, are rather vague, incoherent longings to achieve his destined greatness, Gatsby's are wedded to a concept, to the recreation of a perfect moment in time. *The Last Tycoon*'s Monroe Stahr, as the ultimate dream purveyor, intends to give cinematic life to his visions of the world. Whatever the aim, however, the dream itself constitutes the central fact of the life of each of Fitzgerald's male protagonists. Their pursuit of the dream serves as the vehicle by which Fitzgerald develops the thematic concerns in his novels.

Fitzgerald's recurrent themes tend toward the tragic and certainly evoke the pathos of the human condition. His central characters, those romantic idealists, begin life with high hopes and lofty aspirations, but they inevitably fall far short of their dreams. They are defeated by the fact of time, the vagaries of love, and the human frailties that bedevil our own best selves. "All the stories that came into my head had a touch of disaster in them," Fitzgerald observed of his fiction, noting the sadness that pervades his work. "The lovely young creatures in my novels went to ruin, the diamond mountains of my short stories blew up, my millionaires were as beautiful and damned as [English novelist] Thomas Hardy's peasants" ("Early Success," *The Crack-Up* 87). This "touch of disaster" springs from Fitzgerald's understanding of lost hopes and defeated aspirations, of the passage of time and its attendant losses, of the conflict between art and life, of the meaning of America and its unfulfilled history—the recurrent themes of his fiction.

A poet of lost hopes and defeated aspirations, Fitzgerald locates such circumstances in two different sources, the fact of time and the conflict between art and life, between the spiritual and the material. Both are realities that cause his romantic idealists to falter and thereby experience disillusionment with the world and, in his most fully aware characters, disappointment with the self. Time, for instance, robs human beings of youth and all its promise as well as the wonders of beauty. Youthful heroes such as *This Side of Paradise*'s Amory Blaine and *The Beautiful and Damned*'s Anthony Patch see age as one of their primary assets. The world is all before them, not behind, and they are secure in the knowledge that they have the energy, stamina, talent, and desire to conquer it. Armed with this certainty, Amory especially rebounds from every setback with renewed hope and vigor, propelled by yet another dream. Yet if we see Anthony Patch as the logical extension of Fitzgerald's first protagonist, then we understand the disillusionment that he will inevitably face when he can no longer shrug off the physical toll of endless nights of drunken excess, when he feels every one of his thirty years and knows that time robs him daily of even more of this youth. Gloria Patch may wail, "I don't want to live without my pretty face!" (*Beautiful* 404), but the beauty that she and Fitzgerald's male protagonists so value is as transient as their youth. To Nick Carraway's assertion "You can't repeat the past," Jay Gatsby may counter in utter disbelief, "Can't repeat the past . . . why of course you can!" (*Gatsby* 116), but the truth is that Daisy does indeed have a daughter. Time and change are inevitable. The perfect golden moment is an impossibility. Thus there is in Fitzgerald's fiction the elegaic tone of loss. His characters dream big, but time-bound reality can never correspond to the ephemeral ideal; only the dream dreamed, not the dream materialized, can bring them happiness. Even on that golden afternoon of their reunion, "Daisy tumbled short of [Gatsby's] dreams" (*Gatsby* 101), and for all Kathleen's physical resemblance to Minna, *The Last Tycoon*'s Monroe Stahr cannot escape the fact of his wife's death.

Fitzgerald deepens the disillusionment of self-aware characters such as Stahr and especially *Tender is the Night*'s Dick Diver by placing their personal stories within the context of historical processes. When Dick tours World War I battlefields, where the dead had lain "like a million bloody rugs" (*Tender* 57), he confronts the reality of social and moral changes that have also been wrought by time. In their efforts to fling off what seem to be the empty and outmoded values of the past, which had led to such tragedy, a new generation embraces the promise of freedom and personal satisfaction, only to find itself aimless, rootless, and in a state of perpetual change that denies them the stability of any lasting truths or values. Within the context of historical process, Dick's personal tragedy is thus symptomatic, reflecting the forces of time and change against which he is powerless. These forces eventually defeat all of Fitzgerald's central characters.

Time is not alone, however, in working against the attainment of hopes and dreams. Equally powerful is the internal conflict between art and life, between the spiritual and the material, that undermines the quests of Fitzgerald's protagonists. This conflict is most pronounced in *Tender is the Night*, where Dick Diver, who begins his career as a psychiatrist dedicated to his patients and his profession and with the hope that he can achieve some personal greatness from his work, finds himself seduced away from his best intentions by the ease and beauty made possible by wealth. Increasingly bent on the pursuit of pleasure, which brings him no real joy, Dick without purpose or a dream becomes a mere shadow of his former brilliant self. When he finally begins to analyze himself, he is filled with self-disgust and loathing for what he has become—a man who has allowed himself to be purchased and who has betrayed his own dream of self.

Dick's conflict is to some extent characteristic of all Fitzgerald protagonists. They long for some ideal, sometimes just an ideal of self, but they confuse its attainment with wealth, not money itself, but the ease and beauty that money can buy. In their minds, the rich are indeed different. Their money frees them from an anxious, grubbing existence; it makes possible happiness and confers on them virtue. The monied tones of Daisy's voice convince Gatsby of her perfection. In *This Side of Paradise* Rosalind Connage has purchased ease and self-assurance, Amory knows, with her fortune. Fitzgerald's protagonists desire these same intangibles, and so they fill their wardrobes with a rainbow array of shirts and inhabit villas in the south of France, believing that the trappings of wealth will satisfy their longings. Thus they are doomed to disappointment and disillusionment, for no thing, not even the embodiment of the ideal, can match the conception of the thing. Because Fitzgerald's protagonists only vaguely intuit this truth or are reluctant to acknowledge it if they do, they persist to the end to mingle their dreams with the things of this world, which inevitably fall short of the mark.

This conflict between the real and the ideal and this confusion of virtue or happiness with wealth merge with Fitzgerald's anxieties about time and loss and lie at the heart of his questioning of the meaning of the American Dream. From the beginning of his career, Fitzgerald was a writer grounded in the American scene. From small midwestern towns to cosmopolitan clubs, from the halls of ivy at prestigious seats of learning to the manufactured perfections of the Hollywood dream machine, Fitzgerald's fiction focuses on American manners and mores. Even *Tender is the Night*, a novel set in Europe, is a tale of expatriate Americans who, rather like the Fitzgeralds themselves, choose not to enter into the lives of the locals but to fashion their own native enclaves, their Villas America, on a pristine spot of foreign soil. Fitzgerald responded to the promise inherent in the national myth and lived its contradictions, and his fiction reflects his understanding of it. His evocation of American heroes such as Abraham Lincoln and Ulysses S. Grant, moreover, and of the early settlers who sought in the New World to realize their own dreams and aspirations makes clear his intention to invest his tales with symbolic meaning. America, with its vast promise; America, with its high idealism; America, with its bounty and richness; America, a concept defeated before it is begun by the forces of time and human nature; America is thus Fitzgerald's overarching subject, his greatest theme.

Fitzgerald was not the first novelist to write of lost hopes and defeated aspirations, to lament time and change, or to make America his subject. Indeed, he was not the only novelist of the Lost Generation, a group of expatriate American writers residing mainly in Paris in the 1920s and 1930s. Yet readers respond to his characters and themes through the beauty of the prose itself. Through language vivid and immediate Fitzgerald renders experience with an emotional intensity that conveys understanding. His is a prose of intimate involvement, drawing readers into his characters' lives, responding to the narrative voice, whether earnest or disillusioned, naive or matter-of-fact. Always, too, are the images, which evoke and define without ever explaining. Nick Carraway's first glimpse of Daisy Buchanan and Jordan Baker in *The Great Gatsby*, for instance, utterly fixes them as representatives of their class. Similarly, Carraway's description of Gatsby's car is an evocation of the owner's psyche rather than a recitation of make and model: "It was a rich cream color, bright with nickel, swollen here and there in its monstrous length with triumphant hatboxes and supper-boxes and tool-boxes, and terraced with a labyrinth of windshields that mirrored a dozen suns" (*Gatsby* 68). In the end, Fitzgerald's style—the rhythm of his sentences, the precision of his language, the intensity of his poetic prose—is an elegant signature that defines his fiction as distinctly as his characters and their social world, as precisely as his themes.

These elements of a literary career have confirmed Fitzgerald's status as one of the major American novelists of the twentieth century and sustained his reputation for the more than half century since his death. They testify to his seriousness as a writer who, at his best in novels such as *The Great Gatsby* and, for all its flaws, *Tender is the Night*, fulfilled the promise of his own grand conception of his art. They put into perspective as well the swirl of ideas and images, of influences and experiences from which he fashioned a fictional world that expressed his vision of his own.

This Side of Paradise
(1920)

The novel that launched F. Scott Fitzgerald's career as a writer, *This Side of Paradise*, is also in many respects the novel that Fitzgerald rewrote again and again throughout his career. In the story of Amory Blaine, an idealistic youth in pursuit of an ideal, Fitzgerald explored the themes and characters and experimented with the narrative strategies and techniques that define his vision and characterize his style. *This Side of Paradise*, like the majority of first novels, is not without its flaws and weaknesses. Yet its importance to Fitzgerald's development as a writer is undeniable, and it is "valuable," as biographer Jeffrey Meyers observes, "both as autobiography and as social history" (56). Moreover, with this novel that made his name synonymous with the Jazz Age, Fitzgerald staked claim to territory that simultaneously nurtured and constrained his literary career.

A decidedly autobiographical novel, *This Side of Paradise* recounts the life of Amory Blaine from his wealthy and pampered childhood through prep school and Princeton, charting the course of his moral education, sexual awakening, and romantic disillusionment with life. Amory, a "romantic egotist" (23), has a fine sense of his own immense possibilities and believes that a great destiny awaits him. His heightened conception of self, however, is both his best and his worst quality, providing him with a sense of mission but also convincing him of its easy attainment. Expulsion from college and rejection by the woman he loves eventually lead Amory to discover that his dreams are not enough to ensure his desires, and he grows disillusioned with life. Yet that disillusionment does not cause Amory to lose faith in himself, and the novel ends as it begins—with Fitzgerald's "romantic egotist" in pursuit of his great destiny, beginning yet again the eternal quest that will define his life and existence.

GENESIS AND CRITICAL RECEPTION

Selling out within twenty-four hours of its publication on March 26, 1920, *This Side of Paradise* was an immediate popular success (Meyers 65), capturing the spirit of disillusionment that followed World War I and the hedonistic rebellion that constituted the Jazz Age. It provided its readers, in other words, with a rendering of their own era that validated its contradictions. The critical response, as Jeffrey Meyers notes, was also "surprisingly enthusiastic and generous about the flawed but vibrant novel" (60). Reviewers might quibble with the novel's excesses, its sentimentality and lack of control, for instance, but most could not deny "its originality, its vitality and its style" (Meyers 60). H. L. Mencken, the influential editor of *The Smart Set*, enthused that *This Side of Paradise* is a "truly amazing first novel—original in structure, extremely sophisticated in manner, and adorned with a brilliancy that is as rare in American writing as honesty is in American statecraft" (Bryer, *Reputation* 28). Even Edmund Wilson, perhaps the most influential literary critic of his day and a former classmate of Fitzgerald who became his literary mentor and one of his harshest critics, was forced to concede the novel's appeal in a 1922 review. "I have said that *This Side of Paradise* commits almost every sin that a novel can possibly commit: but it does not commit the unpardonable sin: it does not fail to live. The whole preposterous farrago is animated with life" (29).

Fitzgerald crafted his first novel from stories that he had published as an undergraduate in Princeton University's *Nassau Literary Magazine* and from the draft of a novel entitled "The Romantic Egotist" that he took with him when he left the university in 1917. This rough draft, as literary critic Kenneth Eble observes, "[makes] less of an attempt to create a convincing fictional character than to write a first person account of Fitzgerald's life at Newman [preparatory school] and Princeton" (*Fitzgerald* 43), and a disappointed Fitzgerald was unable to find a publisher for the work. For the next two years he reworked his material and expanded his focus, heavily influenced by Compton Mackenzie's now nearly forgotten novel *Sinister Street*. Eventually he even quit his job writing advertising copy to devote himself to the completion of the novel. When he finally submitted the manuscript to Scribner's in July 1919, Fitzgerald was convinced that he had succeeded in "disciplining the muse." As he wrote to Maxwell Perkins, the Scribner's editor who nurtured Fitzgerald's talent, the new novel, which he now called "The Education of a Personage," was "in no sense a revision of the ill-fated *Romantic Egotist* but it contains some of the former material improved and worked over. . . . But while the other was a tedius [*sic*], disconnected casserole this is a definate [*sic*] attempt at a big novel and I really believe I have hit it" (*Life in Letters* 28). In September 1919, less than a month after the manuscript's submission, Perkins accepted it for publication, and F. Scott Fitzgerald was finally a novelist.

PLOT DEVELOPMENT

Fitzgerald divides the plot of his first novel into two books, each of which contains several chapters dramatizing the significant events in the life of Amory Blaine. Separating the books is a brief "Interlude" that conveys in two letters Amory's experience as a second lieutenant in World War I. The effect of this structure is to suggest that the war separates Amory's life into two distinct halves. Yet the organization of each book is essentially the same: Amory moves forward toward his expected destiny, falls in love with a beautiful woman who disappoints him, plunges into despair but ultimately recovers his essential self, and prepares to advance to the next thing that will take him to his golden future.

Book One, entitled "The Romantic Egotist," focuses on Amory's rootless childhood and Midwestern youth, his years at St. Regis' prep school, and his career at Princeton University. Chapter One, "Amory, Son of Beatrice," makes clear the importance of Amory's mother during her son's formative years. In short, newsreel-like sequences, it also briefly dramatizes his first flirtation and kiss; his two-year exile (or so it seems to him) in Minneapolis, where he develops the code by which he intends to live; his first meeting with Monsignor Darcy, who will become his spiritual father; and his two-year stint at St. Regis'. All of this life, however, is merely a prelude to the first experience that he feels worthy of him—his tenure at Princeton University, which Fitzgerald details in the next three chapters.

Chapter Two, "Spires and Gargoyles," focuses on the high points of Amory's college career. He meets the friends who will help him to learn about himself and his world—Burne Holiday, Thomas Parke D'Invilliers, and Dick Humbird—as well as the woman who will first win his heart—Isabelle Borgé. He achieves success through his literary efforts and his productions for Triangle Club musicals and enjoys the status that they confer upon him. Yet the death of Dick Humbird, killed in an automobile accident at the end of the chapter following a night of drunken carousing, marks as well the end of Amory's ascendancy, proof of which lies in Chapter Three, "The Egotist Considers." There, Isabelle breaks off her relationship with Amory, whose poor academic record causes him also to lose his college honors. Following his father's death, Amory seeks direction from Monsignor Darcy, but he cannot escape his own demons, signified by the appearance of Dick Humbird's ghost at the chapter's end.

The title of Chapter Four, "Narcissus Off Duty," with its allusion to the Greek myth of a youth so enamoured of his own reflection that he fell into a pond and drowned in an effort to embrace his own beauty, relates the fortunate escape of Fitzgerald's "romantic egotist" from a similar fate. Under the positive influence of Burne Holiday, who challenges his notions about society and its values, Amory begins to look beyond his self-absorption. His infatuation with his virtuous cousin, the widowed Clara Page, is similarly redemptive. Now Amory, for whom world war had been previously little more than an historical footnote (62) to his college years, departs from Princeton to take his place in the wide world.

Amory's two-year stint in the army, during which he does indeed see service in Europe, might be expected to change Fitzgerald's hero, and the two letters that convey that experience suggest as much. The first, a letter from Monsignor Darcy to Amory, laments what he knows will be the spiritual death of his young admirer. The second, a letter from Amory to Thomas Parke D'Invilliers, reveals the romantic egotist's newly developed and thoroughly modern cynicism. The product of a new age, the representative of a new generation, baptized by war and thus, as his poem in this section makes clear, cut loose from his moorings and haunted by ghosts (164–165), Amory does indeed seem a changed man. Yet the structure of Book Two, the events of which essentially recapitulate those in Book One, suggests that the essential Amory survives; his cynicism does not run deep.

In Book Two, Fitzgerald details "The Education of a Personage." He shows, in other words, the process by which Amory gathers stature (108). In Chapter One, "The Debutante," Amory again falls in love with a beautiful woman, the self-absorbed Rosalind Connage, who will ultimately disappoint him. In response, dramatized in Chapter Two, "Experiments in Convalescence," he indulges in drunken debauchery, secures and promptly quits an advertising job, and then seeks solace in literary discussions with his friend Tom. Sinking ever deeper into "Young Irony," as the title of Chapter Three makes clear, Amory enters his Edgar Allan Poe period. He explores and, indeed, courts his dark self through his infatuation with Eleanor Savage. Amory's instinct for self-preservation, however, saves him for "The Supercilious Sacrifice" dramatized in Chapter Four. There, Amory, who is drifting without either desire or purpose, assumes responsibility for Alex Connage's sexual misconduct, a gesture that brings him no reward whatsoever. The chapter ends with Monsignor Darcy's death, robbing Amory of his final support.

In Chapter Five, however, "The Egotist Becomes a Personage," Amory, as he had at the end of Book One, regains something of his old optimism, even if a veneer of irony now covers it. In this chapter, Dick Humbird's father offers a ride to the hitchhiking Amory, and the two men, neither of whom recognizes the other, argue politics, economics, and morality as they travel the road together. Amory expresses all the disillusionment of his generation in this confrontation with the previous generation, but ultimately it helps him to renounce beauty and accept himself as he is. And thus, once again, he is ready to take his place in the wide world.

The plot of *This Side of Paradise* is, then, both linear and circular. On the one hand, it moves Amory in a straight line from childhood to adulthood. On the other, the two halves of Amory's life move from optimism through disappointment and disillusionment to a reassertion of self that leads to or anticipates further movement forward. This circularity suggests both the preservation of Amory's essential self and the pattern of his future experiences.

A NOVEL OF APPRENTICESHIP

In both style and form, *This Side of Paradise* is Fitzgerald's novel of apprenticeship. In it the novice writer is clearly striving to demonstrate both his technical virtuosity and his seriousness of purpose. To display his mastery of literary form, for instance, Fitzgerald creates a novel that is a pastiche of poems, letters, lists, and even a play in three acts embedded within a prose narrative. At times the novel's style is almost cinematic. Chapters are divided by subheadings such as "Snapshots of the Young Egotist" and "The Superman Grows Careless" that function as subtitles to what could very well be a newsreel about the life of a famous person. The effect of these various narrative strategies is startlingly original and unabashedly exuberant, conveying the brash self-confidence of both Fitzgerald and his fictional hero. It conveys as well a youthful enthusiasm perfectly in sync with its time and place.

Amory Blaine's life experience is, after all, a story of invention set in a time of change. His conception of himself is so broad as to contain multiple self-images, and experimentation is key to his self-definition. Flaunting convention is also a hallmark of Amory's era, the period of American history known as the Jazz Age. The flappers and philosophers (to use Fitzgerald's term for them) of the time were challenging the manners, mores, and beliefs of the past and forging a new style that reflected their own views about life. Within this context, Fitzgerald's own experiments with style are perfectly natural. Like Amory, Fitzgerald will not be constrained by narrow conceptions of the possible. The novel can be whatever he wants it to be, and he will draw upon any literary form that suits his purpose.

For all its technical virtuosity, however, *This Side of Paradise* is utterly conventional in narrative form because Fitzgerald, perhaps to make clear his seriousness of purpose, grounds his tale in the conventions of a traditional literary genre, the *bildungsroman*, or novel of development or apprenticeship. The *bil-*

dungsroman, a term derived from the German author Goethe's novel *Wilhelm Meister's Apprenticeship*, is a literary form that deals with the development of a young person, usually from adolescence to maturity. Such novels are frequently autobiographical. According to literary critic Martin Swales, the *bildungsroman* "is a novel form that is animated by a concern for the whole man unfolding organically in all his complexity and richness" (14). The classic conception of *bildung* stresses the process by which the hero realizes the physical, intellectual, emotional, moral, and spiritual capacities inherent in his personality. Each stage of the hero's life has its own intrinsic value, but it also serves as the basis for a higher stage of development. Obstacles serve as necessary growth points through which the hero must pass on his journey to maturity. Ultimately, the purpose of that journey is to prepare the hero to accept a responsible role in a friendly social community. Fitzgerald certainly drew upon these conventions as he related Amory's passage to adulthood because *This Side of Paradise* is, in fact, that "definite type of biographical novel" that Amory calls a " 'quest' book" (124). It details his journey from innocence to knowledge of both self and society.

A NOVEL OF MANNERS

Since its publication, *This Side of Paradise* has also been considered a chronicle of the Jazz Age, conveying the styles, themes, and fashions of a generation. As the English novelist and critic Malcolm Bradbury observes, "No writer set out more determinedly to capture in fiction the tone, the hope, the possibility, and the touch of despair of the Twenties" than Fitzgerald (83). The novelist himself explained the source of his tale by saying, "I was certain that all the young people were going to be killed in the war, and I wanted to put on paper a record of the strange life they had lived in their time" (Bradbury 77).

Clearly, then, *This Side of Paradise* is a novel of manners, a literary form depicting the manners and mores of a class of people in a particular time and place. In it, Fitzgerald, as Bradbury explains, "made sure that the Twenties was known as 'the Jazz Age,' that the new goods and chattels, the new expressions and sexual styles, made their way into fiction" (83). Indeed, the automobile, Prohibition, the flapper and the sheik, the new woman and man of the age, all figure prominently in the novel's pages, revealing the profound changes in the attitudes and mores of a modern generation. While it may lack the comic tone characteristic of the novel of manners, conveying its vision with a seriousness that frequently registers as pretentiousness, *This Side of Paradise* does contain, as Meyers notes, "flashes of insight on a number of serious subjects: wealth, class, sex, mores, fame, romance, glamour, success, vanity, egoism, politics and religion" (59).

Fitzgerald deals frankly, for instance, with the new attitudes about sex. At a time when casual kissing was considered immoral and a serious kiss was a prelude to a marriage proposal (185), his flappers, such as Isabelle Borgé and Rosalind Connage, display a boyish toughness that makes them utterly immune to the sexual prohibitions of a previous age. Indeed, their "Victorian mothers" would have been shocked had they "any idea how casually their daughters were accustomed to being kissed" (65). In the section on "Petting" (65–66), which is actually about kissing, and another entitled "Restlessness," Fitzgerald exposes the myth of sexlessness that makes hypocrites of so many American men and women (218), and he is equally honest about attitudes toward drinking and religion as well.

As a novel of manners, *This Side of Paradise*, as Meyers observes, expresses a generation's "revolt against prewar respectability" and "both baptized the Jazz Age and glorified its fashionable hedonism" (59). Chief spokesman for his generation is the novel's protagonist, Amory Blaine. As one of "the chosen youth from the muddled, unchastened world," he will learn "the fear of poverty and the worship of success" (284) that support twentieth-century dreams and ideals.

CHARACTER DEVELOPMENT

The focus of Fitzgerald's *bildungsroman*, Amory Blaine, is a character who in many respects functions as the author's alter ego, or second self. In fact, several months after the publication of *This Side of Paradise*, Fitzgerald called his first novel "a somewhat edited history of me and my imagination" ("Who's Who," *Afternoon of an Author* 61). An incongruous combination of Midwestern yearning and Eastern cosmopolitanism, Amory is filled with a sense of his own potential and convinced that he will achieve it. He is, after all, "armed with the best weapons" (124), like the heroes of the "quest" books he so admires. In Amory's case, these weapons are his own innate intelligence, his ability to please, and, above all, his powerful imagination. Yet these very qualities that should lead to his success also doom him to disappointment and failure, for Amory's is a dream of becoming rather than being (25). For such a person, reality will never correspond to desire.

Early in the novel, in a section subtitled "Snapshots of the Young Egotist," Fitzgerald lays bare "the fundamental Amory" (103), revealing the internal contradictions that make him so fascinating to himself. While Amory considers himself "a boy marked for glory" (25) and frequently wonders why others fail to note his brilliance, his masters at school find him "idle, unreliable and superficially clever" (25), and their analysis is certainly not far off the mark. Extremely sensitive and vain, Amory possesses "neither courage, perseverance, nor self-respect" (27), and he seldom yields to his rather "Puritan conscience" (26). Posturing is "absolutely essential" (35) to Amory because it makes possible others' acceptance, which he craves. He proudly confesses to his mother, for example, following his two years in Minneapolis in his early teens, " 'I adapted myself to the bourgeoisie. I became conventional'" (29). Yet despite shortcomings of character, Amory's charm, poise, and personal magnetism make him "capable of infinite expansion for good or evil" (26). It is this sense of immense possibility that accounts for his attractiveness. Buoyed up by his naive belief in his future self, Amory rides the crests of his triumphs and despairs, pushing ever onward toward his elusive goal. Throughout the novel, Amory is influenced by people and events. He will even make "his nearest approach to success through conformity" (104) at Princeton, but when "his imagination [is] neither satisfied nor grasped by his own success" (104), as it inevitably fails to be, Amory always reverts back to his fundamental self. It is the one certainty in his life.

Amory's choice of schools for his formal education reveals much about his sense of self and his dreams of becoming. Following his peripatetic education traveling about the world with his mother in his youth and his two years in the "crude, vulgar air" (16) of Minneapolis during his early adolescence, Amory determines to complete his preparatory schooling at St. Regis' in Connecticut. He then chooses Princeton over other Ivy League institutions, enrolling at both schools for essentially the same reason: Neither will do more than polish his essential self. St. Regis', a "gentlemen's school" (32), is the perfect antidote to his Midwestern experience because nothing of the democratic sullies its elitism. Similarly, Princeton promises membership in "the pleasantest country club in America" (43). Its gargoyles and spires offer a hallowed "aristocratic" tradition that Amory can claim as his own without too much effort because, in his mind, it is a "lazy" and "good-looking" (33) place, rather like himself.

While Amory's secular education does little more than finish him off, his spiritual education does even less, despite the fact that one of his most important mentors is a priest. His vague Roman Catholicism may provide him with a sense of good and evil, but it primarily enhances his innate dreaminess. The rigors of true spirituality are beyond Amory's capacities and would demand too much of him. By the end of the novel, moreover, he harbors a belief that "there was a certain intrinsic lack in those to whom orthodox religion was necessary" (283). The ideal that he pursues has nothing to do with the church. Rather, Amory makes of its pursuit his own sort of religion.

Two significant figures shape Amory's youth and encourage his dreams: his mother, from whom he inherits "every trait, except the stray inexpressible few, that made him worth while" (11), and Monsignor Thayer Darcy, his spiritual father. Both feed Amory's burgeoning egotism, for reasons that have much to do with their own egos. In Amory, in other words, both intend to realize their own conceptions of self.

Beatrice O'Hara Blaine shapes the romantic background of her son's life. Sensitive, sentimental, and utterly self-absorbed, Beatrice creates for herself a "delightful companion" (12) in Amory. He is someone who shares her own disdain for ideas and mirrors her own dreamy view of life. From Beatrice, Amory derives a "highly specialized education" (13), one, like her own, that had taught her "the number of things and people one could be contemptuous of and charming about" (12) and that valued style over substance, romance over reality. Amory is Beatrice's only and best creation, and while he may indeed harbor "no illusions" (13) about his mother, he cannot deny that he is her second self.

If Beatrice shapes Amory's youth, then Monsignor Darcy shapes his adolescence and young adulthood, and his influence is similar. Like Beatrice, Monsignor Darcy believes in romantic ideals. In fact, he understands and approves of Amory's romantic lost causes such as Bonnie Prince Charlie and the Southern Confederacy (33). Drawn to him by a feeling of instant kinship (32), Amory finds in Monsignor Darcy a spiritual father and a father confessor, someone who shares his idealistic beliefs and who supports his pursuit of them. He is someone, in fact, who provides Amory with "egotistic food for consumption" (109). Above all, Monsignor Darcy helps Amory to clarify his thinking and to understand his self by explaining to him the key difference between a personality and a personage.

The personality, according to Monsignor Darcy, is "active" (108). He seizes the moment and charges ahead with the indiscriminate passion of youth, but without a sense of purpose. The personality "overrides 'the next thing' " (108) because he fails to understand, as the personage does, the necessity of each step. The personage, in contrast, "gathers. He is never thought of," Monsignor Darcy explains, "apart from what is done" (108). In consequence, he accumulates the power and force to attain his goal, for the personage, unlike the personality, uses his experiences "with a cold mentality back of them" (108). This sense of mission, the sign of a keen imagination, distinguishes the personage from the personality. Needless to say, Amory is a personage. His image of himself may be vague and incomplete, but its mere existence is sufficient to harness his energy and drive him toward his dream.

THEMATIC ISSUES

Amory's dream of greatness is linked to an ideal of beauty embodied in the women he loves. Each of them also represents an aspect of Amory's own self, and thus, his pursuit of each underscores the nature of his quest and indeed the very themes of the novel. *This Side of Paradise*, as literary critic Richard Lehan asserts, is a "novel about youth lost to misplaced ideals" (70). It is a novel about disillusionment and loss, the inevitable consequences of the experience of growing older and wiser. Amory's repeated failures to win the women he loves, more than any other element of his life, chart his course to maturity.

Isabelle Borgé, Amory's first real love, is in many respects a lesser version of the Princeton undergraduate who pursues her. Like Amory, she wears a studied mask of "blasé sophistication," "the result of accessible popular novels and dressing room conversation culled from a slightly older set" (72), and "all impressions and . . . ideas were extremely kaleidoscopic" (69) to her. A girl with a reputation for being kissed, Isabelle plays the ingenue to Amory's devoted swain, each enacting an appropriate part in an idealized romance that gives shape to Amory's sophomore year at college. Indeed, their first kiss, which coincides with Amory's realization that his life can never be more perfect than it is at that moment, marks "the high point of vanity, the crest of his young egotism" (94).

That high point, however, coincides as well with the death of Dick Humbird, Amory's Princeton classmate, in an automobile accident following a night of carefree drinking and carousing. Humbird's death, which Amory finds "so horrible and unaristocratic and close to the earth" (92), foreshadows the disillusionments that he will experience when he recognizes that Isabelle "all along . . . had been nothing except what he had read into her" (99). Possessing Isabelle, in other words, is not what he imagined. She has been a dream, a projection of Amory's imagination, and possessing her has convinced him of her insubstantiality. In her own way, she is as sordid as Dick Humbird's death.

Amory's disillusionment following his breakup with Isabelle is merely temporary; it does not deter him from pursuit of his ideal. Having wedded his dream to the wrong person, Amory, under the influence of an earnest classmate, Burne Holiday, simply sets off on a different path to it. That path leads him to a distant cousin, Clara Page, "the first fine woman he ever knew and one of the few good people who ever interested him" (144).

Clara's superior goodness, as literary critic Kenneth Eble observes, "is consistent with the new idealism now infecting Amory" (*Fitzgerald* 47), an idealism born of his new appreciation for Burne Holiday. "Climbing heights where others would be forever unable to get a foothold" (135), Burne is accumulating the experience and gathering the momentum that will lead him to his greatness. Quietly, unobtrusively, but purposefully, he stands in sight of "a land Amory hoped he was drifting toward" (127), and the realization awes him. To discover how Burne has forged his way through the dark wood of his own doubts and fears, Amory engages with him in challenging discussions about biology, religion, economics, and politics, and, in so doing, he rekindles the fire of his own idealism. He recovers his "sense of going forward in a direct, determined line" and even harnesses the "energy to sally into a new pose" (140). Thus, his attraction to Clara's own intense earnestness, which follows on the heels of this transformation, is yet another attraction to his own dreams.

An otherworldly creature rooted firmly to the real, Clara possesses the ability to inspire goodness in others and to cut through the cant of the insincere. Amory pursues her with the unconscious fear that she may indeed accept him (144). The product of a different world, he understands that the ideals that she embodies cannot sustain him. In fact, they are collapsing about him as Europe prepares to launch into a world war that will forever break "all the links that seemed to bind [his generation] . . . to the top-booted and high-stocked generations" (156) of the past. As the embodiment of that past, Clara can never lead Amory to his future, so he must reluctantly part with her. So, too, must he reluctantly part with "the whole heritage of youth" (156) embodied in Princeton's spires and gargoyles. That much he also knows.

Despite the collapse of the past, of the old moral values and the old attitudes and beliefs, the fundamental Amory returns from Europe. Almost immediately he attaches his dream to yet another beautiful woman, Rosalind Connage. With her *"fresh enthusiasm, her will to grow and learn, her endless faith in the inexhaustibility of romance"* (175), she is Amory's true alter ego, but she possesses already the one thing that Amory has always lacked and that he has always desired—the wealth and position that signify success. In Rosalind, Amory believes that he will achieve the fulfillment of his dream, but that belief proves as ephemeral as the dream. He may be able to woo her, but he can never hope to win her. Like his dream, she will remain ever beyond his reach.

Perhaps to underscore the futile nature of Amory's pursuit of Rosalind, Fitzgerald creates a farce, a clever theatrical performance, to chronicle the rise and fall of his young egotist's dreams and hopes. Amory and Rosalind play out their brief but intense love affair in a first act characterized by witty banter, a second act (several hours later) in which they declare their love, and a third act (five weeks later) during which they mouth the platitudes of renunciation. Their love, Rosalind regretfully proclaims, is simply too beautiful to bear the ugliness of life (198–199). Their love, as the form of its dramatization more aptly suggests, is superficial, insubstantial, and a source of tragedy only to the self-absorbed lovers.

Rosalind's rejection of Amory, more than any other life experience, dashes his hopes and sends him spiraling down toward the abyss of despair. Without the woman to whom he had attached his dream, he can believe in nothing, neither religion, politics, the idea of progress, nor even heroes, men of distinction of the sort he imagined himself one day to be. As Amory explains to Tom D'Invilliers, his roommate and fellow Princetonian, the war had "killed individualism out of our generation" (216), and a destructive cynicism—brittle, brilliant, and born of their losses—now pervades the world.

In this state of mind, Amory begins his flirtation with Eleanor Savage, a woman whose dangerous beauty embodies yet another ideal to pursue. If Clara represents Amory's attraction to the good, then Eleanor signifies the appeal of its opposite: "Eleanor was . . . the last time that evil crept close to Amory under the mask of beauty, the last weird mystery that held him with wild fascination and pounded his soul to flakes" (225). Headstrong and reckless, Eleanor barely conceals a tendency toward self-destruction, and Amory finds it fascinating because it matches his own sense of reckless despair. Together, Amory and Eleanor "see the devil in each other" (225), their minds are so perfectly paired. In fact, as Fitzgerald's allusions to Edgar Allan Poe make clear, they are like Roderick and Madeline Usher, the ill-fated twins in Poe's "The Fall of the House of Usher." They are dangerously close to narcissistic self-destruction, victims of their own egotism.

Amory, however, who has always lacked courage and the will to persevere, does not follow Eleanor to the edge. For a long, glorious summer, he attempts "to play Rupert Brooke" (234), the English poet whose lament for an innocence lost serves as an epigraph to the novel, by adopting his elegiac attitude toward life and love. Yet he cannot maintain this pose indefinitely, and on the day that Eleanor courts her destruction by charging on horseback to the brink of a cliff and allows her mount to plunge to its death in her place, Amory, a horrified spectator, is released from the spell of his own dark self.

Clearly, Amory's efforts to wed his desires to an ideal embodied in a beautiful woman are misguided. Frail humanity cannot bear such weight. Moreover, the romantic, as Amory confesses to both Rosalind and Eleanor, truly does not wish it to. The ideal is both living and elusive and would lose its power to inspire if it were ever contained or attained. It is the quest for the ideal that gives meaning to life. In fact, "if living isn't a seeking for the grail," Amory tells Mr. Ferrenby, the representative of the old order, in the novel's final chapter, then "it may be a damned amusing game" (281). Thus, the romantic "hopes against hope that [things] won't last" (181). Granted, disappointment and disillusionment may follow the collapse of a dream, but such setbacks are only temporary. Romantics, like Amory, eventually recover their fundamental selves and experience again the thrill of desire. This is the pattern of Amory's life and loves, and it is this pattern that ultimately reveals the themes of *This Side of Paradise*: the power of the imagination, the idealism of youth, and the tragic waste of human potential in pursuit of the wrong dreams.

SYMBOLISM

Amory's idealistic quest for the ideal plays itself out against the backdrop of a changing world order, one that leaves his generation "grown up to find all

Gods dead, all wars fought, all faiths in man shaken" (284) forever. Traces of the vanquished past, however, pervade *This Side of Paradise*, providing the novel with its most haunting symbol, the ghost. These projections of the mind, born of doubts and fears, delusions and desires, signify the presence of the past, and Amory and his Princeton classmates do battle daily with them. Yet they are unable and perhaps unwilling to vanquish them completely.

Amory's first encounter with the presence of the past perhaps explains his ambivalence about the ghosts that haunt his life and mind. Amory finds himself in a hotel room with Asia, a woman of brief acquaintance, and dangerously on the verge of succumbing to the debaucheries of Broadway. Watching his seduction by evil is the pale ghostly presence of the devil, embodied, Amory comes to realize, in the image of Dick Humbird, who was killed in an automobile accident, a sad victim of his own excesses. Amory, who has been reluctant to join the party and never intended going so far, reacts wildly to the vision. He escapes the clutches of Asia and runs blindly into the shadows of night. Calling aloud for someone "good" and "stupid," the two qualities "somehow intermingled [for him] through previous association" (120), Amory instinctively seeks his salvation in the "pile on pile of inherent tradition or some wild prayer from way over the night" (120).

Dick Humbird's ghost, as it turns out, is a curious combination of good and evil. On the one hand, it represents the excesses of youth, the seductive power of pleasure, and the rejection of conformity. Humbird dies, after all, following a riotous adventure in New York. On the other hand, it functions in an odd way as a sort of conscience. Confronted with this image of his own dark self, Amory withdraws from the edge, as he does later in a similar situation with Eleanor. As much guardian angel as evil demon, then, Dick Humbird's ghost evokes a fundamental morality that connects Amory to the past and thereby saves him from self-destruction.

Amory and his Princeton classmates joke about the ghosts that haunt their lives, laughing that they can be easily dispatched with a stick (139). Burne Holiday, however, is more realistic about the need to face them. Any imaginative person, Burne tells Amory, is bound to have demons, to "[people] the woods with everything ghastly" (134). By an effort of will, however, it is possible for such a person to master the horrors in the dark. The trick is to stick one's imagination into the dark and to recognize that the horrors are self-created (134). Yet in the end, Amory comes to believe that present fears are the product of previous experience and that the vague, insubstantial thing that is a human being is itself little more than a ghost. In fact, as he bids good-bye to Mr. Ferrenby late in the novel, Amory reflects with amazement, "What ghosts were people with which to work!" (281).

The ghost in *This Side of Paradise* is, then, a trace of the past, an image of the future, and a constant reminder of the diminished thing that is humanity. Yet Amory's final reflection about the ghost's significance clearly reveals the ambivalence at the heart of Fitzgerald's hero and novel. On the one hand, it reflects the cynicism of the new generation loosed from its moorings and dedicated to nothing so much as its own success. On the other hand, diminished thing or not, humanity is something with which to work, and therein lies its promise. Amory, by the end of the novel, may be alone in the "labyrinth" (267, 268), seemingly lost in the maze of his own disillusionment, but when he emerges from its tangled pathways (that is, when he thinks his way through his own confusion), he will find again in his fundamental self the will to dream on.

A FEMINIST INTERPRETATION

This Side of Paradise, as Malcolm Bradbury asserts, "follow[s] the period vogue for young man's novels" (84), and Amory Blaine's world is indeed a masculine one, filled with the sort of male camaraderie that relegates women to supporting roles. Certainly women figure prominently in Amory's life, but primarily as idealized conceptions of desire. Seldom does Fitzgerald render the reality of their lives or the complexity of their thoughts. His treatment of women may seem inconsequential to many readers, but to the feminist critic, who looks at literature through the lens of gender roles and gender expectations, it raises serious issues about Fitzgerald's world and serious questions about his vision.

To understand the perspective of the feminist critic, we must first consider the word "feminism," a term everyone recognizes but one that few can define clearly and with uniform agreement. Feminist criticism does not include all literary criticism written by women, since not all women are feminists, and it does not include all criticism written by feminists because they may view a literary work from any theoretical perspective. The characteristic common to feminist criticism is its concern for the impact of gender on reading and writing. To determine that impact, it examines not only the concerns of literature, but also sociological, political, and economic ideas. "The feminist critique," as literary critic Elaine Showalter notes, "is essentially political and polemical" ("Poetics" 129), and thus it suggests alternatives to tradition.

Histories of feminist criticism usually divide it into three broad phases. The first involves analysis of patriarchal culture, a term for the institutions, attitudes, and beliefs of a society dominated by men. It examines as well the woman as reader of works by men and by other women, exploring the way in which "the hypothesis of a female reader changes our apprehension of" the literary text (Showalter, "Poetics" 128). This critique has led to enlightening new interpretations of classics previously evaluated only by male critics with tradi-tional patriarchal attitudes. Some critics, however, caution against the poten-tial dangers of such readings, arguing that the social and historical contexts of a literary work are essential to understanding the author's choices.

The second phase of feminist literary criticism has concerned itself with women as writers giving expression to the female experience through their work. This focus led to the recovery of many forgotten works by women and to a new understanding of the struggles women writers faced to express their own visions and experiences in a patriarchal society that discounted them.

Both of these phases of feminist criticism constitute what in recent years has been termed "gender studies." Both also share the idea that gender difference determines much about a person's life experience and thus about one's means of communicating, reading, or writing. A third phase of feminist criticism fo-cuses on the similarities between men and women and argues that emphasizing differences is a tactic used by men to exclude and oppress women. These critics stress instead the humanity of all people, regardless of gender. They believe that the only way to achieve equality is to deny that fundamental differences be-tween men and women exist.

Whatever the critical stance, feminist critics do seem to share one impor-tant idea about literary criticism: the impossibility of achieving objectivity. For years, critics believed that the author's personal history, the social expectations of his or her time, and the historical events that transpired during the author's life had no bearing on understanding literary works. Feminist critics believe that such objectivity is impossible. Instead, they promote subjectivity, responses based on experience and belief. They recognize that every reader brings both aspects to the literary work and thus understands literature from a personal perspective.

The women in *This Side of Paradise* are primarily projections of Amory Blaine's desire. In their beauty Amory sees an image of perfection that repre-sents the fulfillment of his dreams. As he tells Rosalind, the primary object of his desire, "Beauty means the agony of sacrifice and the end of agony" (192). It is, in other words, an ideal that gives hope and meaning to his world and thereby one worth suffering to attain.

As objects of desire, Fitzgerald's women are expensive commodities. Money makes possible their beauty, draping it in fashionable frocks, adorning it in glit-tering jewels, and allowing its object to worry, as Rosalind confesses to Amory, only about "whether my legs will get slick and brown when I swim in the sum-mer" (199). Money is the price of possessing them. Rosalind, for example, breaks off her relationship with Amory because she knows that poverty will de-stroy the beautiful illusion that is its basis. Without the trappings of material wealth, Rosalind will be a different sort of woman, not the sort that Amory could love (197–199).

Ever the romantic, Amory is unwilling to accept Rosalind's clearsighted assessment of their situation, yet she is correct in her understanding of her worth. She knows, as the majority of the novel's women do, that her human value is extrinsic, not intrinsic; it resides in the superficialities of her manners and appearance rather than in the quality of her thought and actions. She is "Rosalind Unlimited," on offer to the world: "Fiftyone shares, name, good-will, and everything goes at $25,000 a year" (178). This knowledge makes her hard and brittle, impervious to Amory's appeals, however much she would like to indulge her own romantic desires and marry him.

Rosalind's understanding brings into sharp relief truths that have been largely implied in Fitzgerald's characterizations of Beatrice Blaine and Clara Page and foreshadows the dark significance of Eleanor Savage. Each woman, in her own way, is a symbol of blighted possibility. Filled with dreams of their own, they discover few avenues of experience open to them because they are expected to fulfill the dreams of others. In consequence, they grow selfish or cynical as a defense against their own disappointment.

Beatrice Blaine, Amory's mother, is a clever woman, perhaps not as clever as she thinks, but aware of her world and mistress of it. Educated as a girl in the nuances of that world by traveling throughout Europe, she can make small talk with cardinals and queens and has learned "to prefer whiskey and soda to wine" (12). Despite its expense and novelty, hers has been, in other words, an education in style rather than substance, one "barren of all ideas" (12), more, certainly, than would be afforded most girls but less than her male counterparts could expect. Such an education, however, leaves Beatrice little more to do than marry well (which she does), produce an heir (which she does), and cultivate her own selfishness (which she does). "Weary" and "sad" about her own life (12), she plays the hypochondriac to control her existence and escapes into alcohol when she can bear it no longer (16). Untutored in any meaningful occupation or beliefs, Beatrice is the pathetic product of a previous generation. Given the changing world into which Amory and the women he loves are born, the expectations for them might be different. But only in matters of sexuality do Rosalind or Eleanor seem more free than Beatrice, and such freedom is little compensation for almost equally shallow existences.

While Rosalind grows as selfish and manipulative as Beatrice under the influence of her own knowledge of blighted possibility, Eleanor Savage, as her name suggests, grows wild and cynical. "One of those people who go through the world giving other people thrills" (231), Eleanor and Amory meet in the midst of a tumultuous thunderstorm that foreshadows their brief, but intense and wickedly frightening relationship. A girl with a past (235), Eleanor is rebellious and recalcitrant, and her most passionate outbursts are focused on the injustices of her sex. "Oh, why am I a girl?" she rages to Amory. "You can do anything and be justified—and here I am with the brains to do everything, yet tied to the sinking ship of future matrimony" (240). Marriage, perhaps, Eleanor could accept, but the cost of her groom is high: "I'm too bright for most men," she proclaims, "and yet I have to descend to their level and let them patronize my intellect in order to get their attention" (240).

Eleanor's assessment of her life may lack humility and certainly indicates a lack of courage because she seems unwilling to reject the expectation of marriage. It does not, however, lack truth, and the proof lies in the experiences of Clara Page, a widow with two small children and no intention, at the age of twenty-six, of marrying again. As docile as Eleanor is wild, Clara is goodness personified, and she has the ability to inspire others, including Amory, to her own example (141). While her marriage may have been happy, she seems to suffer little pain about its sad end (144); her two daughters are adequate compensation for her loss (if loss it actually were). Widowhood, in fact, quite suits Clara, for it has allowed her to have her own life.

From the age of sixteen, Clara had lived a "harried life . . . and her education had stopped sharply with her leisure" (143). Given her background and her age and present situation, it seems likely that marriage had been a refuge for her, perhaps the only option out of a difficult situation. This implication gains force when Clara confides to Amory that "if it weren't for my face I'd be a quiet nun in the convent" (149). Beauty may have saved her from physical hardship, in other words, but it has prevented her from having the life she might have preferred. In this context, widowhood is indeed liberating because it frees her from the gender expectations under which Eleanor chafes. Clara does not have to conceal her intelligence and wit to win a husband. Instead, she can selfishly be herself.

Fitzgerald's women provide adequate proof that the generational changes so liberating to Amory and his Princeton classmates left virtually unchallenged expectations for women. Granted, the new woman embraced a sexual freedom that was still considered shocking, and she developed a rather polished veneer, a sort of masculine toughness, to distinguish herself from the soft femininity of a previous age. She became, in other words, the flapper or the vamp epitomized by Isabelle and Rosalind. Yet, despite her "liberation," the new woman is still expected to give herself to marriage, and she remains the projection of male desire, as the attitudes of Amory and his classmates make patently clear. If beauty is the commodity on sale, then Fitzgerald's women remain quite willing to pay the price. Their world is, after all, a gentleman's club, and they are its exclusive members. If it has taught them nothing else, their privileged education has taught them this lesson.

In the end, of course, Amory can only be disillusioned by the collapse of his ideal. Embodied as it is in human imperfection, it is, in fact, bound to fail, and so he renounces beauty. "Weak" and feminine, it is a deception that inevitably "leered out at him with the grotesque face of evil" (283), an evil more potent than the "strong phallic worship" (283) he is also beginning to doubt. Its renunciation may prevent him from being "a certain type of artist," but it will, he believes, permit him to become "a certain sort of man" (283). The choice sets Amory once more on his quest for his own possibility.

This Side of Paradise is not a great novel, but like its hero, it promises much. Amory takes himself so seriously that his emotions, as Richard Lehan correctly observes, "are heightened to the point of outrageous sentimentality or they are cynical to the point of pretension" (67). They could certainly be tempered by a good dose of irony. In fact, Fitzgerald will himself eventually pronounce his novel "one of the funniest books since [Oscar Wilde's *The Picture of*] *Dorian Gray* in its utter speciousness" (*Dear Scott/Dear Max* 245). Fitzgerald's style, moreover, is self-consciously literary, clearly the work of a novice, and his characters are clichés. None of them, including Amory, has much depth. Yet taken on its own terms, *This Side of Paradise* does indeed capture the hopes and fears of a generation faced with the challenges of modernity, and it stakes out the territory that Fitzgerald will explore in subsequent novels.

4

The Beautiful
and Damned
(1922)

If in *This Side of Paradise*, Amory Blaine's quest for life's meaning is a paean to possibility, then in *The Beautiful and Damned* Anthony and Gloria Patch's descent into self-absorbed paralysis is a dirge to disillusionment and human waste. F. Scott Fitzgerald's second novel is, in other words, the perfect complement to his first. In his first novel, Fitzgerald had captured the spirit of an age in the adolescent posturing of a romantic egotist determined to possess the grand destiny that he knew awaited him. A tale of yearning, it was in its exuberance a novel that defined a new era in and announced a new perspective on American life through its hero's efforts to discard an outmoded set of values and to recast their replacements according to his own vision. It ends at the beginning, just at the point where Amory is prepared to move forward into the wide world beyond Princeton's spires and gargoyles.

The Beautiful and Damned begins at that ending. Anthony Patch, its protagonist, or central character, is ready as well to embrace his destiny. He is not, however, prepared to step beyond the rarified atmosphere of his own insular world to attain it. Preferring instead to wait for his destiny to happen, Anthony sits in ironical judgment of the world, unwilling to exert himself because he sees such effort as futile and unable because he lacks the courage to do the "next thing" (*Paradise* 68). To do so would be to acknowledge the ordinary, to accept limitation. *The Beautiful and Damned* is thus an exploration of life's meaninglessness and of the decay of character that results from such a point of view.

Set in the same prewar to postwar period (1910–1920) of Fitzgerald's first novel, *The Beautiful and Damned* charts the journey of a degenerating hero and a disintegrating marriage, the result of squandered talent and reckless freedom. Harvard educated and an aspiring aesthete, Anthony Patch spends his golden youth waiting for the inheritance that will make possible the life that his wit and style deserve. When he finds his spiritual twin in Gloria Gilbert, Anthony, for the first and only time in his life, pursues the object of his desire until he attains it. Their marriage, which begins as a glamorous performance based on the premise that they will one day meet their wonderful destiny, soon deteriorates into an alcoholic nightmare, and both Anthony and Gloria find themselves imprisoned in their false illusions. Unable and unwilling to discard their dreams, they spiral ever downward into dissipation, squandering their youth and beauty in moral carelessness. By the time the elusive inheritance comes, they and their marriage are empty shells, and the money can do nothing but gild their surfaces. It cannot save them, in other words, from their own damnation.

GENESIS AND CRITICAL RECEPTION

In style, tone, and intent, *The Beautiful and Damned* is far different from *This Side of Paradise*. Although they share certain perspectives and character types, "the earlier novel," as biographer Jeffrey Meyers asserts, "is witty, flippant and lighthearted, the later . . . ponderous and tragic, twice as long, less 'literary' and more static" (85–86). Fitzgerald's own description of the novel's plot may provide some clue to these differences. "My new novel," he wrote to Charles Scribner, his publisher, in August 1920, "called 'The Flight of the Rocket,' concerns the life of one Anthony Patch. . . . He is one of those many with the tastes and weaknesses of an artist but with no actual creative inspiration. How he and his beautiful young wife are wrecked on the shoals of dissipation is told in the story" (*Life in Letters* 41). Although the novel's plot, as Fitzgerald acknowledged, was "sordid" (*Life in Letters* 145), that very quality, as his shipwreck metaphor suggests, seemed to have fired his imagination. This novel, as its working title suggests, was intended to examine a brief but intense ascent of power, one that contained in its rise its inevitable fall. In its conception, *The Beautiful and Damned* was a darker novel than *This Side of Paradise*. It demanded a different style, a different tone.

One of the stories that Fitzgerald published in 1922, "The Diamond as Big as the Ritz," gives some evidence of the tragic vision that shaped his perception of the world during the composition of *The Beautiful and Damned*. The story of the fall of the richest family in the United States (if not the world), the Washingtons, it is a fable cast as a fantasy, a cautionary tale about the underside of great wealth. When John T. Unger, the story's protagonist, accepts his friend Percy Washington's invitation to visit his family home during their summer holiday from school, little does he suspect the fate that awaits him. Set amid a Montana landscape that language such as "gigantic bruise," "poisoned sky," and "coagulated into dark" (*Short Stories* 185, 186) makes eerily menacing, the Washington mansion sits atop an intricate maze of subterranean passages, including a deep pit covered by an iron grating in which Percy's father keeps imprisoned any unfortunate aviators who violate his airspace. The reason for such extreme behavior is the need to protect the secret about the source of the family's wealth—an enormous diamond that cannot be sold without destroying the economic foundations of the world. The diamond has conferred upon the Washingtons tremendous, but useless, wealth. It has also led to their moral corruption. Percy's grandfather had murdered his brother, "whose unfortunate habit of drinking himself into an indiscreet stupor" (*Short Stories* 194) threatened the family secret, and his sisters take as a matter of course, as Unger learns too late, the fact that any friends invited to visit their home will never leave it.

Unger, however, who falls in love with Percy's sister Kismine, is more fortunate than the Washingtons' other school chums. Initially dazzled by their wealth, he gradually understands that it has trapped and corrupted the family. In fact, he even witnesses Percy's father offering a futile bribe to God to save them from destruction. When the diamond mountain explodes, Unger escapes his intended fate, or kismet, with Kismine, who has so little regard for property that she inadvertently stuffs her pockets with rhinestones rather than diamonds as they flee the conflagration, thereby rendering them poor but virtuous at the story's end. Fitzgerald, however, undercuts any of the story's optimism by making it clear that Unger has only half-learned the lesson of the Washingtons: Without the diamonds to sustain them, a disillusioned and despairing Unger knows that he will be unable to love Kismine for more than a few years.

Greed obscene and corrupting is the destructive force in "The Diamond as Big as the Ritz." The Washingtons' great wealth brings them neither happiness nor security, and it perverts the very notion of culture and of human values such as freedom and autonomy. This perspective lies at the heart of *The Beautiful and Damned* as well, exemplified in the progressive coarsening of Anthony and Gloria Patch and the inevitable deterioration of the grand illusions that even money cannot sustain. The story's satiric and ironic edge also corresponds to a similar tone, or authorial stance, in the novel. The Washingtons, as their name implies, evoke America's founding fathers just as Adam Patch, as the analysis of his character will make clear, evokes the first man in the mythic New World that signifies America for its Puritan forebears and their descendants. Fitzgerald's evocation of this mythical dimension transforms his works into allegories, or stories with a moral, about the American Dream. In effect, Fitzgerald condemns the vulgarization of the dream, the perverse corruption in the greedy pursuit of wealth and material possessions of its highest ideals and sustaining vision, and thus both works make clear the development of his thinking in the aftermath of his first phenomenal success. In two short years, he knew already its inevitable cost.

Published on March 4, 1922, *The Beautiful and Damned* secured for Fitzgerald both popular and critical success. In *The Smart Set*, H. L. Mencken praised its "fine observation" and "penetrating detail" (Bryer, *Reputation* 107), and John Peale Bishop, one of his former Princeton classmates whose opinion Fitzgerald valued, concluded his review in the *New York Herald* by observing, "Fitzgerald is at the moment of announcing the meaninglessness of life magnificently alive" (Bryer, *Reputation* 74). Perhaps the most spirited review, however, and certainly the most unique, was penned by Fitzgerald's wife Zelda, the model for Gloria, the novel's "Beautiful Lady without Mercy," a second working title.

Writing in the *New York Tribune*, Zelda urged readers to purchase the book so that Fitzgerald could buy a new overcoat and she could have the expensive gold dress and platinum ring with complete circlet that she desired. She then revealed that her husband had, with her permission, incorporated into the novel edited portions of her diary and playfully complained, "Mr. Fitzgerald—I believe that is how he spells his name—seems to believe that plagiarism begins at home" (Bryer, *Reputation* 111). Zelda's review made patently clear what critics certainly recognize about Fitzgerald's fiction—its autobiographical nature.

Indeed, *The Beautiful and Damned* reflects many elements of Fitzgerald's own marriage to Zelda. She was, of course, the model for Gloria Patch, although as Fitzgerald lovingly explained to their daughter Scottie years later, "We had a much better time than Anthony and Gloria had" (*Life in Letters* 453). That "better time," in fact, fueled by the wealth and sudden fame that followed the publication of *This Side of Paradise*, defined their early married life. Raucous parties, madcap behavior, wild and well-publicized pranks, and drinking, always drinking, made Scott and Zelda the very models for Anthony and Gloria Patch. The facts of their lives—their life in Westport, Connecticut, where they spent their first months of marriage, a quarrel by the railroad tracks, an offer to star in the film version of *This Side of Paradise*, Zelda's decision to have her first abortion (Meyers 87–88)— Fitzgerald transmuted into the stuff of fiction and mined for their meaning and significance. What he found were dissolution, decay, and the bleak demise of perfection in the hedonistic attempt to escape meaninglessness.

PLOT DEVELOPMENT

The plot of *The Beautiful and Damned* is linear, mirroring Anthony and Gloria Patch's relentless march toward degeneration. Each of the novel's three books, which are themselves divided into three chapters, dramatizes a segment of their lives. There are few deviations in the straightforward movement of the events, perhaps because Anthony and Gloria are so constituted as to be ever looking to the future. They know that a bright destiny awaits them, and they live always in expectation of it. Indeed, the plot's very symmetry reinforces this view.

Book One focuses on the certainties of youth. Chapter One, entitled "Anthony Patch," introduces Fitzgerald's twenty-five-year-old protagonist, or central character, and his two college friends, Maury Noble and Richard (Dick) Caramel. Two brief flashbacks relate the events of Anthony's formative years and the chief influences on his character: his grandfather, the self-made millionaire Adam Patch, and the appeal of an ideal of Beauty, the physical manifestation of which Anthony discovers in Chapter Two. In that chapter, Fitzgerald renders his "Portrait of a Siren," twenty-two-year-old Gloria Gilbert, who captures Anthony's heart. Their courtship is the focus of Chapter Three, "The Connoisseur of Kisses." Although Anthony is intent on winning Gloria, he engages in a flirtation with Geraldine Burke, an usher at a motion picture theater. Gloria similarly enjoys the attentions of Joseph Bloeckman. Following a temporary break-up of their relationship when Gloria refuses to kiss Anthony a second time, they reunite in the certainty of their love.

Book Two moves the Patches from the sureties of youth to the complexities of adulthood. That journey begins in Chapter One, "The Radiant Hour," with all the promise of a beautiful future that an engagement and wedding signify. Within the first six months of their marriage, however, Anthony and Gloria discover the irritation of living with each other's flaws. Indeed, as they travel across the country on their honeymoon trip, already disappointment creeps into their marriage. After concluding their wedding trip with a disastrous visit to Washington, D.C., and to Robert E. Lee's Arlington, Virginia, home, the Patches drive about the affluent New York suburbs in a dilapidated automobile, searching for a home of their own, one that suits their vision of themselves, but they can only afford to rent a gray house in an unfashionable suburb. Diminished expectations come all too soon and are all too real for the Patches.

Chapter Two, entitled "The Symposium," is the novel's center. Their lives a continual drunken party lived in expectation of Anthony's inheritance, Anthony and Gloria struggle financially to maintain their lifestyle. Anthony rouses himself briefly to take a job, but abruptly quits it. Shortly thereafter, he and Gloria have a terrible argument, and during a long, alcohol-fueled philosophical discussion, Maury Noble articulates some unpleasant truths about life—and Gloria—to Anthony. Their marriage will never be the same following this confrontation, and any hope of repair is dashed in Chapter Three, "The Broken Lute," when Adam Patch, who has become a moral reformer, interrupts a drunken party at his grandson's home. At Adam's death, Anthony and Gloria learn that their worst fears have indeed come true: They have been disinherited. By their third wedding anniversary, Anthony has been drafted into the army, and their marriage is floundering on the shoals of dissipation and disappointment.

The first two chapters of Book Three, each of which focuses primarily on one of the marriage partners and not the united couple, structurally reinforces the apparent collapse of the Patch relationship and their lives. In Chapter One, "A Matter of Civilization," Anthony endures basic training in the expectation that he will rise to the rank of officer. Then, what is for him a casual affair with a local working-class girl, Dorothy Raycroft, leads to unforeseen complications and a careless breach of military discipline. Reduced in rank by the war's end, Anthony returns to Gloria, only to discover that she, too, has been living another life. The central event is detailed in Chapter Two, "A Matter of Aesthetics." Her twenty-ninth birthday approaching, Gloria determines to pursue Joseph Bloeckman's, now Black's, offer of a screen test. The successful owner of Films Par Excellence, however, cannot erase the physical effects of careless living from her once beautiful face, and when he offers her not the ingenue's part, but the role of a rich widow, Gloria is devastated. Only their mutual misery and disappointment and their legal efforts to reverse the terms of Adam's will unite Anthony and Gloria.

One year later, however, in the novel's final chapter, "No matter!," Anthony and Gloria achieve what they believe is their vindication. Although Anthony has alienated his old friends Maury Noble and Dick Caramel and suffered a beating at the hands of Joseph Black, he triumphs in court and secures his long-anticipated inheritance. The novel ends with a careworn but fur-draped Gloria and a wheelchair-bound Anthony, mere shells of their former selves, sailing away to the life that they always knew would be theirs, beginning yet another episode in their relentless passage into the future. As Fitzgerald's linear plot has made clear, there is simply no turning back for the Patches.

CHARACTER DEVELOPMENT

The chief player in this drama, Anthony Comstock Patch, possesses every advantage for success. The grandson of a self-made millionaire and one of the wealthiest men in America, he lives in expectation of inheriting that fortune and is thus secure in his future. His innate intelligence polished by a Harvard education and European travel, he needs only to choose a career to make it his. "Cheerful, pleasant, and very attractive to intelligent men and to all women," he expects "one day [to] accomplish some quiet subtle thing that the elect would deem worthy" (3). Expectation, clearly, is a key element of Anthony's character, and this quality makes him yet another of Fitzgerald's romantic ego-tists. In the deep recesses of his soul, Anthony, too, knows "the faint winds, the illusions, the eternal present with its promise of romance" (329).

In these basic outlines of character, Anthony is virtually an extension of *This Side of Paradise*'s Amory Blaine, and thus his life completes the *bildungsroman*, or novel of development or education (defined more fully in Chapter 3), begun in the previous work. Yet as literary critic Milton R. Stern observes, "Anthony Patch, the romantic egotist, is hardly the avatar of Amory Blaine, the person-age; his career is not the one promised by the materials and life-story intro-duced in *This Side of Paradise*" (*Moment* 115). Anthony's education ends, in other words, not in self-knowledge and vocation, the traditional outcomes of *bildung*, but in self-deception and aimlessness.

Anthony's chief difference from Amory lies in his attitude toward life. Whereas Amory is all seriousness and lacks any sense of irony, Anthony wears his like a badge of honor. Irony is, for Anthony, "the final polish of the shoe, the ultimate dab of the clothes-brush, a sort of intellectual 'There!' " (3) that dis-tinguishes him from the merely clever of his world. Irony gives Anthony's char-acter an edge, something that Amory's never developed. It makes him cynical and contemptuous of ordinary life. Although his ironical attitude is little more than a pose when Anthony is twenty-five, the point at which his tale begins, it hardens into pessimism as he expends the promise of his own life in eight brief years.

Anthony also lacks the resiliency of Amory. Whereas Amory's disappoint-ments are inevitably followed by yet another attempt to achieve his bright des-tiny, Anthony's inevitably reveal a failure of nerve and imagination that aborts almost any purposeful action. Early in their marriage, for instance, Gloria dis-covers her husband's weakness when she awakens one night to find Anthony, a victim of his own night terrors, telephoning the house detective to investigate a sound at their hotel window, fifty feet above a "sheer fall" (159) to the street. Shamed by his cowardice, she is, however, more keenly disappointed by his fabrication of a lie to explain his actions (157–161). Years later, Anthony's fail-ure of nerve is compounded by his failure of imagination. As they drift into debt and dissolution, he can think of no way to save them. Anthony's repeated "What am I going to do!" (210) is the refrain to their existence, but he seems to think that someone other than himself will write the verse and tune. From time to time, Gloria will intimidate him into action, such as his inept attempt at sell-ing "Heart Talks" bonds (377–388), but ultimately, his own solution to tem-porary poverty—pawning his watch, at which he also fails miserably—reveals just how impoverished he has become. In Anthony, failure of nerve and imagi-nation becomes paralysis of hope and action.

Wealth and the promise of greater wealth make Anthony an "ineffectual idler" (211). Contemptuous of all work because nothing is worth the effort, he dabbles at a writing career, producing an essay on medieval history for an esoteric journal and several short stories that are rejected by every publisher (300–303). He also rejects his grandfather's offer to become a war correspondent (206) and quits within days a job as a stock broker (228–231). Even his military service Anthony fails to take seriously and as a result finds himself demoted in rank and denied admission to officers' training school (350). It does not matter that his friends are fashioning their own careers or that he is frequently bored by his leisure. To Anthony, the very notion of material success is "appalling," for it represents compromise and limitation (231).

When he meets Gloria Gilbert, Anthony finds the "something" (55) that he has wanted in his life. In her he sees the "path of hope" (55), "the end of all restlessness, all malcontent" (107). The pampered daughter of a Midwestern businessman and his ineffectual wife, Gloria takes "all the things of life for hers to choose from and apportion, as though she were continually picking out presents for herself from an inexhaustible counter" (62). Selfish and self-centered, she has the courage to seize the moment, the passion to live, and the "unwavering indifference" (116) to be utterly herself. Like *This Side of Paradise*'s Rosalind Connage, she is the epitome of Beauty, which inhabits her form at birth (27–30); she is an ideal of perfection "*for, in her, soul and spirit were one—the beauty of her body was the essence of her soul*" (27). In Gloria, Anthony finds his spiritual "twin" (131), and he simply must possess her "triumphant soul. . . . She was beautiful—but especially she was without mercy. He must own that strength that could send him away" (116). Bewitched like the knight-errant in John Keats's poem "Les Belle dan Sans Merci" (the beautiful lady without mercy), to which Fitzgerald obviously alludes in this passage, Anthony, for the first and only time is his life, musters the force of character to capture the object of his desire, which, ironically, leads to his damnation.

Gloria may be the embodiment of Anthony's ideal, but she is also lazy, childish, and completely self-absorbed. Nibbling gumdrops to relieve boredom (48), she is her favorite topic of conversation (48, 60, 61), and she asks nothing more from life than to be the center of her world. As she confesses to Anthony, "I want to just be lazy and I want some of the people around me doing things, because that makes me feel comfortable and safe—and I want some of them doing nothing at all, because they can be graceful and companionable for me" (66). During their honeymoon, Anthony discovers that Gloria has not lied. Their hotel rooms littered with soiled lingerie, stockings, dresses, and pajamas, Gloria simply cannot be bothered to rouse herself to ring for the maid to collect their laundry (163–165). She also has temper tantrums when she is crossed. On one occasion, when she is served a tomato stuffed with chicken salad rather than celery, Gloria pounds her fists on the table and complains bitterly that she cannot eat "stuff" (161). Resisting like a recalcitrant child Anthony's best efforts to cajole her into good humor, she sullenly picks at the salad, only to discover, to her husband's silent glee, that she can indeed eat it and that she may, in fact, like it (161–162).

Throughout their marriage, only Gloria's beauty changes. The essential elements of her character remain intact. Her aimlessness, for instance, causes her to postpone the offer of a screen test until her faded beauty makes impossible the role of ingenue that she envisions for herself (403–404). Similarly, self-love lies behind her decision to abort her pregnancy (203–205). Child-bearing is simply too real, too earthy, for Gloria's ethereal beauty (392). Even as they drift toward ruin, Gloria feels cruelly abused because she cannot have the gray squirrel fur coat that is all the fashion that season (389–390). The "wise and lovely Gloria," Maury Noble, Anthony's former classmate, proclaims in one of the novel's key scenes, was "born knowing" what he himself only recently learned: "the tremendous importance of myself to me, . . . the necessity of acknowledging that importance to myself, . . . and the painful futility of trying to know anything else" (257). It is this knowledge that gives Gloria her edge, that makes her the perfect counterpart to her husband.

Because neither Anthony nor Gloria represents reality for each other, their marriage is doomed from its beginning. Anthony wishes to possess an ideal; Gloria simply wants the freedom to be that ideal and expects her husband to make it possible. The conflict between these competing desires surfaces shortly after their honeymoon, when they make their only real attempt to settle into conventional life in the gray house. One lazy summer day, Anthony determines to bend Gloria to his will because he believes that "for a whim she had deprived him of a pleasure" (198). For once, Anthony, who feels that he always submits to his wife's desires, intends to make Gloria do as he wishes, to make her feel his power as he feels hers: "Then Anthony knew what he wanted—to assert his will against this cool and impervious girl, to obtain with one magnificent effort a mastery that seemed infinitely desirable" (197). Their struggle for dominance escalating, Anthony finally seizes Gloria's arm and prevents her from boarding the train that will take her home in victory, but his triumph is costly.

Although Anthony is convinced that Gloria will eventually "admire him for his dominance" (199), he has failed to understand the nature of his own desire. Gloria's appeal is her selfishness, her imperviousness to the will of others. When he bends her will to his, he destroys the very thing that makes her desirable: "it was yet problematical whether Gloria without her arrogance, her independence, her virginal confidence and courage, would be the girl of his glory, the radiant woman who was precious and charming because she was ineffably, triumphantly herself" (201–202). Gloria, who understands the essence of her appeal, knows immediately the consequences of her defeat: their love will be forever changed (202). At some future point, Anthony will realize that what he possesses is a human incarnation of the ideal, not the ideal itself, and he will despise her for her reality and himself for his self-deception. For her part, Gloria will despise him for knowing. Given this foundation, the Patches' marriage must inevitably fall victim to the same cynicism that destroys their every chance for happiness.

As the novel's central characters, Anthony and Gloria carry the weight of and give focus to its developing themes, yet Fitzgerald peoples *The Beautiful and Damned* with secondary characters who reiterate what Milton R. Stern calls the novel's "universe of values" (*Moment* 150). Stern argues that "all the commentary [on the lives of Anthony and Gloria] is provided by only those who participate in and stand out in no way from the drift and pointlessness and irresponsibility of the lives commented upon" (*Moment* 134), and his observation hits the mark. In fact, none of the secondary characters embodies an alternative life that is anymore meaningful than the Patches'.

Adam Patch, the founder (as his name implies) of the family wealth, for instance, represents the world that his grandson despises. Had he been less skilled or less fortunate, he could have been, in fact, nothing more than the grubbing huckster embodied in Sammy Carleton, the salesman who pitches "Heart Talks" pamphlets in a "get-rich-quick" scheme. A ruthless opportunist who has managed to turn everything from service in the Civil War to marriage to financial advancement, Adam amasses a fortune on Wall Street and then hypocritically "consecrates the remainder of his life to the moral regeneration of the world" (4). In this effort, Anthony is his greatest failure. Try as he does to intimidate his grandson into conventional occupation, he cannot do so because Anthony, rejecting the actualities of his society, is impervious to his grandfather's "subtle and sanctimonious browbeating" (16). The teeming masses may consider Adam a "fine example of an American" (94), but to Anthony he is merely a cantankerous impediment to his grandson's beautiful future.

Despite his fortune, Adam's inability to reform his grandson renders his life virtually meaningless. His wealth should have guaranteed him happiness, it should have ensured control, and it should have given significance and value to his life and actions. Anthony's rejection of his world, however, reduces all for which he had worked and all for which he had stood to the squalid grubbing it was at the beginning of his career. When Adam interrupts one of the Patches' riotous parties, he confronts this truth and is repelled by it. Yet his mean-spirited disinheritance of Anthony and the subsequent legal battle for control of his fortune do nothing to reverse it.

The lives of Anthony's closest friends, Maury Noble and Richard (Dick) Caramel, prove equally empty, despite their seeming success in the world. The ironically named Maury Noble is a hopeless cynic who believes only in meaninglessness. Because the universe and society lack purpose, he intends upon leaving Harvard "to use three years in travel, three years in utter leisure—and then to become immensely rich as quickly as possible" (43). He is, in his own way, as self-centered as Gloria, and his philosophical justification of his actions in the "Symposium" at the novel's center makes clear this connection (251–258). Maury spends his three years of leisure as a constant companion to Anthony and Gloria, drinking and carousing with a wild abandon that nearly matches their own, but as they spiral downward into dissolution, Maury begins his pursuit of riches. When the Patches next hear of their friend, in the pages of "Town Tattle," Maury is a successful businessman engaged to marry a wealthy Philadelphia socialite (409). According to Dick Caramel, he has become "a sort of tight-fisted aristocrat" (419), and Anthony, at their final meeting, experiences the full force of this new persona when Maury delivers a cutting blow.

At a chance encounter in front of the Biltmore Hotel, a drunken Anthony desperate for money accosts his friend with the intention of asking for a loan. Maury's "inscrutable feline silence" (433), however, renders Anthony speechless. Before he can compose himself, his friend has helped his companion, a woman wearing an ermine coat, into a waiting taxi, bid a polite farewell to Anthony, and left him standing on the pavement. To Anthony, his expression through the window seems not to have changed "by a shade or a hair" (433). True to form, the former cynic, now cynical aristocrat, will not respond to the plight of another for it does not matter to him. Like Gloria, Maury acknowledges only the imperatives of self, and values such as compassion and sacrifice are meaningless to him. His snub of Anthony is thus neither vindictive nor cruel; it is merely the logical outcome of his cynicism.

Dick Caramel, Anthony's other college mate, offers yet another study in self-deception and moral compromise. Less jaded than either Anthony or Maury, perhaps because his intelligence is facile and superficial, Dick spends a year upon graduation in the slums of New York, following some vague notion of the value of service. Eventually concluding that his efforts would never do more than make "sow-ear purses out of sows' ears" (75), he moves uptown from his room at the Y.M.C.A. to pursue his dream of becoming a writer. Before long, his first novel, "The Demon Lover," has made him both rich and famous, and deservedly so as far as Dick is concerned.

Dick begins his writing career in the belief that art matters (23), but such words from his mouth, as both Anthony and Maury realize and Dick never will, are empty platitudes. A man of good nature but limited imagination, he is a mere recorder of others' lives and witticisms. If his first novel has any merit at all, it is because it chiefly documents the lives of Anthony and Gloria and the new generation that they represent. Fame and fortune are the true lures for Dick, and in their pursuit, he produces a string of novels that are as sticky sweet as his name, all the while clinging to his belief that what he writes does indeed matter. By the novel's conclusion, his deterioration into self-deceived hack writer complete, Dick can smugly claim the high moral ground. After all, as he tells Anthony, "There's nothing I'd violate certain principles for" (420). The irony of his assertion is lost only on himself.

One other secondary character, Joseph Bloeckman, offers evidence of the meaninglessness at the center of all the lives in *The Beautiful and Damned*. An immigrant Jew who "had begun his American career as a peanut vender [*sic*] with a travelling circus" (96), Bloeckman is, by the age of thirty-five, the vice president of Films Par Excellence and the epitome of the American dream of rags to riches. Not surprisingly, given his own rise to fortune, it is Bloeckman who pronounces Adam Patch an American example. In an industry that had discarded "dozens of men with more financial ability, more imagination, and more practical ideas" (97), Bloeckman, by all appearances, seems to have prevailed not because he is talented, but because he is capable of transforming himself. From peanut vendor to "side-show ballyhoo" to "proprietor of a second-class vaudeville house" (96–97), Bloeckman, who understands the popular mind, becomes what he needs to be in the world, even if that means denying what he is and was.

Bloeckman has the position and wealth to gain entry into the world of Anthony and Gloria, but any hopes he has of winning the golden girl can be no more than that. His "bland and consciously tolerant smile of an intellectual among spoiled and callow youth" (100) is a pose that fools nobody. To Gloria, he is "Blockhead" (99), and Anthony smugly pronounces him "underdone" (94). Within several years of the Patches' marriage, however, Bloeckman can hold his own with them for emptiness: "and now the three sit like overoiled machines, without conflict, without fear, without elation, heavily enamelled little figures secure beyond enjoyment" (213). By the time both Gloria and Anthony seek his assistance, he has surpassed them.

As Joseph Black, "a dark suave gentleman, gracefully engaged in the middle forties" (397), Bloeckman is definitely "done." With confident assurance, he can arrange a screen test for the fading Gloria (395–404); with equal aplomb, he can deliver two smashing jabs that dislodge Anthony's teeth and send him sprawling upon the plush carpet of the Boul' Mich' (437). An entrepreneur of illusion, a manufacturer of stars, Bloeckman is himself his greatest creation, so his thrashing of Anthony should matter. Yet the circumstances of their tiff suggest otherwise. That drunk Anthony still has the ability to unmask Bloeckman simply by proclaiming his Jewishness suggests, in fact, that Joseph Black has as much substance as his predecessor. Bloeckman/Black is a hollow man, with only a facade to transform.

If the characters in *The Beautiful and Damned* sound relentlessly bleak, perhaps that is because they are. Corrupted by wealth, false ideals, or their own paralyzing cynicism, none of them has the capacity to grow or change. For most, an aimless pursuit of sensation substitutes for an authentic living of life. With Anthony, we wonder what he ever saw in Gloria. Indeed, we wonder that Anthony was meant to be the hero of the novel, for as that term is generally applied, he has nothing of the heroic about him. Yet the emptiness and meaninglessness of these lives clearly serve Fitzgerald's thematic purpose. Compromised and flawed, they are examples of wasted potential. Moral carelessness and the ravages of time seal their doom.

THEMATIC ISSUES

The epigraph to *The Beautiful and Damned*, "The victors belong to the spoils," with its ironic twist on the conventional cliché, and the novel's very title make clear Fitzgerald's thematic intention. In this world, nothing is what it appears to be. The beautiful, who seem to have within their grasp all that could give life ease, pleasure, and the freedom to enjoy it, know neither goodness nor truth. They are damned by their own cynicism to meaningless pursuit of ease and pleasure. Their spoils in a very real sense spoil them, making them prisoners to their vanity and selfishness. They may in the end have captured the tangible trappings of success, but the price has been high. Proof of this point lies in the novel's final glimpse of Anthony and Gloria Patch.

In the last scene, a sable-coated Gloria and wheelchair-bound Anthony are sailing to vindication in Europe on *The Berengaria*. After years of wrangling in the courts, Anthony has won his lawsuit to reverse his grandfather's will, and the money that had always constituted their future is theirs, and with it the life that they had imagined. Their victory, however, is hollow, for it has not altered their essential selves. Nor has it erased the traces of their dissolution. Nothing, in fact, can conceal the fact that Anthony and Gloria have spent their youth and beauty, their only currency, in vain pursuit of what they already possessed.

Fitzgerald filters the scene through the perceptions of a young couple newly in love who are also making the voyage to Europe. The young couple might very well have been Anthony and Gloria but stand now as a reminder of what they will never be again. The strategy, a shift in point of view, allows Fitzgerald to pronounce judgment on the Patches by relegating them to secondary roles in their own drama. Removed as physical presences from the stage of their greatest triumphs and tragedies, they are little more now than grist for gossip. Removed as centers of consciousness, they are rendered tawdry and tainted by an objective perspective. The shift in point of view thus makes clear how far the Patches have fallen.

The young woman's assessment of Gloria is especially telling because it evokes one of the novel's central metaphors, cleanliness. Throughout *The Beautiful and Damned,* cleanliness is the hallmark of the beautiful, a positive value that stamps it authentic and makes it priceless. As the epitome of Beauty, Gloria is the chief focus of the metaphor. Shortly before their marriage, for instance, Gloria tells Anthony that one of the reasons she loves him is because he is "so clean. You're sort of blowy clean, like I am," she goes on to explain, not like Dick, who is "clean like polished pans." They are instead a second sort of clean: "You and I are clean like streams and winds. I can tell," Gloria concludes, "whenever I see a person whether he is clean, and if so, which kind of clean he is" (131). Cleanliness, to Gloria, is natural and good, and those who lack it, especially women, who "soil easily" (235), are somehow tainted: "Always intensely skeptical of her sex, her judgments were now concerned with the question of whether women were or were not clean. By uncleanliness she meant a variety of things, a lack of pride, a slackness in fibre and, most of all, the unmistakable aura of promiscuity" (234–235). Her anxieties about cleanliness quickened, perhaps, by a nagging fear that the endless party of her marriage is debasing her own freshness, Gloria believes that she can at least avoid contamination by others.

It is ironic, then, that the quality the young woman on the ship first attaches to Gloria is uncleanliness. "I can't stand her," she tells her companion. "She seems sort of—sort of dyed and *unclean,* if you know what I mean. Some people just have that look about them whether they are or not" (448). Only thirty, Gloria, without the "placid confidence of beauty" (472), can do nothing more than simulate it. She may dress it in sable or revive it with bottled color, creams, and unguents, but she cannot conceal the truth. Nor can she be saved from her own judgments.

The objective perspective on the Patches renders ironic not only Gloria's final appearance but also Anthony's final reflections. His thoughts focused on the "insufferable tribulations" (448) he had survived, Anthony smugly congratulates himself for refusing "to submit to mediocrity" and believes himself "justified in his way of life" (449). After all, "the very friends who had been most unkind have come to respect him, to know he had been right all along" (449), and he has, in fact, "[come] through" (449). Yet the man who sits "bundled" (447) in a wheelchair, his mind snapped and his physical independence sapped, obviously lacks the ability to understand his situation clearly or to evaluate himself honestly. The names of Maury Noble and Dick Caramel, for example, are conspicuously absent from the list of visitors who called to bid them bon voyage, in all probability because the "friends" who came called not to acknowledge his *good* fortune but rather in deference to his *fortune*. To the end, Anthony remains a self-deceived poseur, as empty as his philosophy.

The novel's final scene thus makes clear the themes encapsulated in its title and epigraph. It suggests as well a corollary theme: the waste of potential in moral carelessness. Certainly, *The Beautiful and Damned* bears traces of the Naturalism, a literary movement of the late-nineteenth and early twentieth centuries, that Fitzgerald admired in contemporary writers such as Frank Norris and Theodore Dreiser. In their novels, characters were generally the pathetic victims of circumstances and forces over which they had little control and even less understanding. At times, something of this attitude enters Fitzgerald's work. The Patches' downward spiral, for instance, seems to assume a life of its own and gather momentum as it falls. No matter what they do, life conspires against them. The postwar economy shrinks their income as it increases their expenses; the lawsuit drags on interminably in the courts. Fitzgerald's emphasis on environmental determinism, on the role of society in shaping the individual's self and destiny, also bears the traces of Naturalism. At one point, for example, the narrator records that Gloria "was being bent by her environment into a grotesque similitude of a housewife" (424), and Anthony argues that "Aristocracy's only an admission that certain traits which we call fine—courage and honor and beauty and all that sort of thing—can best be developed in a favorable environment, where you don't have the warpings of ignorance and necessity" (407). Yet, in spite of this tendency, Fitzgerald never really compromises his vision that Anthony and Gloria are responsible for their lives.

Every squandered opportunity in their lives, in fact, results from their choices. Anthony, for instance, rejects any number of job offers, and Gloria can blame only herself for postponing her screen test. Contemptuous of mere existence, they choose instead to be "the noisiest and most conspicuous members of the noisiest and most conspicuous party at the Boul' Mich', or the Club Ramée, or at other resorts much less particular about the hilarity of their clientele" (296). If others criticize their choices, no matter. Gloria, in fact, takes as her tenet "not to be sorry, not to loose one cry of regret, to live according to a clear code of honor toward each other, and to seek the moment's happiness as fervently and persistently as possible" (226). Eventually, however, the consequences of their choices make them careless of themselves and others. Too many drinks on too many nights sap Gloria's beauty. Too little regard for personal integrity leads Anthony to his "inevitable" affair with Dorothy Raycroft (324). Because they choose stasis in a world of change, failure is inevitable, and all their dreams are wasted.

The novel's biting irony and its bleak tone make clear Fitzgerald's judgment of Anthony and Gloria. One of his letters to Zelda, however, also sheds light on his intention. In the letter, written in 1930, when his wife was again under the care of psychiatrists, Fitzgerald regretfully assessed their life together, concluding with a provocative acknowledgment about his novel and their lives: "I wish the Beautiful and Damned had been a maturely written book because it was all true. We ruined ourselves—I have never honestly thought that we ruined each other" (*Life in Letters* 189). In admitting that his novel may not have been "maturely written" and then coupling that admission to an assertion of personal responsibility, Fitzgerald may have been suggesting a lack of control of his thematic perspective. Because Anthony and Gloria win their lawsuit and acquire thirty million dollars, for instance, Fitzgerald may have seemed to absolve them of responsibility for their ruin. His own assertion of responsibility, however, especially given the novel's autobiographical element, suggests that Anthony and Gloria were intended to bear responsibility for their lives, too.

Behind the Patches' degeneration lies what literary critic and Fitzgerald's former Princeton classmate Edmund Wilson calls their ironical pessimism (32), an attitude that strips life of its meaning. It is also deeply rooted in knowledge of time and change, a fact of existence that makes everything in life mutable and elusive. Anthony's contempt for the conventional lies in his desire for the ideal, but the ideal, he is all too painfully aware, always just exceeds his grasp, disappearing in an instant of time. Robbed of hope, Anthony dons the mask of the cynic until it is ingrained into the fiber of his being. *The Beautiful and Damned* offers a hard examination of this attitude and ultimately a repudiation of it, developing yet another of Fitzgerald's themes.

Early in the novel, Fitzgerald establishes the fact of Anthony's blighted idealism in a scene that emphasizes the appeal of beauty and the despair that results from its elusiveness. Having spent the day in leisurely reading followed by the "drowsy content" (17) of a warm bath, a self-satisfied Anthony prepares to meet Maury and Dick for dinner at the Ritz when "a spot of brilliant color on the roof of a house" (18) arrests his attention. The "spot" Anthony discerns is "a girl in a red negligee, silk surely, drying her hair by the still hot sun of late afternoon. . . . Sitting on the stone parapet beside her was a cushion the same color as her garment and she was leaning both arms upon it as she looked down into the sunny areaway" (18). Captured in an instant of time, the image gives Anthony "a sudden impression that she was beautiful" (18), and he indulges himself by watching her for several minutes.

The impression of beauty briefly transforms Anthony's perspective, heightening his appreciation of the world but inspiring something more, "something not accounted for by the warm smell of the afternoon or the triumphant vividness of red" (18). Anthony recognizes that the girl's appeal resides in her "distance" (18), that she is, in other words, an object of desire, and her beauty the promise of a dream. "Yet for a not altogether explained second," he acknowledges, "posing perversely in time, his emotion had been nearer to adoration than in the deepest kiss he had ever known" (18).

Anthony's response to the appeal of beauty clearly underscores his essential idealism. He is as much a romantic as Amory Blaine. At this point in his life, when he puts on his irony with his jacket and tie, he can also, like Amory, rebound from a recognition that the ideal is both elusive and ephemeral. Turning back to the window just prior to his departure, Anthony now sees the bright spot of color with different eyes. Standing upright with her hair tossed back from her face, the beautiful woman is "fat, full thirty-five, utterly undistinguished" (19). An instant of time had captured Beauty, but the next instant has released it. The ideal has become mere dross. Nevertheless, an undaunted Anthony sallies forth to meet his friends singing the refrain to beautiful ladies that has provided the background accompaniment to the scene, clearly implying his faith in the reality of some other bright spot of color. Over time, however, as his irony hardens about him like a shell, Anthony cannot retain that faith. The fact of time prevents him from doing so.

From his youth, Anthony has known the tyranny of time in the face of death. An orphan at the age of eleven, he understands that "life was a struggle against death, that waited at every corner" (7), and he has lived daily throughout his youth with the vivid incarnation of this truth. His grandfather, Adam Patch, at age seventy-five, is a living cadaver and the very specter of death:

The span of his seventy-five years had acted as a magic bellows—the first quarter-century had blown him full with life, and the last had sucked it all back. It had sucked in the cheeks and the chest and the girth of arm and leg. It had tyrannously demanded his teeth, one by one, suspended his small eyes in dark-bluish sacks, tweaked out his hairs, changed him from gray to white in some places, from pink to yellow in others. . . . Then through his body and his soul it had attacked his brain. (14)

Time, clearly, has been Adam's enemy. No amount of money or will to power is capable of arresting its progress.

Given the fact of time and its inevitable consequences, the ideal, Anthony comes to recognize, can only ever be ephemeral, as fleeting as the moment. This knowledge accounts for his pessimism. This knowledge strips life and human action of meaning. This knowledge prompts Anthony's "loneliness" (93) and results in his aimless drift: "It was a self-absorption with no comfort, a demand for expression with no outlet, a sense of time rushing by, ceaselessly and wastefully—assuaged only by that conviction that there was nothing to waste, because all efforts and attainments were equally valueless" (93). At times, Anthony, "regretting, weakly and secretly, the collapse of an insufficient and wretched idealism," longs for "the old rubbish" (56); at times, he is even "haunted by the suggestion that life might be, after all, significant" (284). Vague nostalgia for a past that never was, however, because it was always already changing, is not enough to overcome Anthony's belief that "desire just cheats you" (341).

In the gray November of her twenties, Gloria, too, knows the tyranny of time because it robs her of Beauty, the foundation of her existence. Beauty has been the only source of meaning in her life. It has given her leave to be selfish and thereby "to weave about her immeasurable illusions, immeasurable distances, immeasurable light" (392). As the epitome of the ideal, she has "wanted to exist only as a conscious flower, prolonging and preserving itself" (392–393) because only in the moment of perfection can the ideal exist and with it her chance for happiness. Yet in the end, Gloria, like Anthony, must admit the fact of time. She must acknowledge that "her beauty was all that ever failed her" (393), and when she does, she, too, feels the vacuum produced by lost idealism. Even her "penchant for premonitions and her bursts of vague supernaturalism" (187) can do nothing more than help her counterfeit belief.

If Anthony and Gloria were different characters, their story could be tragic. Their belief in the ideal could be heroic, their pessimism the result of genuine struggle. But Anthony and Gloria lack humanity and the values attached to it: integrity, honor, compassion, courage. At their lowest point, for instance, they suffer alone together, unable even to care about each other. They also lack the capacity for moral growth. In fact, they confuse the aesthetic and the moral, the sentimental and the profound, and believe to the end that their innate superiority authorizes them to sneer at convention and reject conformity. Because Anthony and Gloria are these characters, their story is merely pathetic and their lives unworthy of pity. In their character lies their damnation, and Fitzgerald never flinches from that truth.

A MARXIST INTERPRETATION

As a record of the period in American history known as the Jazz Age, *The Beautiful and Damned* reveals the class consciousness and class pretensions of a generation facing enormous social change and thus provides the Marxist critic with a field for fertile study. The Marxist critic focuses on the relation between literature and history, emphasizing particularly the social and economic factors that, according to the philosopher Karl Marx (1818–1883), drive historical change. Like feminism, with which it shares some basic tenets, Marxism is not a single theory. In fact, several different schools of Marxist critics exist, and "all of them," according to cultural critic Arthur Asa Berger, "base their criticism on varying and sometimes conflicting interpretations of Marx's theories and how they can be applied to analyzing culture in general and, more specifically, literary texts, works of elite culture, popular culture, and the mass media" (41). To understand Marxist criticism, a brief explanation of the concepts that serve as its foundation is necessary.

Marx believed that historical transformations occur through a dialectic, or development, throughout the stages of thesis, antithesis, and synthesis. Each historical force, according to Marx, calls into being its Other so that the two opposing forces negate each other and eventually give rise to a third force that transcends its opposition.

In Marxism, the ultimate moving force of human history is economics or, perhaps more specifically, political economy. This term encompasses political and social issues as well as economic factors. Each society, according to Marx, bases its culture upon its means of production, the techniques by which it produces food, clothing, shelter, and other necessities of life, and the social relations these methods create. For example, an economy based on manufacturing demands a division of labor, cooperation among workers, and a hierarchical system of managers. These economic demands in turn shape the social relations of the people. From this basic premise, Marx argued that major historical changes occur as a result of economic contradictions, what might be termed class consciousness and class conflict. The source of the French Revolution of the 1790s, for example, was conflict between the aristocracy and the middle classes.

In Marxist thought, the economic base gives rise to and shapes the superstructure, which consists of all the institutions of the society, such as the church, the education system, the art world, and the legal system. Generally, the ideology, which includes literature, conforms to and supports the culture's dominant means of production. Economic conditions alone, however, are not sufficient to explain the development and effect of its institutions. Human agency, or individual consciousness, is active in these institutions as well.

Marxism is primarily a political and economic philosophy, not a guide to understanding literature. As a result, Marxist criticism takes a variety of forms, including analyzing for an understanding of class consciousness and class conflict. Fitzgerald's presentation of American society between the world wars lends itself readily to a Marxist critique. As an imitation of the culture that helped to produce it, *The Beautiful and Damned* reveals the social, political, and economic forces that uphold the privileged world—significant aspects of which are class consciousness and class conflict.

Representatives of the *nouveau riche*, a class of newly rich Americans whose wealth was the consequence of capitalism and not the gift of tradition and inheritance, Anthony and Gloria reveal the anxieties inherent in their status in their own class consciousness and class pretensions. Their fathers and grandfathers were businessmen who had earned their fortunes in trade. They created their own class, their own society, when they were prevented by the representatives of old money from joining the exclusive gentlemen class. The trappings of wealth thus sit uneasily on their shoulders. They may graduate from Harvard and take tea at the Ritz, but such activities, they are all too aware, will never transform them into Van Rennsalaers or Rothschilds or any of the other families of New York's elite Four Hundred. This awareness heightens their own sense of class distinction, making them contemptuous of the very class from which they arose.

Anthony's brief tenure at the firm of Wilson, Hiemer, and Hardy makes patently clear his attitude toward the working class. There, Anthony eats in the employees' lunch room (230) and struggles in vain to learn the "romance of finance" (229), but the labor of the industrious clerks who ply their trade in the hope of attaining success seems to Anthony only unproductive and pointless "striving toward an incomprehensible goal" (229–230). They are deluding themselves if they think that the occasional triumph of one of their number is anything more than luck. Yet such stories, the "gypsy siren to content them with meagre wage and with the arithmetical improbability of their eventual success" (230–231), fuel their dreams and drive their existence. In a matter of weeks, Anthony cannot bear the "appalling" (231) prospect of conforming to this world, with its narrow conception of life and its vision of success embodied not in the freedom to be, but in the building of "triumphal palace[s]" (230), and quits the job. He believes he is made for so much more than this.

Anthony's contempt for the working class makes his affair with Dorothy Raycroft particularly despicable. Beyond the obvious moral issues of his adultery, the affair, with its callous disregard for the integrity of another human being, transforms Dot into a mere thing of use, no different from a table or chair. At nineteen, her reputation tarnished already by rumors of promiscuity, Dot clerks at a jewelry store in the small southern town near the military base where Anthony takes his basic training. Neither intelligent nor clever, she is the kind of person to whom "things happened" (326), and she has little to commend her but a beauty as vague and insubstantial as her thoughts. But in her "lilac gown of frailest organdy" (325), she offers Anthony escape from his own diminished self: "The girl promised rest; the hours in her company each evening alleviated the morbid and inevitably futile poundings of his imagination" (325). Within the darkness of the Bijou Moving Picture Theatre, a fitting site of unreality and manufactured illusion, Anthony drifts into his equally self-deceptive affair with Dot.

Before his marriage to Gloria, Anthony had engaged in casual flirtations with knowing New York working girls, chiefly, it seemed, to amuse himself with a sense of his own superiority. Yet the objects of those flirtations, as his relationship with Geraldine Burke makes clear (85–93), suffered no damage. After all, an usher at a movie theater could hardly expect to become a permanent fixture in a life such as his; she could be quite content, in fact, to amuse herself with him. But an unsophisticated tea shop girl like Dot, to whom Anthony misrepresents his status and who he allows to follow him upon his transfer to another base, is a different matter. Anthony bears responsibility for his callous mistreatment of Dot, yet he would never admit to that fact. Instead, when she appears on his New York doorstep on the day of his expected legal triumph, he threatens to kill this tangible reminder of the tawdry and conventional world that he despises (444–446).

Gloria's disdain for the masses is no less intense than Anthony's, as she reveals during a brief stop in Washington, D.C., on their honeymoon trip. Finding the city symbolic of the country's democratic ideals to be full of "pomp without splendor" (165), they cross the Potomac River in a bus crowded with other tourists for a sightseeing trip to the home of General Robert E. Lee in Arlington, Virginia. The "hot, unprosperous people" (165–166) making the journey particularly arouse Gloria's ire during a brief stop at the zoo, where their "perspiring offspring" imitate the caged monkeys (166). Their behavior at Lee's mansion, where they leave "a trail of peanut shells through the halls" (166), convinces Gloria (if any convincing were needed) that they lack the ability to appreciate what should be the "poignancy" of a decayed monument to past glory but is instead a trumped-up restoration complete with a "Ladies Toilet." "How many of these —these *animals*," Gloria rages to Anthony, "get anything from this, for all the histories and guide-books and restorations in existence?" (167). To the Patches, the working classes are beneath contempt. Their lack of breeding makes them incapable of ever appreciating history and culture. They are fit only for the basest of amusements, and they transform everything into a base amusement.

The Patches' incipient racism is further evidence of the class consciousness that serves as the backdrop to *The Beautiful and Damned*. From the "icy-hearted Scandinavian" who depresses Gloria to the chattering but "exceedingly efficient" Tana (193) to the "big-boned Irish woman" whose talk of Sinn Fein Gloria despises (288), the Patches employ a string of ethnic domestics, but only the Englishman Bounds, a proper manservant, adequately represents their self-image. During his military service, Anthony rubs shoulders with Poles and Italians, indeed the whole polyglot population of America (including some home-grown yokels and Southern blacks). All are prepared, despite their immigrant status and marginal position in American society, to defend a country not yet theirs and are poorly treated for their efforts (331). Yet the experience does nothing to democratize Anthony. Ethnics, people of color, and the working poor are merely stereotypes to the Patches, and contact with them does nothing more than confirm their prejudices. On the rare occasions when Anthony and Gloria take any notice of them at all, they are either dismayed by the "slow, upward creep of this people," in this case, Jewish shopkeepers (283), or drawn by the picturesque qualities of their impoverished existence to transmute them into art objects for their enjoyment (283, 413). Even at their lowest, Anthony and Gloria hold themselves above the many faces of Americans. Certainly that is the point when Anthony hurls the word "Jew" as an epithet in the face of Bloeckman.

The Patches' attitudes are clearly intended to represent those of their class. Maury, Dick, and others of their set hold similar biases and, because they also reflect the authorial voice, reveal a disheartening truth about America's democratic ideal: Everyone, it seems, is aware of class distinctions and strives, in consequence, to attain higher status than his or her neighbors. Everywhere in New York, for instance, are clubs that "[imitate] with a sort of shoddy and mechanical wistfulness the glittering antics of the great cafés in the theatre district" (69). There, "the credulous, sentimental, underpaid, overworked people with hyphenated occupations: book-keepers, ticket-sellers, office-managers, salesmen, and, most of all, clerks" (69) gather in imitation of the rich or the bohemian, of any class with more status than their own. Once there, they engage in petty games of one-upmanship, the women pretend they are "slumming" (70), and everyone is anxious to make the right impression.

Fitzgerald's New York is teeming with such "abandoned people" (70), who know, in the deep recesses of their souls, that they are indeed abandoned. What makes them particularly disturbing to the Patches and their set, who have their own anxieties about class, is that they embody the very flux that makes their status so precarious: "They were forever changing classes, all of them—the women after marrying above their opportunities, the men striking suddenly a magnificent opulence: a sufficiently preposterous advertising scheme, a celestialized ice cream cone" (71). If luck and pluck can transform a Jewish immigrant from peanut vendor to motion picture mogul, then Anthony and Gloria have every reason to be concerned about their own precipitous decline from a luxurious uptown apartment to an undistinguished flat in the "dim hundreds" (405). Social security of the sort that the Patches expect clearly is something beyond their control.

Fitzgerald's depiction of class consciousness ultimately challenges the democratic ideals of American culture and the very myth of America as a New World. Envisioned by its Puritan forebearers as a New Eden, America embodied promise. It was an opportunity for the New Adam to create anew a perfect society founded on sound moral principles. Those principles, as translated by the founding fathers in the seminal documents of American government, included "life, liberty, and the pursuit of happiness," to which was eventually wedded the democratic ideal "to all." These high ideals, however, as Fitzgerald's

Adam clearly conveys, have by the turn of the twentieth century been translated yet again to signify economic opportunity and the pursuit of wealth. The American Dream becomes a dream of material success, and that dream, as Fitzgerald presents it, is virtually bankrupt. Even those who attain it are damned.

In his review of _The Beautiful and Damned_, Edmund Wilson argued for the novel's "moral importance." "The hero and the heroine . . . are creatures," Wilson claimed:

Without method or purpose: they give themselves up to wild debaucheries and do not, from beginning to end, perform a single serious act; but somehow you get the impression that, in spite of their fantastic behavior, Anthony and Gloria Patch are the most rational people in the book. Wherever they come in contact with institutions, with the serious life of their time, these are made to appear ridiculous, they are subjects for scorn or mirth. We see the army, finance and business successively and casually exposed as completely without point or dignity. The inference we are led to draw is that, in such a civilization as this, the sanest and most honorable course is to escape from organized society and live for the excitement of the moment. (34–35)

That "truth," as Wilson calls it, gives Fitzgerald's novel the sharp edge of social criticism, and his critique clearly cuts both ways. Anthony and Gloria and their set offer little to recommend them, but then neither do those who aspire to their status. Corrupted by a dream that is itself a corruption, they chase an illusion that destroys them, whether they know it or not, by rendering their lives meaningless.

Fitzgerald's America is a chaotic mass of teeming humanity and promises unfulfilled. The gap between desire and actuality has been eroded into an uncrossable chasm. Every character in his world settles for less, and therein lies the tragedy of Anthony and Gloria, indeed, of all the immigrants and workers of every race and color who, like them, dream of something more. In this critique, _The Beautiful and Damned_ thus stands as the foundation for Fitzgerald's greatest novel, _The Great Gatsby_.

5

The Great Gatsby
(1925)

The Great Gatsby is F. Scott Fitzgerald's triumph. It is, in fact, an American masterpiece. The story of a poor boy who in pursuit of a dream transforms himself into the image of success, *The Great Gatsby* captures in a work of conscious artistry all the yearning desire and anguished disappointment of its hopelessly romantic hero. Gatsby's story is, however, more than the story of an individual. It is, in fact, the story of America. Gatsby's dream is the American Dream; his successes and failures are America's successes and failures. And in this correspondence, Fitzgerald creates his own version of national tragedy. The promise of a dream lies at the heart of Fitzgerald's American classic, but it is a dream corrupted by money and betrayed by carelessness. *The Great Gatsby* stands as a haunting elegy to its passing.

Set amid a world of glittering wealth during an era, the Jazz Age, that Fitzgerald had claimed as his own, *The Great Gatsby* chronicles the life of a dreamer whose pursuit of an ideal saves him from corruption. As James Gatz, a poor boy from the Midwest, he had dreamed of attaining the wealth that would ensure his success and had even invented a self to accompany it, Jay Gatsby. At seventeen, he sets off to become that self. His journey leads him to a military training camp near Louisville, Kentucky, where his officer's uniform gives him entry to the world of Daisy Fay, who comes to embody, in her beauty and purity and essential aloofness, his dream. For Gatsby, to possess Daisy is to possess the ideal.

When Daisy breaks their engagement to marry Tom Buchanan, Gatsby devotes all his efforts to reclaiming his "golden girl" (127). Amassing a fortune as a bootlegger and stock-sharper or speculator, he settles in West Egg, Long Island, across the bay from the Buchanan mansion and there, night after night, hosts lavish parties to which he hopes to lure Daisy. Frustrated in his efforts, he enlists the help of Daisy's cousin, Nick Carraway, a tenant on his estate, to arrange a reunion that nearly fulfills his desire, but possessing Daisy is not enough. Gatsby must also reclaim the past, and to do so, Daisy must deny her love for her husband Tom. When Daisy fails Gatsby once again, she destroys his dream and then carelessly sets in motion the events that will lead to his death. Great in conception, Gatsby falls victim to a dream that can never be attained in a reality tainted by gross materialism, cold indifference, and moral corruption.

GENESIS AND CRITICAL RECEPTION

Fitzgerald conceptualized his third novel as early as June 1922 with the conscious awareness that he may have been squandering his talent and the determination to reveal himself as the artist he knew he could be. So concerned was Fitzgerald to announce his new artistic seriousness that he insisted in 1924, even before the novel's completion, that its jacket have no "signed blurbs" that would compare this work to his others. "I'm tired of being the author of *This Side of Paradise*," he asserted to his editor, Maxwell Perkins, "and I want to start over" (*Life in Letters* 84).

Nearly another year would elapse before the novel was complete because Fitzgerald, at least in part at the suggestion of Perkins, revised major portions of the text when it was already in galley proofs. Aspects of plot and characterization—how to get his characters to New York and thereby create the conditions for the automobile accident that kills Myrtle Wilson, Tom's lover; how to reveal Gatsby's past without destroying his mystery; how, in fact, to make Gatsby as fully realized a character as Tom Buchanan—prompted Fitzgerald to restructure some portions of the novel and rewrite others (*Life in Letters* 86–89, 91–92, 94–96). Even the novel's title caused Fitzgerald problems. Although he submitted the manuscript with the title *The Great Gatsby*, he considered several others, including "Gold Hatted Gatsby," "The High-Bouncing Lover" (both references to the novel's epigraphs), "Among Ash-Heaps and Millionaires," "On the Road to West Egg," and "Trimalchio in West Egg." When he finally decided on a title, "Under the Red, White, and Blue," and cabled it to Perkins, it was too late to change the plates without delaying publication, so Fitzgerald, in need of money, settled for his original title (*Life in Letters* 85, 95, 98).

During the novel's three-year evolution, Fitzgerald tested some of his material in the short stories that he was writing to support his family. "The Diamond as Big as the Ritz" (1922), "Winter Dreams" (1922), "The Sensible Thing" (1924), and "Dice, Brass Knuckles & Guitar" (1923) bear striking similarities in plot, theme, and characterization to *The Great Gatsby*. So, too, does the story "Absolution" (1924), which "was to have been the prologue of the novel," Fitzgerald informed Perkins, "but it interfered with the neatness of the plan" (*Life in Letters* 76). This *Gatsby* cluster of stories, among his most accomplished, reveals Fitzgerald's efforts to come to terms with his material and to extend his scope beyond his previous work.

In "Winter Dreams," for instance, Dexter Green, a poor boy from the Midwest, falls in love with Judy Jones, a beautiful and wealthy young woman who epitomizes the "glittering" (*Short Stories* 221) world to which he aspires. Aware of his attraction and the power it gives her, Judy cruelly manipulates Dexter, treating him "with interest, with encouragement, with malice, with indifference, with contempt" (*Short Stories* 228). After she rejects him, Dexter becomes engaged to and then abandons another young woman whose only flaw is that she is not Judy Jones. Years later, a disillusioned Dexter learns that Judy is unhappily married and that her beauty, like his dreams of perfection, has faded with time. The knowledge takes from him any vestiges of hope that remain alive: "He had thought that having nothing else to lose he was invulnerable at last but he knew that he had just lost something more. . . . The dream was gone. Something had been taken from him. . . . Even the grief he could have borne was left behind in the country of illusion, of youth, of the richness of life, where his winter dreams had flourished" (*Short Stories* 235–236). A tale of lost hopes and illusory dreams, "Winter Dreams" certainly anticipates the essential themes of *The Great Gatsby*, and so, too, does its emphasis on money and class as insurmountable impediments to the fulfillment of desire.

"The Sensible Thing" reveals a similar working out of *Gatsby's* themes and subject. In this story, George O'Kelly, armed with an engineering degree, is struggling to achieve success in New York in the insurance business so he can marry the girl of his dreams, Jonquil Cary. When Jonquil grows nervous about his prospects, she breaks off their engagement. It is, after all, the "sensible thing" (*Short Stories* 295) in the circumstances. A year later, when a lean, tanned, and successful George O'Kelly, of Cuzco, Peru, calls on Jonquil on his way to another engineering project in New York, the joy of his reunion and eventual reconciliation with Jonquil registers as a diminished thing: "Yet he knew that that boy of fifteen months before had had something, a trust, a warmth that was gone forever. The sensible thing—they had done the sensible thing. He had traded his youth for strength and carved success out of despair. But with his youth, life had carried away the freshness of his love" (*Short Stories* 300). He might now marry this "rare" creature for whom he had struggled to make his own, but he knows, even as he embraces her, that "April is over, April is over. There are all kinds of love in the world, but never the same love twice" (*Short Stories* 301). Time, "The Sensible Thing" makes clear, takes the freshness from the bloom. The late summer chrysanthemum, George recognizes when he and Jonquil visit a neighbor's garden, has its own beauty, but its difference from that of the jonquil of spring is cause for regret. This sad understanding of the nature of time, with its accompanying sense of loss, echoes another of *Gatsby*'s major themes, and thus the story provides further evidence of the development of Fitzgerald's thinking during the novel's gestational period.

Fitzgerald's apprenticeship with these stories served him well. So, too, did the advice of his editor, Maxwell Perkins, whose reservations, particularly about the characterization of the title figure, prompted Fitzgerald to flesh out his sketchy portrait (*Life in Letters* 87–88, 91, 125). Fitzgerald's reading during this period, particularly the novels of Joseph Conrad, also had a tremendous influence on his new novel. From such works as *Heart of Darkness* and *Lord Jim* Fitzgerald learned lessons about point of view and narrative structure that helped him gain control of his material. Whereas his previous novels had been loosely constructed and largely autobiographical, *The Great Gatsby* is unified and imaginative; its themes are evocatively conveyed in its symbols and figurative language. Fitzgerald credited the influence for these advancements to Conrad. Whatever the source of his creative growth, Fitzgerald was confident that he had found his vision. "It represents about a year's work and I think it's about ten years better than anything I've done," he wrote to the Irish critic Ernest Boyd in February 1925. He was, however, apprehensive about public reaction to it (*Life in Letters* 105).

When *The Great Gatsby* was published on April 10, 1925, Fitzgerald had, in fact, "done something really my own" (*Life in Letters* 84). Its language, structure, and themes demonstrated the artistic control and seriousness of purpose for which he had been striving, justifying his claim to Harold Ober, his agent, that "Artisticly [*sic*] its [*sic*] head and shoulders over everything I've done" (*Life in Letters* 81). The poet T. S. Eliot even praised the work in a letter to Fitzgerald, asserting that it was "the first step that American fiction has taken since Henry James" (*The Crack-Up* 310). Yet neither the critics nor the public knew quite what to make of Fitzgerald's masterpiece, and the novel sold disappointingly, barely recouping his advance (Meyers 130).

Typical of the reviews were Edwin Clark's assertion in the *New York Times Book Review* that *The Great Gatsby* was "a curious book, a mystical, glamourous story of today" (Bryer, *Reputation* 200) and Fanny Butcher's judgment in the *Chicago Daily Tribune* that the novel was "bizarre" and "melodramatic" and even, "at moments, dime novelish" (Bryer, *Reputation* 196–197). Even H. L. Mencken, one of Fitzgerald's previous champions, could muster only qualified praise for the new work. "*The Great Gatsby*," Mencken wrote to Fitzgerald, "fills me with pleasant sentiments. I think it is incomparably the best piece of work you have done. Evidences of careful workmanship are on every page. The thing is well managed, and has a fine surface. My one complaint is that the basic story is somewhat trivial—that it reduces itself, in the end, to a sort of anecdote. But God will forgive you for that" (Fitzgerald, *Correspondence* 158). Isabel Patterson, however, writing in the *New York Times Herald Tribune Books*, noted the novel's "almost perfectly fulfilled intention. There is not one accidental phrase in it," she praised, "nor yet one obvious or blatant line" (Bryer, *Reputation* 201). It would take another generation to accord Fitzgerald's novel the acclaim it deserved.

PLOT DEVELOPMENT

The self-conscious artistry of *The Great Gatsby* distinguishes its every element, but perhaps nowhere is it more apparent than in the novel's complex plot or the arrangement of events. *This Side of Paradise* and *The Beautiful and Damned* are linear narratives; they start at the beginning and work in logical sequence to a conclusion, chiefly through a series of discrete episodes in the protagonist's life. The plot of *The Great Gatsby*, in contrast, shifts back and forth in time and place, beginning well after the events that the novel chronicles and ending there as well. For all its narrative shifts, however, the plot is tightly constructed; each chapter is organized around a significant event that strips bare the novel's illusory world and gradually unmasks its title character to expose its meaning and significance. Literary critic Milton R. Stern argues that the novel's plot is "organized around a series of parties" (*Moment* 188), while biographer Robert Sklar focuses on the novel's circular motion, including not only Nick Carraway's "voyage from the old center of the world to the new, and a returning homeward," but also "the circle of nature, the life-giving and life-ending cycle of the seasons" (176). Both are correct, for the novel is indeed one of patterns and parallel relationships. All give shape to what is essentially a sensational tale of love and betrayal.

Chapter One focuses on the Buchanan dinner party, where Nick Carraway, the narrator, reestablishes his acquaintance with his cousin Daisy and her husband Tom, a former college mate, and meets the golf champion Jordan Baker. The chapter places the Buchanans within their East Egg world of smugly genteel privilege but reveals as well the cracks in its foundation, the adultery, deceit, and violence that the beautiful facade covers. In immediate contrast, Chapter Two opens with Fitzgerald's symbolic evocation of the modern world, his description of the Valley of Ashes, above which brood the sightless eyes of Doctor T. J. Eckleburg, and then focuses on the antithesis of the Buchanans' party, the drunken affair at Myrtle Wilson's pretentious New York apartment.

The affair exposes the pathetic aspirations of the middle class in their crude efforts to participate in the East Egg world. Fitzgerald depicts the zenith of those aspirations in Chapter Three, the party at Gatsby's mansion. There, in West Egg, the *nouveau riche*, a newly rich middle class energized by their success, engage in an ostentatious orgy of consumption as they look longingly toward East Egg respectability. In Chapter Three, Gatsby also makes his first appearance in the novel.

Fitzgerald's strategy in these first three chapters is masterful. He maps the socioeconomic geography of his story, introduces not only his cast of characters but also major symbols and metaphors, and, perhaps most importantly, creates a context in which a character as improbable as Gatsby seems probable. By the time Gatsby makes his appearance, readers are as intrigued by this mysterious figure as his guests. Like Nick Carraway, they know only rumors and innuendo about him, including stories that he had been a spy and that he once murdered a man. He may even have studied at Oxford University. This figure of romantic speculation and vast contradiction seems little more than a figment of the imagination. He could be anybody or nobody. Thus, his first quiet and unassuming appearance in the novel takes Nick—and the reader—by surprise (51–53). In an instant, Fitzgerald makes possible anything and everything about Gatsby.

Once Gatsby enters the drama, Fitzgerald begins to unmask him. Chapter Four centers on a luncheon in New York, where Nick meets one of Gatsby's business associates, Meyer Wolfsheim, and then takes tea with Jordan Baker. Both occasions serve as opportunities to reveal Gatsby's story, but even here, in doing so, Fitzgerald takes care not to expose too much and weaves in enough of the fantastic and contradictory to maintain Gatsby's mystique. On the drive to New York, for instance, Gatsby tells Nick about his Midwest origins, his life as a "young rajah" in Paris, Rome, and Venice "collecting jewels, chiefly rubies, hunting big game, painting a little, things for myself only, and trying to forget something very sad that happened to me long ago" (70), and his military service, for which he was decorated by every Allied government, even "little Montenegro" (70). Even Nick can hardly believe Gatsby's tale (70). Wolfsheim, however, confirms Gatsby's status as an "Oggsford man" (76), and Jordan, who picks up Gatsby's narrative later in the day, relates the "something very sad" in Gatsby's life—his blighted love for Daisy (79–83). Suddenly, Gatsby "[comes] alive" for Nick (83), as he does for the reader. Chapter Five, the reunion of Gatsby and Daisy at the tea party in Nick's bungalow, is the novel's emotional and structural center. Here, Fitzgerald brings the past into the present in an almost timeless moment that suggests the possibility that Gatsby's dream may come true. In the broken clock, the healing rain, and Gatsby's dazzling display of success, the cascade of multicolored shirts, Fitzgerald creates the symbols that give meaning to the scene. Here as well, Fitzgerald powerfully evokes one of the novel's central themes—time's mutability, the fact of change and death—and in so doing foreshadows the tragic consequences of this reunion, which are the focus of the novel's remaining chapters.

Chapter Six parallels Chapter Three in all but one key aspect: point of view, or the perspective from which readers see the events. In Chapter Six, Gatsby hosts another of his famous parties, and Daisy finally comes. Now, what had been merely dramatized in Chapter Three is judged, and from Daisy's point of view, the vulgarity of Gatsby's party is offensive and appalling (113–114). This crucial judgment, which reiterates the point of an earlier scene in the chapter, Gatsby's snub by Tom and his riding companions, makes clear the East Egg perspective on their West Egg "wannabes" and suggests the impossibility of Gatsby's dream.

In Chapter Seven, the novel's climax, Fitzgerald weaves together the many threads of his narrative, but especially his themes and symbols. In the enervating heat of late summer, Daisy, Gatsby, Tom, Nick, and Jordan motor to the Plaza Hotel, where a devastating confrontation strips Gatsby of his dream. Then, in the Valley of Ashes, the violence and horror that have resided beneath the pleasing facades of the Eggs come appropriately to the surface as Daisy, at the wheel of Gatsby's car, strikes and kills Myrtle Wilson, Tom's lover, and leaves others to clean up her mess. Chapter Eight, which ends in Gatsby's murder, and Chapter Nine, which focuses on his funeral and ends with Nick's retreat to the Midwest of his origins, allow Fitzgerald to fill in the gaps of Gatsby's life and, through Nick's lyrical evocation of the American Dream, to connect his fate to the history of a country and thereby tie the knot that holds together the threads of his thought.

While the plot of *The Great Gatsby*, in its barest outline, may be, as Mencken observed, "somewhat trivial," Fitzgerald's handling of its various threads is masterful and, as literary critic Henry Dan Piper demonstrates in his analysis of the manuscript's multiple drafts (137–154), the result of painstaking revision. Parallel scenes serve to emphasize contrasts; repeated patterns of symbols and imagery evoke meaning. Fitzgerald's decision to distribute Gatsby's monologue throughout the narrative controls his readers' perception of the title character, and so, too, does his decision to frame his story with the judgments of Nick Carraway, the novel's narrator. In fact, Fitzgerald's decision to make Nick the narrator may have been his most crucial. Not only does it allow him to use Nick's growing friendship with Gatsby to link together the novel's various episodes, but it also allows him to maintain necessary distance from his material through control of the point of view.

POINT OF VIEW

In *The Great Gatsby*, Fitzgerald's manipulation of the point of view, or the perspective from which readers view the events, gives further evidence of his artistic maturation. In his previous novels, Fitzgerald had used the third-person omniscient point of view. The narrator, in other words, possessed the ability to relate the thoughts and feelings of any of the novel's characters and knowledge of both past and present, thereby giving readers a privileged position from which to observe and evaluate the action. In Fitzgerald's early novels, those third-person narrators became his voice, and that voice was the voice of his central characters, with whom he clearly identified. Amory Blaine and Anthony Patch were Fitzgerald; he had, to some extent, lived their lives. Consequently, it was difficult for him to distance himself from their experiences and thereby evaluate them objectively.

In *The Great Gatsby*, however, Fitzgerald steps back from his central character by creating a first-person narrator. As the "I" of the story, Nick Carraway is both a participant in and an observer of Gatsby's fate, but he does not possess the privileges that result from a third-person point of view. Nick must struggle to understand Gatsby. Moreover, as a character in the novel and not just a voice, Nick must have a distinct identity separate from Gatsby's. He may be sympathetic to Gatsby and may even harbor in his own heart Gatsby's desires and emotions, but he must be true to himself. Nick may ultimately give voice to Fitzgerald's ideas (and indeed he does), but unlike Amory or Anthony, he speaks with the authority of his own experience as well. As a result, his judgments carry added credibility.

One other aspect of Nick's narratorial stance, its retrospective nature, helps Fitzgerald maintain distance from his material. Nick is clearly narrating events that occurred more than two years prior to the novel's present moment, so he has had the benefit of time to reflect on and evaluate the experience. That fact gives added weight to his judgments and, by implication, to Fitzgerald's. It also makes probable Nick's lyrical elegy at the novel's conclusion. The leap from Gatsby's dream to the American Dream could have seemed unearned had Fitzgerald allowed Nick to make it at the time of the events. The immediacy of his emotions would have colored his vision and clouded his judgment. In hindsight, however, as the result of conscious intellectual effort, Nick's mythologizing of Gatsby's experience is earned and therefore believable.

CHARACTER DEVELOPMENT

Nick's credibility as a narrator is not at issue in *The Great Gatsby*, as it sometimes is with first-person narrators, because Fitzgerald endows him with a number of admirable character traits and virtues, especially honesty, as Nick confesses to the reader (64). While Nick's disarming assertion may smack of boasting and thereby undermine his credibility, his actions throughout the novel certainly justify his self-assessment. Before Nick returns to the Midwest, for instance, he insists upon seeing Jordan Baker to end their relationship honorably. While it would have been easy for him to avoid the "awkward, unpleasant" (185) encounter (and most people would have done so), Nick must be honest with her and explain his reasons for his actions. Nick may be willing to excuse dishonesty in others, as he does with Jordan's deceptions (63), but he will not tolerate it in himself. In fact, when Jordan accuses him of dishonesty at their final meeting, his reply cuts all their ties: "I'm thirty. . . . I'm five years too old to lie to myself and call it honor" (186). Clearly, Nick's honesty encompasses self-assessment, making him an anomaly among the novel's self-deceived cast of characters.

Two other virtues shape Nick's perception of the novel's events: his tolerance and his sense of responsibility. Nick is aware that his has been a life of privilege and that economic security has made it possible for him to scorn the false and pretentious. Yet he is also aware, as his father had cautioned him, that his class brings with it certain expectations of decency. This awareness, as he himself admits, may be snobbish (6), but it also makes him tolerant of others' behavior. After all, they may not have benefited from similar advantages (5). Nick's inclination "to reserve all judgements" (5) does not, however, prevent him from judging. In fact, he insists on judgment based on very clear standards of duty, honor, and responsibility that are the "fundamental decencies" (6) associated with his father's world.

Unlike the other guests at Gatsby's parties, Nick, who has actually been invited to attend (45), feels compelled by good breeding and manners to seek out his host and extend him the courtesy of formal greeting and appreciation (46, 49, 57). He is also dismayed by Tom's infidelity and Daisy's seemingly casual acceptance of it (19–22) and is shocked to realize that greed could compel Meyer Wolfsheim to fix the World Series. (As if fearful of being corrupted by his contact with Wolfsheim, Nick demanded to pay the bill at this luncheon.) And it is, of course, Nick who assumes responsibility for Gatsby's funeral. All around him are "careless" (63) people who use and abuse others, who are both irresponsible and insensitive, without "care" in every sense, but Nick will not allow himself to be careless. Eventually, he will not forgive the quality in others either. Invested with "fundamental decencies" (6), Nick thus becomes the moral center of *The Great Gatsby*.

As one of the novel's careless people, Tom Buchanan stands in sharp contrast to his former Yale classmate Nick. A crude, arrogant man who cares nothing for ideas, Tom is not above using the brute force of his physical strength to intimidate and even subdue others. With one biting retort he can silence his wife; with one sharp blow he can break the nose of his lover (41). Five years before the novel's events, he had taken possession of Daisy Fay; he had purchased her, as it were, for the cost of an expensive string of pearls (80). Now, bored and complacent, his aggressive physicality straining against the proprieties, he strikes Nick as a man who "would drift on forever seeking a little wistfully for the dramatic turbulence of some irrecoverable football game" (10).

Tom's physical strength serves as a metaphor for what Robert Sklar aptly notes is his "real strength, his imperishable strength, . . . the power of his social standing" (190). He may, within months of his marriage, be responsible for an automobile accident that leaves his companion, a chambermaid, with a broken arm (82), he may be supporting a mistress in New York, and he may even conceal one murderer and assist another, but he does so with the certainty that his money, which has conferred respectability on him, insulates him from the consequences of his actions. Indeed, the arrogance with which Tom proclaims the superiority of the Nordic race makes clear all that he takes for granted (18).

With the security that comes from possession of an East Egg mansion, Tom can, in all seriousness, rail against the "Coloured Empires" (17) and defend "family life and family institutions" (137) without ever seeing the hypocrisy of his adultery or the hatefulness of his prejudice. In a modern world where the traditional values and the accepted social order appear to be turning upside down, Tom sees "himself standing alone on the last barrier of civilization" (137), fulfilling his duty to uphold the systems that uphold him, and never once does he question his fitness for the job. He is a denizen of East Egg; social standing alone has conferred on him the right.

Daisy Buchanan, the object of Gatsby's desire, is equally certain of "her membership in [the same] rather distinguished secret society" (22), and the knowledge has made her little more than a passive spectator on life. Her first appearance in the novel emphasizes this aspect of her character. When Nick enters the Buchanan drawing room on a warm, windy summer evening, she and her female companion are lounging on "an enormous couch. . . . Their [white] dresses were rippling and fluttering as if they had just been blown back in after a short flight around the house" (12). While the passage's verbs and images give the impression of movement, the two living beings in the scene, Daisy and Jordan Baker, in their white dresses, are eerily lacking any vitality. Lounging on the couch, they could be wax figures or marble statues; they seem so cool and lifeless. Only Daisy makes an attempt to rouse herself at Nick's entrance, but she abandons the half-hearted effort, offering instead her hand and her smile as if this should be a quite sufficient greeting.

Fitzgerald extends this initial impression of Daisy's passivity in subsequent scenes and flashbacks. As this scene develops, for instance, Daisy rather "helplessly" appeals to Nick when Jordan suggests that they do something to mark the summer solstice. "What'll we plan?" she asks. "What do people plan?" (16), she wonders, her questions making clear Daisy's lack of imagination and implying a willingness to follow rather than to lead. Those qualities account as well for her marriage to Tom. Under the influence of alcohol, she can muster the courage to toss in the waste bin the pearl necklace that had been his wedding gift to her and to call off the ceremony, but a half hour later, cold sober, the pearls around her neck, she is the radiant guest of honor at her bridal dinner. However much she loves Gatsby, she cannot bear to wait for him. A pearl necklace is hers now (80–81). Given the essential nature of her character, Daisy's willingness to abandon Gatsby and follow Tom once again in the aftermath of the hit-and-run accident ultimately comes as no surprise. The comfort and security of her money and position ensure all that she wants from life. Gatsby unmasked is too frightening a reality for Daisy.

Paired with Daisy in her whiteness, Jordan, too, draws strength from her wealth and social standing. Yet there is an aggressive edge to Jordan that makes her different from Daisy. Her "hard jaunty body" (63) is the sign of a ruthlessness that manifests itself in basic dishonesty. When Jordan lies about leaving the borrowed car, Nick remembers a rumor that she had cheated in her first big golf tournament and realizes that this woman is incapable of playing fair. Jordan develops a "universal skepticism" (84) that excuses her behavior and then depends upon her social standing to protect her from exposure. She is quite willing to enjoy the Buchanan hospitality so long as it demands nothing of her, but when things go wrong, she does not want to be bothered. Lending support is too dangerous a reality for Jordan. It might, after all, involve her in some scandal.

It is Jordan who clarifies for Nick the essential amorality of the representatives of East Egg when she defends her reckless driving. When Jordan drives dangerously close to some workmen, Nick admonishes her to be careful. In the exchange that follows, Jordon dismisses Nick's warning, indicating that other drivers should stay out of *her* way. Tom, Daisy, and Jordan are indeed careless, and they can afford to be. They have learned to expect somebody else to take care, to clean up after them and to feel for them. Rarely can they muster any emotion beyond indignation; remorse is a foreign concept to them because to know such a feeling is to acknowledge responsibility. At Myrtle's death, for instance, Tom feels little more than a twinge of self-pity (187), and he feels positively justified by Gatsby's murder (187), when, in fact, he bears some responsibility for both. Decency and morality, as Jordan implies, are for other people, those who cannot afford not to care. Against their hard aggressiveness, calm indifference, and cool insolence, the Myrtle Wilsons and Jay Gatsbys of the world do not stand a chance.

On the surface at least, Myrtle Wilson, Tom's lover, might seem to possess the qualities that could help her to escape the impoverishment of life in the Valley of Ashes. As coarse and aggressive as her lover, Myrtle is Daisy's antithesis in every way but one: she, too, would like to inhabit the Buchanan mansion. Daisy's passivity, for instance, which is born of possession, is countered by Myrtle's animal vitality, which is born of dispossession. A fleshy woman in her mid-thirties, Myrtle lacks physical beauty, and yet her sensuous vitality attracts Tom and even emboldens her to make eye contact with her lover in the presence of her husband (30). A woman such as Myrtle should survive and indeed prosper by the sheer force of her physical presence, yet her own intense yearning for the Buchanan world makes her its pathetic victim.

Wherever she goes, Myrtle seems to have only one refrain, "I want." On the day that Tom, Myrtle, and Nick go to her New York love nest, the first thing she does on alighting from the train is to buy magazines and personal toiletries. Not yet content with her purchases, she "wants" and buys a dog, a mongrel breed like herself (31–32), and at the apartment, she announces the "list" of cheap and tawdry items with which she intends to indulge herself. The sheer breathlessness of her acquisitiveness is astounding, and so, too, is the triviality of her desires. Myrtle's vision is so limited that if she had Daisy's money, she would spend it on garish items like a mechanical ashtray (41) or a vulgar automobile like the taxi in which she deliberately chooses to ride (31). Myrtle is as tasteless and pretentious as her New York apartment. Yet Fitzgerald leaves her some measure of our sympathy, which he denies Tom and Daisy, and thereby subtly connects her to Gatsby. A victim of her own pathetic yearning, Myrtle has aspired to the Buchanan world and, given her limited imagination, sought to achieve it through material possessions. In itself, her yearning for something more in her life is both human and understandable; thus, we can forgive her vulgarity. Yet Myrtle is also the victim of the very world to which she aspires, and the Buchanans' irresponsible use and abuse of her are reprehensible. When she lies dead in the road, her chest torn open to expose her heart, Myrtle touches the sympathetic chords in our own hearts, for we all know her longing. Certainly Gatsby did.

If Nick Carraway is the moral center of *The Great Gatsby*, then Gatsby is its symbolic center. A self-made man—indeed, a self-invented man—Gatsby epitomizes the American Dream. His story, as Fitzgerald gradually unfolds it, is a tale of desire, a dream of possibility, a quest for an eternal moment of perfection conducted by a hero whose energy and imagination and unfailing belief nearly empower him to succeed. As great as his conception of himself and his willingness to commit to his aspirations, Gatsby is, nevertheless, a fraud, a man whose identity shifts with the sands in order to be what he must. He is "Mr. Nobody from Nowhere," as Tom calls him (137). It is this complexity and these contradictions that make Gatsby far more than a romantic dreamer, far more than a simple bootlegger.

Gatsby emerges from the rumors and innuendo and his own conflicting stories of self to embody possibilities that ultimately save him from contempt. As James Gatz, a poor boy growing up in the Midwest, Gatsby had already begun to plot his course to success. At his son's funeral, Mr. Gatz shares with Nick a tattered copy of "Hopalong Cassidy"; on the back cover Gatsby had printed his daily schedule and a list of resolves for his improvement. That list gives evidence of both the deliberateness of that young boy's quest and his conception of how to conduct it. In addition to exercise, work, and sports, he was also committed to self-improvement through reading. Like Ragged Dick, the rags-to-riches hero of Horatio Alger stories, or the original American self-made man, Benjamin Franklin, whose *Autobiography* advocated just such a course of self-improvements, young James Gatz intended to achieve his success by hard work and self-reliance. He also was ready to seize any opportunity and to take advantage of luck. He recognized the importance of creating an image. If he were to be a success, he must look successful.

When his opportunities come, James Gatz is indeed ready for them. On the day that the yacht of the self-made millionaire Dan Cody drops anchor in Lake Superior's Little Girl Bay, for instance, Jay Gatsby is born. Several years later, world war and a military uniform gain him admittance to the world of Daisy Fay, and when, later still, Meyer Wolfsheim offers to make use of this "Oggsford man," Gatsby is willingly made (179). Opportunism is ingrained in Gatsby's character, and it supersedes any moral quibbles about means to the end. Dan Cody, after all, had served as his model of success, and Ella Kaye, the woman who legally cheated him of Cody's inheritance, had rounded out his education (107). The path to bootlegging and stock-sharping had been paved by others before him, so Gatsby, too, takes what he wants, including Daisy.

With his wealth, Gatsby purchases everything but respectability. He acquires a mansion in West Egg, an outlandish automobile (68), a library of fine books (49–50), and a wardrobe of multicolored shirts (97–98). As the host of a perpetual round of parties, Gatsby is indeed the "Sheik of Araby" (83). What saves him from being another Myrtle Wilson, however, is his dream. Gatsby's purpose is not merely to amass a fortune with which to purchase things, but to amass a fortune with which to purchase things that will prove him worthy of attaining Daisy. Like Amory Blaine and Anthony Patch, Gatsby, too, has "wed" his dreams to a beautiful woman who embodies for him all that life could ever offer (117). Gatsby is, then, more than a crass materialist. He is a romantic idealist.

Gatsby's idealism elevates him above every character in the novel except Nick, but it also, rather ironically, makes him vulnerable to the vicious barbar-

world, a barbarity to which he contributes. From the moment that
cklessly strikes Myrtle with his car, Gatsby has no intention of allow-
to pay for her actions. While he may conceal the evidence (169), he
make no attempt to run from the crime, as do Tom and Daisy. In fact, there is
a certain inevitability about his actions following the accident that clearly suggests Gatsby's willingness to die. His solitary vigil outside the Buchanan mansion on the night of the accident, for instance, is a wasted effort to protect
Daisy from the only man who really can protect her, and the day after the accident, he lounges in his swimming pool for the first and only time that summer
as if waiting for the thing he knows is going to happen. In a world of careless
disregard for others, Gatsby ultimately proves himself a man of principle by
sacrificing himself to his ideal.

Yet Gatsby's sacrifice is wasted on the careless Buchanans of the world.
Gatsby simply does what they would have expected. It is wasted as well because
his ideal is ultimately so much less than it could be. In choosing Daisy, Gatsby
accepts the limitations of the Buchanan world and settles for wealth and social
standing. This choice destroys him.

In some ways, Jay Gatsby remains the seventeen-year-old boy with the energy and purity of a dream that is from its conception limited by immaturity
and inexperience. Against the brute force of Tom Buchanan, Gatsby simply
collapses. When, in the hotel room at the Plaza, Tom attacks Gatsby's self and
exposes it as a facade, he leaves Gatsby and Daisy with nothing but the truth
about himself.

THEMATIC ISSUES

Because Gatsby serves as the novel's symbolic center, his fate reveals the thematic issues that resonate through *The Great Gatsby*, and because Nick serves as
the novel's moral center, his judgments provide the perspective from which
readers understand them. Given this connection, the relationship between the
characters bears some consideration. While Nick forthrightly admits that he
disapproves of Gatsby (6), who represents everything he scorns, he asserts, just
after he has recounted his final words to Gatsby, "They're a rotten crowd
. . . you're worth the whole damn bunch put together" (162). These contradictions indicate the complexity of the relationship between Nick and Gatsby.
Nick can never excuse Gatsby's corruption; he can never forget that he earns his
money from illegal activities and is in his own way as amoral as Jordan and the
Buchanans. Yet Nick's growing sympathy for Gatsby takes root in the deep recesses of his own heart, where he harbors some of Gatsby's own desires and
emotions. Nick, too, has a capacity for "infinite hope" (6). He wants to believe
in Gatsby's quest, in the purity of a dream that can lead to greatness. When

Tom, for instance, during the confrontation at the Plaza, accuses Gatsby of lying about his Oxford connection, Nick is genuinely elated that Gatsby's answer proves him wrong (136). For just a moment during this confrontation, Gatsby gets the better of Tom, and Nick takes hope that a dream, however fragile, can withstand reality, however brutal. Nick, therefore, from their common chord of hope, will forgive Gatsby his corruption. He, too, is a Midwesterner, and he can relate to this "story of the West" (184), a story, in effect, of misplaced longing, as Gatsby's fate so clearly proves.

As a "story of the West," *The Great Gatsby* completes the critique of American society that Fitzgerald had been conducting, but without its equivalent depth and maturity of vision, since the publication of his first novel. Nick, Gatsby, Daisy, Tom, and Jordan are all in their own ways reverse pioneers. Instead of making their way west to the land of opportunity and promise, the traditional American journey, these Midwesterners go east, seduced by its constant motion that suggests possibility. By 1925, the year of *The Great Gatsby's* publication, the West is settled, and the Midwest seems, to Nick, a place of dull conformity, respectable towns, and repressed emotion, a place that had been chronicled by Sinclair Lewis in *Babbitt* (1922) and *Main Street* (1920) and Sherwood Anderson in *Winesburg, Ohio* (1919).

For a Midwesterner, the East, epitomized by New York City, seems a land of enchantment, mystery, and beauty. As Nick and Gatsby cross the Queensboro Bridge into Manhattan on the day of their luncheon with Wolfsheim, Nick thinks anything could happen, "even Gatsby" (73). A place of mobility, the East is now the new West. It promises the opportunity to make quick and easy money in the stock market and, with the price of admission, to purchase social standing.

Fitzgerald uses this shift in both physical and psychic geography to explore the nature of the American Dream itself, and what he finds is its corruption by money. As an ideal, the American Dream had once been a dream of self. The freedom and openness of the vast American landscape had promised the opportunity to be. Unfettered by rigid boundaries, unchained from the past, American pioneers could, like Gatsby, create themselves. In time, however, that dream of self became a dream of success. The opportunity to be became the opportunity to be rich, and the goal of life became not self-fulfillment, but the acquisition of the trappings of economic success. Daisy's "voice is full of money," Gatsby tells Nick (127), and its seductive power corrupts his dream just as surely as the sirens' song of money and power that issues forth from the financial centers of the East corrupts the dreams of countless Americans. Money, it seems, can buy anything in this world, from a dog leash of leather and braided silver to an easy life and a new identity. For the right price, and with the right currency, even Daisy is for sale. Money, then, has changed the nature of the American Dream; it has destroyed its finest conception. The result is *The Great Gatsby* world of diminished things, and that world reflects Fitzgerald's tragic awareness of loss, given what it has become.

Fitzgerald heightens Nick's sense of the dark underside of this reality by juxtaposing to it images of death and the grotesque. Nick notices, for instance, on his journey into New York with Gatsby, a hearse, the sight of which evokes the transient nature of this reality. The Valley of Ashes and the billboard eyes of Doctor T. J. Eckleburg also serve as constant reminders of this dark reality, and West Egg, as Nick finally comes to see it, reminds him of a surrealistic painting of death by El Greco (185). The adjectives in his description of this painting—"sullen," "cold," "lustreless," "grotesque"—emphasize the "quality of distortion" (185) that Nick associates with the East, and the anonymity of the human figures in the painting and the landscape itself suggest the very namelessness and placelessness that also characterize the East. Nobody seems to have a name at Gatsby's parties; everybody seems identified instead by appearance or by occupation or, more tellingly, by automobile, the very symbol of rootlessness and mobility. What emerges from these images is a world with a glittering veneer that conceals the rottenness beneath.

The novel's symbolic geography also makes clear that the distinctions between East and West are largely matters of appearance rather than substance, and Fitzgerald emphasizes the point in his use of the Long Island setting. Despite their physical similarities, the "wingless" souls who inhabit the Eggs draw vast distinctions between them (9). West Egg, like the Midwest, is the less fashionable promontory. It glitters with the spoils of new money and dances with the raw energy of desire. There Gatsby lives in his spacious, hotel-like mansion, a place as temporary as its occupant. East Egg, in contrast, is stately and dignified, clearly reflecting its sense of itself. There the residents are rooted to the past and linked to history. The Buchanans, for instance, live in a Georgian Colonial mansion that seems an extension of its immaculate lawn, so covered is it in ivy (11). Yet Nick's experience and Gatsby's fate demonstrate that the Eggs' "wingless" residents, who lack the ability to soar above their own limited perceptions, have mistaken appearance for substance. East Egg is the center of old money and genteel respectabilities, the place that the *nouveau riche* of West Egg, energized by their desire, seek to emulate. As Fitzgerald makes clear, however, the only real difference between them is that one group has what the other wants, and what both want is not worth having. It brings nobody any real satisfaction because it is not what is truly wanted.

Fitzgerald drives home this point through the development of a second major theme, time, with its accompanying attendants, mutability and loss. Gatsby's dream of Daisy involves more than simply reclaiming her. He wants as well to redeem the five years that have separated them. He wants, in fact, to erase the past. Nick is astounded by this aspect of Gatsby's quest and simply cannot believe that his friend is serious about it. Gatsby insists, however, that he can "repeat the past" (116). Gatsby expects Daisy to tell Tom that she never loved him (116). He, in turn, is going to restore everything to its former state; only by redeeming the past can he find his ideal. This is the nature of Gatsby's true quest, and it is doomed to fail from the beginning.

What Gatsby seeks to recover is a timeless moment of perfection, and the closest he comes to it is his reunion with Daisy in Nick's bungalow. Preparations for that reunion begin in a moment of disjointed time when Nick returns to West Egg at two in the morning following his meeting with Jordan. An agitated Gatsby is clearly waiting for his arrival, killing time, as it were, until he learns whether Nick will help him achieve his dream. Their ensuing conversation centers on issues of time: when the meeting shall take place, how long it will take to have Nick's grass cut. On the day of the reunion, time again preoccupies Gatsby. He arrives at Nick's bungalow hours before the scheduled event and then, two minutes before the appointed hour, announces that he is returning home. Finally, at the moment of their meeting, Gatsby and Daisy do indeed seem to slip out of time because a broken mantle clock, on which Gatsby rests his head, presides over the occasion, no longer ticking off the minutes and hours as they inevitably pass (91). Like the lyrics of the song that Klipspringer plays for them on the piano, their reunion seems to take place "In the meantime, / In between time" (101). Yet, throughout it all, Gatsby is indeed aware of time's passing. He knows, for instance, exactly the number of years that have separated them (92), as well as the number it has taken to make possible this reunion (95). Nick even senses that Gatsby, in his intense anticipation, is overwound like a clock (97). At the novel's emotional center, the fact of time underscores every aspect of the occasion. References to time dominate *The Great Gatsby*, making clear its reality and its inevitability, much as Gatsby might like to believe otherwise. Perhaps one of time's most poignant manifestations is Pammy, Daisy's daughter. When Gatsby actually meets her, he stares at the child in disbelief (123), unable to comprehend her reality. Daisy's child, however, is a fact of time, a fact that no amount of "fixing things" can change, and her existence foreshadows Gatsby's inevitable disillusionment when Daisy fails to redeem time for him during the confrontation at the Plaza (137–140).

Even if Daisy had denied those years, she would not have been able to give Gatsby what he desired because it (if it ever existed) was already gone. Gatsby wants the dream, the illusion, but it is wedded to a human reality that is bound by the process of time to change and mutability. As much as Gatsby seeks to deny that process and its effects, he cannot. In fact, even his dream has changed over time, embellished by his own desire to the point that it could never exist. Eventually, Gatsby's loss of his illusion destroys him.

Nick, however, is saved from Gatsby's fate by both his undertaking and his acceptance of time's inevitabilities. Throughout the novel, Fitzgerald has associated images of death and decay with Nick, suggesting his awareness of time's reality. He emphasizes the point, however, when he imposes on him his thirtieth birthday on the day that Gatsby's world collapses at the Plaza. At thirty, his youth gone, Nick anticipates with some trepidation the adult realities that he must face: "Thirty—the promise of a decade of loneliness, a thinning list of single men to know, a thinning brief-case of enthusiasm, thinning hair" (143). The repetition of the word "thinning" makes clear that diminished possibilities are the reality of adulthood, but with Jordan leaning on his shoulder, Nick finds temporary reassurance that they can wait. That reassurance, however, vanishes in the aftermath of the hit-and-run accident and Gatsby's murder. On his thirtieth birthday, Nick must accept change or, like Gatsby, be destroyed.

In the aftermath of Gatsby's death, Nick retreats from the East and all that it embodies, returning to the Midwest of his birth because it represents moral certainty and connects him to a sense of place. He is drawn there, perhaps by memories of other homecomings from prep school and college when, in Chicago's Union Station, he and his old acquaintances, who were making similar journeys, would match invitations with the easy familiarity and pleasing comfort that comes of shared histories and experiences. Then, as the train bore him ever closer to the heart of home, he would feel in the air a vivid sense of place and identity with the Midwest (184). For Nick, the Midwest is a certainty epitomized by the Carraway house, still called by its family name, and he draws strength and satisfaction from that certainty. The Midwest may be staid, respectable, and even a little complacent, but Nick has come to see that there may be nothing wrong with these qualities. At the very least, they ensure decent behavior, and behind such behavior may actually lie true human feelings.

Nick's return to the Midwest makes clear Fitzgerald's judgment of *The Great Gatsby* world of careless cruelty and counterfeit realities. It also ties together the novel's major themes. In its final elegiac paragraphs, a chastened Nick reflects on the larger meaning of his experience and makes clear the connection between Gatsby's story and the national myth of the American Dream. Behind *The Great Gatsby* world lie the traces of the new world that had "flowered once for Dutch sailors' eyes" (189). Like Gatsby, those sailors had gazed on possibility and been awed by it. For Gatsby and those sailors, the enormity of the challenge—to dream a dream, to imagine a world equal to its promise—was beyond the capability of any human being, so even at the moment of discovery, that bright new promise had already disappeared. Bound by time to mutability and loss, each generation struggles, nevertheless, to dream a world of perfection into existence again. That effort, that dream, is both the hope and the tragedy of the human experience and the American myth.

SYMBOLISM AND FIGURATIVE LANGUAGE

In his most fully realized artistic achievement, Fitzgerald creates a rich pattern of evocative language and some equally provocative symbols to carry the weight and meaning of his ideas. Some, such as the novel's symbolic geography and the many references to time and death, have been discussed in the Theme section; another, the metaphor of carelessness, has been analyzed in the section on Character Development. Other equally important poetic devices resonate with meaning in *The Great Gatsby* and provide further evidence of the degree to which Fitzgerald crafted his novel to achieve his purpose.

In East Egg and West Egg, Fitzgerald creates a symbolic geography that clearly evokes the novel's mythic landscapes, and he uses houses to reveal the lives and values of the people who inhabit each territory. Linking the Eggs with New York City is an equally important geographic feature, the Valley of Ashes. A symbol of the modern wasteland that T. S. Eliot had so powerfully dissected in his 1922 poem *The Wasteland*, the Valley of Ashes is a place of poverty and desolation, a vast nothingness that mocks the efforts of the people who inhabit and traverse it daily (27). Here, in a gray, insubstantial landscape that looks as if it were a thriving reality, live the George and Myrtle Wilsons of the world. Poor and seemingly disenfranchised, they long to escape to the Eggs or the city, but their poverty denies them that possibility. George, the proprietor of a garage and thereby the purveyor of mobility, ironically cannot even afford the price of the automobile that would make possible his escape to the West (130).

Brooding over this barrenness are the eyes of Doctor T. J. Eckleburg, which in *The Great Gatsby*'s materialistic world are the rather appropriate remnants of an advertising billboard for an oculist. To a world of the blind, those eyes promise new vision, but now dim, they mock the very notion of clearsightedness. In their suspension in space, from which they stare inscrutably down on the comings and goings that constitute life in the Valley of Ashes, they also represent the God of this world. When George, for instance, accuses Myrtle of adultery, he forces her to look out the window at the eyes of Doctor T. J. Eckleburg, insisting they know and see everything: "You may fool me but you can't fool God! . . . God sees everything" (167). His neighbor, Michaelis, cautions him that it is only an advertisement, not a god, so George should not expect answers from him. In fact, those who inhabit this contemporary wasteland should expect no answers because they have lost the very idea of God if they confuse a billboard for a deity, the material for the spiritual.

Fitzgerald elaborates on the nature of *The Great Gatsby* world and its inhabitants by making the automobile a major symbol in the novel. It functions in two ways. It is first a status symbol, revealing the social identity of its owner. The Buchanans, for instance, secure in their status, drive a tasteful blue coupe that George Wilson, too poor to own any car, would like to purchase for resale (130). To him, it represents the promise of mobility and offers a chance to escape his no-status existence. Gatsby's auto, which Tom likens to a "circus wagon" (128), is as gaudy and ostentatious as his mansion and his parties (68). Gatsby takes pride in his automobile, as he does in all his possessions because it signifies the wealth that he believes legitimizes his claim to Daisy. Yet its sheer audacity, as Tom's comment makes clear, will prevent him from moving to East Egg. He may have wheels, but they transport the wrong sort of chassis.

The automobile also emphasizes the restlessness of those who inhabit *The Great Gatsby* world. These characters are in constant motion, moving back and forth across the landscape on journeys that seem to have no real purpose other than to relieve boredom. Their perpetual motion rather ironically leads them to no destination, no satisfaction. Instead, it increases their opportunities for lethal carelessness. The automobile accident following one of Gatsby's parties (58–60) clearly foreshadows Daisy's hit-and-run encounter with Myrtle. Both drivers are equally oblivious to the potential power of their motion. They must simply move.

Restless and careless, the inhabitants of *The Great Gatsby* world are also brutally animalistic, even cannibalistic, and Fitzgerald dehumanizes them by linking them to other living creatures and plant life with their names. Meyer Wolfsheim, Gatsby's business associate, is certainly the most important character developed in this way; his name, of course, signifies his predatory nature. This gambler, however, preys unabashedly on humans. In fact, he wears cufflinks made of human molars. The owl-eyed man who admires Gatsby's books because he sees through the appearances to the magnitude of his attempt also bears an appropriate name (49–50). Nick's list of guests who attended Gatsby's parties, however, offers the most telling evidence of the pervasiveness of such people in *The Great Gatsby* world: the Leeches, the Hammerheads, the Catlips, James B. ("Rot-gut") Ferret, Clarence Endive, and S. B. Whitebait. The guests at Gatsby's parties seem hardly human, and by including on the list guests whose names evoke America's past, for instance, Stonewall Jackson Abrams and Mrs. Ulysses Swett, Fitzgerald effectively diminishes the greatness of their historical associations (65–68).

As this whole cluster of symbols and metaphors clearly suggests, *The Great Gatsby* world is a barren wasteland in which nothing of value can thrive. Its inhabitants are cruelly callous creatures who rapaciously devour themselves and others. In such a world, Gatsby's dream and his life have about them the unreality of the carnival, yet another of the novel's metaphorical patterns. His salons and verandas "gaudy with primary colors" (44), and his raucous parties likened to amusement parks (45), Gatsby is for a time a modern Trimalchio (119), an allusion to the vulgar parvenu of the Roman satire *The Satyricon*, by Petronis.

By the end of the novel, however, "the whole caravansary," as Nick r
"had fallen in like a cardhouse at the disapproval in [Daisy's] eyes" (12
universe of ineffable gaudiness," Gatsby's dream, and hence his world, is
"founded securely on a fairy's wing" (105), and neither stands a chance of survival in the modern wasteland.

The Great Gatsby is rich with color symbolism and light and dark imagery as well. The green light at the end of Daisy's pier, for instance, beckons Gatsby forward to her white and gold world of belonging. Moonlight and starlight illuminate this world and thereby suggest its dreamlike quality, which the sun's searing heat destroys. Gatsby's dream, for instance, shrivels to nothing on summer's hottest day. Flowers also figure prominently among the novel's metaphorical patterns. Both Myrtle and Daisy, for instance, have floral names suggestive of their natures. Daisy's name combines with the novel's color symbolism to evoke the white and gold colors of wealth. In his analysis of *The Great Gatsby*, Milton R. Stern examines fully the evocative details and language patterns that contribute so much to the novel's central issues and aptly concludes that "Fitzgerald's methods of organization revolved around a series of associations between details and the idea of betrayal, repeated until the idea takes on the life of its own style" (*Moment* 267). Daisy never blossoms for Gatsby, and the green light, which had once seemed so close, loses its enchantment and becomes again merely "a green light on a dock" (98). Beneath appearances and surface details there does indeed lie another reality, one that does, in fact, betray Gatsby and his dream. Fitzgerald's complex pattern of symbol and figurative language ultimately forms a poetry of loss that reveals these truths.

A MYTHOLOGICAL INTERPRETATION

Just prior to his murder, Jay Gatsby confides the remainder of his history to Nick Carraway, who realizes then the significance of his friend's grail-like quest. Like the knights of old, Gatsby had sought something greater than the thing itself, an ideal that would restore order and meaning to his life. Nick's metaphor suggests an alternate critical approach to *The Great Gatsby*, one that focuses on the mythological aspects of Gatsby's tale. Closely connected to the psychological approach to literature outlined in Chapter 6, mythological criticism seeks to explain the motives underlying human behavior. Unlike psychological criticism, however, it finds its answers not in the biological sciences, but in religion, anthropology, and cultural history. To arrive at their conclusions, myth critics thus examine the archetypes and archetypal patterns—the shared images, formulas, and types—upon which writers draw to give order and a frame of meaning to their personal perceptions and visions.

Myths, according to scholars of religion and anthropology, make concrete and particular a special perception of human beings or a worldview; they are a symbolic language through which primitive people express themselves and interpret natural events. Found at the beginnings of every culture, myths are part of every literature. They differ from legends because they rely less on historical background and more on the supernatural; they differ from fables because they are less concerned with teaching a moral lesson and because they are the product of a society rather than the creation of an individual. Collective and communal by nature, myths bind a tribe or a nation together in that people's common psychological and spiritual activities.

A dynamic creation, myth transcends both time and place; it unites the past, or traditional modes of belief, to the present's current values and reaches toward the future in its expression of spiritual and cultural aspirations. Furthermore, although every culture has its own distinctive mythology that may be reflected in its legends, folklore, and ideologies, myth is, in the general sense, universal. In fact, the mythology of all groups, as scholars such as Sir James Frazer, Claude Lévi-Strauss, and Joseph Campbell have demonstrated, centers on certain common motifs or themes: They attempt to explain creation, divinity, and religion; to probe the meaning of existence and death; to account for natural events; and to chronicle the exploits of cultural heroes. They also share certain images, called archetypes, that tend to elicit comparable psychological responses and to serve cultural functions. Water, for instance, is universally associated with the mystery of creation; fertility and growth; the cycle of birth, death, and resurrection; and purification and redemption.

Writers, the myth critic believes, draw consciously or unconsciously upon these archetypes to express their own unique responses to the world and simultaneously to connect their visions to some universal response that resonates in the minds of readers. The myth critic seeks to discover the universal understanding through analysis of the work's archetypes. As dramatic or narrative embodiments of a people's perception of the deepest truths, myths thus serve as a useful lens through which to examine literature, and mythological critics, who believe that literature is informed by these preliterary constructs, or understandings, find in it traces of primordial ritual and ceremony, collective memory, unconsciously held value systems, and general beliefs.

One of the most pervasive myths centers on the hero and functions as an archetype of transformation and redemption. In *The Hero with a Thousand Faces*, Joseph Campbell explains that the myth of the hero typically follows a three-part pattern of separation, initiation, and return. In the first part of the myth, the hero must venture forth from his ordinary existence to undertake a quest; its successful completion will result in the salvation of his kingdom and perhaps marriage to the princess. Complicating his journey is a series of tests and obstacles that he must overcome and that signify his passage from ignorance and immaturity to social and spiritual adulthood. The second part of the hero's quest thus serves as an initiation into the larger community; his integration marks the third phase, the return (30). Sometimes in his quest the hero becomes the scapegoat for the sins of others and must be sacrificed to achieve his ends, but despite his fate, the hero is clearly identified with the welfare of his tribe or his nation. His mysterious adventure confers on him a life-affirming, life-restoring power which he bestows on his people.

When Fitzgerald says of Gatsby that he had "committed himself to the following of a grail" (156), he evokes one of the most famous adventures of Arthurian myth—the quest of the Holy Grail. According to legend, the Grail was a vessel used by Christ at the Last Supper, and thus it was linked with the sacrament of communion and "endowed," notes historian Geoffrey Ashe, "with supernatural properties of the Christian kind. It was a source of healing and inspiration and visions, and its finding, or 'achievement,' was a transcendent mystical experience" (173).

Following the death of King Arthur, several of his knights-errant seek to discover and to retrieve the Grail. Without its king, Britain had fallen into a dark and sterile period, and Arthur's knights sought the Grail to restore life to their land and people. Gawain is one of the first knights to venture forth in search of the Grail, and Galahad, Lancelot's son, achieves it fully. Perceval, the Great or Noble Fool, however, is the principal Grail-seeking knight, and his representation as the Great Fool serves in many ways as a prefiguration of Gatsby's.

The Great or Noble Fool is, like Gatsby, a man of humble birth and rude country ways who meets, wins the favor of, and spends a romantic night with a beautiful aristocratic woman. Arriving at court, the hero is subjected to cruel mockery by the king's entourage and forced to assume a menial position in the royal household, where he suffers ridicule for his unpolished habits. When the lovely lady of his dreams comes under threat, however, the Great Fool seizes the opportunity to prove himself worthy by serving as her champion when everyone else runs in fear of the evil being who has her in thrall. His reward for destroying the evil threat is the lady's hand in marriage.

In one of the myth's most popular versions, the legend of Sir Parzival, a rendition of the Perceval tale by the German poet Wolfram von Eshenbach, the hero ultimately renounces worldly fame and fortune as well as sexual love to dedicate himself to the quest of the Holy Grail. Although it is an unattainable goal in the material world, Parzival, who has been purified by long years of self-denial and simple life, is eventually rewarded with a vision of the Grail as he dies and ascends to heaven.

In his pursuit of Daisy, who represents the good, the true, and the beautiful to him and to whom he has "forever wed his unutterable dreams" (117),

Gatsby, too, resembles a medieval knight-errant in quest of the Grail. If he can reclaim Daisy, he will in some way redeem time. He will make real an ideal that his "extraordinary gift for hope" (6) has sustained in the face of both material and spiritual privation. That dream of Daisy, Gatsby's grail, has fueled his every action since she was lost to him: For Daisy, Gatsby reinvents himself. He must be worthy of his grail.

The Great Gatsby world, however, is far different from the medieval world. Material success rather than high ideals and sacrificial gestures is the measure of *The Great Gatsby* hero. The whim of a Daisy, who will marry any Tom for the price of a pearl necklace, is insubstantial in comparison to the deep and abiding love of a Guinevere for her Lancelot, however adulterous the passion. *The Great Gatsby* world is built on a foundation of bootleg gin, penny stocks, and cufflinks crafted from human molars, and its nightmare landscapes—the sterile Valley of Ashes, the chaotic distortions of New York, the riotous debaucheries at Gatsby's mansion—are the truest images of its reality. Rather than lead the ascetic life of a Parzival, Gatsby revels in his rainbow cascade of shirts and his monstrous Rolls Royce. When he finds his grail, it brings death rather than life, despair and disillusionment rather than faith and hope. Fitzgerald's evocation of the Grail myth, whether conscious or unconscious, thus serves as an ironic counterpoint to modern realities. It underscores the superficial values and the inhumane nature of twentieth-century America, a world that its Puritan forebears had once invested with all the bright hopes of a New Eden.

Those hopes, which Fitzgerald also evokes, most significantly in the novel's final paragraphs, offer the myth critic yet another avenue for exploration because the myth of the American Dream is one of the informing beliefs related to the uniqueness of American culture. The central facet of this myth is the belief in Edenic possibilities, the hope that Paradise could be re-created not in the next world and not out of time, but in the here and now of a new continent, a New World. Europeans from the time of its first settlement saw America as a land of hope and opportunity, a place where men and women could escape centuries of poverty, misery, and corruption and start anew in a land undefiled. Here, in this New World, human beings could satisfy their mythic yearnings for a New Eden. They could re-create a paradise on earth.

In such a New World, a New Adam would also be possible. Cut free from the corrupting influences of European society, this New Adam (for it is chiefly an Adam who figures in the myth, an Adam free from the moral compromise of an Eve), is, as R.W.B. Lewis describes him in his study *The American Adam*, "a radically new personality, the hero of the new adventure: an individual emancipated from history, happily bereft of ancestry, untouched and undefiled by the usual inheritances of family and race; an individual standing alone, self-reliant and self-propelling, ready to confront whatever awaited him with the aid of his own unique and inherent resources" (5). James Fenimore Cooper's Natty Bumppo in his series of Leatherstocking novels is the frontier version of such a hero. His civilized counterpart is the Self-Made Man, the hero of a corollary myth of the American Dream—the Dream of Success. Such a hero is a direct descendent of Benjamin Franklin, who entered Philadelphia with little more than wit, ingenuity, and the will to succeed and through pluck, luck, and the cultivation of some key virtues rose from rags to riches. Horatio Alger's nineteenth-century hero Ragged Dick also represents him, and so, too, does Fitzgerald's Jay Gatsby.

Guided by his "Schedule" and list of "General Resolves" recorded on the fly-leaf of his ragged copy of "Hopalong Cassidy" (181), James Gatz transforms himself into Jay Gatsby, following the footsteps of that mythic American hero who achieves the American Dream of Success. That achievement demonstrates the continued vitality of the myth in American cultural life more than two hundred years after the first versions appeared. Yet in many ways, Gatsby's success is only an illusion. His mansion, for instance, sits in the less fashionable West Egg but is out of place in either of the Eggs, a fact that suggests its owner's uncertain status in the world. Similarly, Gatsby's possession of Daisy, in whom he has invested all his hopes and dreams, is never more than temporary. He may have the money to purchase the trappings of success, but clearly it is the wrong currency with which to purchase the thing itself. Gatsby's death thus suggests the bankruptcy of the American Dream of Success, for a dream based on material wealth, which is, after all, both transient and mutable, ultimately offers no firm foundation and is bound to collapse of its own lack of substance.

The mythic dimensions of *The Great Gatsby* clearly confirm the novel's thematic issues and perspectives. Gatsby is at once a knight-errant intent on rescuing the flower of chivalry from the brutal ogre who possesses her and a self-made man who believes in the power of his vast fortune. He is at once the romantic idealist whose quest of his grail will redeem the past and transform the future and the crass materialist for whom possessions signify success. Both of these myths lie behind the strivings of Jay Gatsby, yet in the end, neither can sustain him. Contemporary America has moved too far away from its foundational hopes and beliefs, and Gatsby, caught between two conflicting ideologies, is simply no match for the casual carelessness of people oblivious to any.

6

Tender is the Night
(1934)

Tender is the Night is F. Scott Fitzgerald's self-proclaimed "confession of faith" (*Life in Letters* 252). A "troubled and troublesome book," as Malcolm Bradbury aptly terms it (90), which exists in two versions, it tells the story of a man of promise destroyed by both his own goodness and the seductions of expatriate life on the French Riviera in the gaudy spree following World War I. In doing so, it exposes the dark underside and the high cost of that spree in terms both personal and social; the psychic disorder of its central characters, Dick and Nicole Diver, mirrors the chaos, disintegration, and sexual confusion of an increasingly violent and perverse world. *Tender is the Night* is thus the story of a generation gone bust on its own promise, its own excesses.

Set amid the hedonistic pleasures of the French Riviera and at the Swiss psychiatric clinics that catered to its victims in the heady days of the late 1920s, *Tender is the Night* charts the tragic romance of a charismatic American couple, Dick and Nicole Diver, who have virtually created and certainly epitomize stylish expatriotism. A promising young psychiatrist at the time of his marriage, Dr. Richard Diver was destined for a brilliant career until he fell in love with and unwisely married a beautiful and wealthy patient. From that point, Dick devotes all his personal and professional talents to his wife-patient's well-being, creating a buffer of ordered calm on the edge of teeming chaos that, for a time, shores up her battered psyche. Nicole's treatment, however, more than tests her husband-doctor's expertise. As he moves farther and farther away from the promise of his early career and finds himself more and more compromised by his conflicting desires, more and more corrupted by Nicole's world of careless wealth, Dick sinks into alcoholism and despair. By the time he effects her cure, he has paid the price with his own self, fading into obscurity as Nicole gleams bright in her ascendancy.

GENESIS AND CRITICAL RECEPTION

Fitzgerald abandoned at least two versions and several drafts of *Tender is the Night*, which he had confidently begun in 1925, but in 1932, he committed himself to a "General Plan" for the book and determined to fulfill it. "The novel should do this," began that "General Plan": "Show a man who is a natural idealist, a spoiled priest, giving in for various causes to the ideas of the haute Burgeoise [*sic*], and in his rise to the top of the social world losing his idealism, his talent and turning to drink and dissipation. Background one in which the liesure [*sic*] class is at their truly most brilliant and glamorous" (Mizener, *Paradise* 307–308). Despite the most troubling personal circumstances, Zelda's collapse into schizophrenia and his own battle with alcoholism, Fitzgerald completed his fourth novel two years later very much according to that plan, but it was not the book he had envisioned in 1925. Nor was he convinced at its publication that he had yet quite found its proper form.

In 1925, Fitzgerald had confidently proclaimed to his editor, Maxwell Perkins, that his next novel would be "something really NEW in form, idea, structure—the model for the age that [James] Joyce and [Gertrude] Stien [*sic*] are searching for, that [Joseph] Conrad didn't find" (*Life in Letters* 108). Its subject matter—matricide, "concerning . . . such a case as that girl who shot her mother on the Pacific coast last year"—promised to be as "highly sensational" as *The Great Gatsby*'s, he confided to Harold Ober, his agent, a year later, when he had completed one fourth of the projected work (*Life in Letters* 140–144). Yet as biographer Robert Sklar has aptly noted, "His conception of what he ought to write—a model for the age, yes, and also a work to vindicate himself after *The Great Gatsby*'s disappointing popular reception—held him like an anchor to plans and ambitions that were far removed from his own talent and inclination" (249). Hundreds of discarded manuscript pages, the labor of intermittent bursts of writing during the next seven years, provide evidence supporting Sklar's assertion.

Scholar Matthew J. Bruccoli has examined those pages, and in his study *The Composition of* Tender is the Night, he identifies three major versions of the novel, each of which underwent multiple drafts. The first version, which was variously titled "Our Type," "The Boy Who Killed His Mother," "The Melarkey Case," and "The World's Fair," told the story of Francis Melarkey, a young Hollywood technician who was intended to kill his mother. The

Melarkey version occupied Fitzgerald from 1925 through 1930, the period of his most self-destructive behavior, although he did briefly interrupt work on this story of matricide to begin a second version, untitled and no more than two long scenes, in 1929. This Kelly version introduced a young actress named Rosemary. The Melarkey version had featured background characters named through various revisions Abe and Mary Grant and Seth and Dinah Piper. These couples would be rechristened in the third version that Fitzgerald began writing in 1932, having finally clarified for himself his novel's intention and focus in his "General Plan." Initially titled "The Drunkard's Holiday," then "Doctor Diver's Holiday," and finally *Tender is the Night*, the third version salvaged much of the Melarkey version in Book One, but its focus from the beginning was tragedy of a different sort than murder. Dick Diver's tragedy of failure was a subject about which Fitzgerald could indeed write with authority.

The troubled composition of *Tender is the Night* was further complicated by Zelda Fitzgerald's own literary ambitions. In 1932, while she was a psychiatric patient at Johns Hopkins University Hospital in Baltimore, Maryland, Zelda composed her own autobiographical novel, *Save Me the Waltz*. In the story of Alabama Beggs, she faithfully chronicled her own childhood and marriage, her husband's early success, the birth of her child, travels in Europe, a brief affair with a French aviator and her husband's retaliatory affair, and her passion for dancing and the end of her brief ballet career. Although he was reluctant to prevent its publication, fearing that disappointment would set back his wife's fragile recovery, Fitzgerald was also deeply distressed by the work because he regarded it, especially in its original draft, as preempting the material that he was using in his novel-in-progress. In a letter to his wife's psychiatrist, Fitzgerald complained that, after he had outlined the approach to his new novel and read a chapter to her, Zelda had tried "to write it herself" (*Life in Letters* 220–221). Although Zelda had agreed that her husband should publish his novel before she began "another extended piece," Fitzgerald also knew that she had just completed a play set, like his novel, on the Riviera. Feeling his livelihood threatened and his talent compromised, Fitzgerald could not prevent his bitterness from sounding in his words. "Imagine a painter," he struggled to explain, "trying to paint on canvasses each of which has a sketchy vulgarization, in his own manner, lined across it, by the companion within whose company he first observed the subject—at the painter's expense" (*Life in Letters* 220–221).

Under the circumstances, Fitzgerald's completion of his novel was itself an act of faith, but one without the rewards for which he had hoped. Published on April 12, 1934, *Tender is the Night* was an artistic success but a commercial failure. In the *New York Times*, John Chamberlain praised Fitzgerald's "craftsmanship, his marvelous sense of what might be called social climate, his sheer writing ability" (Bryer, *Reputation* 294). The Irish critic Mary Colum found the novel flawed, but nevertheless lauded Fitzgerald's "distinctive gifts—a romantic imagination, a style that is often brilliant, a swiftness of movement, and a sense of enchantment in people and places" (Bryer, *Reputation* 286). And the critic who had acclaimed *The Great Gatsby*, Gilbert Seldes, concluded that Fitzgerald "has stepped again to his natural place at the head of the American writers of our time" (Bryer, *Reputation* 293). Fitzgerald's friends and fellow writers, including James Branch Cabell, Robert Benchley, John Peale Bishop, and John Dos Passos, responded appreciatively to the novel, confirming to some extent Fitzgerald's own sense of his achievement.

Fitzgerald had certainly invested much of himself in his novel, turning the euphoric highs and poignant lows of his own marriage and career into the lives of his fictional characters and endowing their story with his own tragic sense of waste and loss. *Tender is the Night* is thus his most deeply personal novel. Yet he drew as well for inspiration on the lives of Gerald and Sara Murphy, to whom he dedicated the novel, and, as Robert Sklar has demonstrated, on his reading of Oswald Spengler, Karl Marx, D. H. Lawrence, and Carl Gustav Jung for the historical and psychological perspectives that would give meaning and significance to personal experience (257–265).

In the Murphys, for instance, Fitzgerald found his models of gracious and cultured expatriate life. From their Villa America on the French Riviera, which was a haven from the crass and corrupt (until it became fashionable), they dispensed "love & encouragement," Fitzgerald confided to Sara, and "clung to the idea of dauntless courage" (*Life in Letters* 288). For Fitzgerald, the Murphys were, as literary critic Milton R. Stern observes, "living examples of the old virtues and the old graces, of civilization wrought to an exquisite turn through work and courage, courtesy and politeness. . . . At the same time, they were representative to him of the new world that emerged from the ruin of the Victorian time that in self-deluded ways opened the doors to . . . gaudy cosmopolitanism, graceless money, and callous power that supplanted and destroyed . . . the graciousness the Murphys personified" (*Moment* 295–296). This paradox certainly lies at the heart of Fitzgerald's depiction of the Divers and their world at the Villa Diana, which is at once both sublime and corrupt.

Fitzgerald may have come to understand the source of that paradox—the relationship between money and class—from his reading of Marx's *The Communist Manifesto* (1848) and Spengler's *Decline of the West* (1932), both of which offered a sense of historical process to this relationship. Certainly the language of the novel's "General Plan," with its references to the "haute Burgeoise [*sic*]" and the hero's "rise to the top of the social world," suggests a Marxist understanding (for discussion of Marxist theory see Chapter 4) of social class and its connection to economics. Spengler, moreover, with his emphasis on money as the source of contemporary civilization's distinctive character, provided Fitzgerald with a philosophical basis for his own concern with money, particularly its corrupting effect.

Fitzgerald's deepening social and historical consciousness may also have been influenced by his reading of D. H. Lawrence and Jung. In Lawrence's *Fantasia of the Unconscious* (1922), for instance, which Fitzgerald recommended to Maxwell Perkins in 1930 (*Life in Letters* 187), the English novelist focused on some of the same psychological and moral issues of contemporary civilization that fascinated his American counterpart, especially the role of sex as a cultural determinant. In Jung's *Psychology of the Unconscious* (1916), in which the Swiss psychologist argued for the social rather than biological foundations of human behavior, Fitzgerald may have found confirmation of some of his own perspectives about society's effect upon character. Whatever the particular influence of his reading, which was wide ranging and heavily theoretical during the period of *Tender is the Night*'s composition, Fitzgerald "had found in Lawrence, Jung, and Spengler the 'data' for a deeper understanding of his own social and fictional world" (Sklar 264). He had found as well a philosophical foundation that would support and give meaning to his deeply personal story.

One of Fitzgerald's best (if not the best of his) short stories, "Babylon Revisited," also anticipates in theme and tone some of the key elements of *Tender is the Night*. First published in February 1931 in the *Saturday Evening Post*, "Babylon Revisited" tells the story of Charlie Wales, a man who confesses that he "lost everything [he] wanted in the boom, and not the bust" (*Short Stories* 633). During that period of gay abandon, he and his wife Helen had lived an extravagant and hedonistic expatriate life in Paris, a city that, as the story's title suggests, represents a modern Babylon. In the Bible, Babylon was a place of decadence, corruption, and, for the Jews who were exiled there, enslavement. One night, when her flirtation with another man goes too far, a drunken Charlie locks Helen out of their apartment and does not respond to her calls for admittance from the snow-covered pavement because he has passed out on the bed. Shortly thereafter, Helen dies of the pneumonia she developed that night, and Charlie, overcome by grief, guilt, and an overwhelming sense of responsibility for her death, leaves their daughter with his sister-in-law and her family and quits Paris to rehabilitate himself. A year and a half later, having recovered his health, battled his alcoholism, and recouped his fortune, a "chastened" (*Short Stories* 625) Charlie returns to Paris to reclaim his daughter, his Honoria. Yet his sister-in-law, who holds him responsible for Helen's death and resents the fact that she and her husband had lived a pinched existence while the Waleses enjoyed their extravagance, is unconvinced about his rehabilitation. When two of Charlie's former acquaintances, the drunken and parasitic Duncan Schaeffer and Lorraine Quarrles, make an unwelcome appearance at her flat, she refuses to relinquish the child to him. Bitterly disappointed, Charlie returns to the Ritz bar, where he had left his address and thus contributed to his own destruction, trying to convince himself that "they couldn't make him pay forever" (*Short Stories* 633).

A sense of loss pervades "Babylon Revisited." Charlie is nostalgic for the heady days that preceded the stock market crash and the Great Depression that ended the gay, glorious spree and regretful because he had "spoiled this city for [himself]" (*Short Stories* 618). And the story's circular structure, its beginning and ending at the Ritz bar, suggests that Charlie is trapped by his own past. He may now be "functioning" and "serious"; others may now be attracted to his "strength" and want "to draw a certain sustenance" from it (*Short Stories* 623), just as some of the characters in *Tender is the Night* feed on Dick Diver's vitality. He may, in fact, have genuinely reformed. Certainly the story's metaphor of payment suggests that Charlie, unlike so many of his former acquaintances, has paid and continues to pay for his irresponsibility. Yet without his Honoria, who is the visible, tangible proof of his rehabilitation, to sustain him, Charlie risks slipping back into his old self-destructive habits. The story resolves itself in irresolution: Is Charlie changed or merely self-deceived? Has he paid sufficiently the price of moral carelessness? Only for Charlie are the answers certain.

"Babylon Revisited" is thus a sad tale of reckoning. It examines the inevitable costs of irresponsibility and self-deception and exposes the self-destructive nature of each. In it, Fitzgerald renders Charlie's fate with compassion, never flinching from an honest presentation of his hero's weaknesses, yet sympathetic to his love of his daughter and his genuine efforts to reform. This theme, this tone, Fitzgerald transferred to his novel-in-progress at the time, *Tender is the Night*, making "Babylon Revisited" a compressed version of the larger work.

PLOT DEVELOPMENT

Fitzgerald may have found the philosophical underpinnings for Dick Diver's story of failure, but he was never entirely satisfied with the structure of its parts. In fact, four years after the publication of *Tender is the Night*, he suggested to his editor that its structure was a reason for its commercial failure. The novel's "true beginning," he wrote to Perkins, the tale of Dick's psychiatric career in Switzerland and his fateful meeting with Nicole, had been buried in its center (*Life in Letters* 374). Fitzgerald offered to restructure the work for publication of a collection of his novels, but never completed such a revision himself. In 1952, however, literary critic Malcolm Cowley did edit the novel according to Fitzgerald's stated intention, giving it a chronological structure by making the flashback with which Book Two begins the novel's opening chapter. Readers thus have two versions of *Tender is the Night*, further complicating an already troublesome novel.

Literary critics, of course, argue about the merits of each version, but Fitzgerald's own comments about the novel at the time of its publication, rather than in hindsight and to justify publication of a new edition, certainly give preference to the 1934 version. In a letter to influential literary critic H. L. Mencken just two weeks after *Tender is the Night*'s publication, Fitzgerald acknowledged that the first part of the book lacked the "deliberate intention" that characterized every other part of the novel, primarily because it had been developed over the years from varying plans. Despite this weakness, Fitzgerald concluded that he would not have changed the plan if he were to write it again (*Life in Letters* 256). *Tender is the Night* may have been flawed, but at its publication, it told the story that Fitzgerald intended and as he intended to tell it, with a certain structural complexity that upon examination does indeed fulfill both a rhetorical and a thematic purpose.

Tender is the Night begins at the chronological midpoint of its plot, in 1925, when Dick and Nicole Diver to all appearances reign supreme on their immaculate stretch of beach on the French Riviera. There, Dick meets a teenage movie actress, Rosemary Hoyt, with whom he shares a romantic infatuation that threatens to destroy his marriage and precipitates his wife's mental breakdown. Fitzgerald risked alienating the reader's sympathy for Dick, his central character, with this beginning. To counteract that effect, he shifted the novel back in time to 1917, when Dick, a medical student in Zurich, shows all the promise of a brilliant professional career, thereby rekindling the reader's sympathy for his protagonist and fanning the flames as he went on to provide the complicated circumstances of Dick's marriage to Nicole. The narrative continues into the present of 1925 and then moves beyond to Dick's partnership in a Swiss sanatorium, his brief affair with Rosemary five years after their initial flirtation, Nicole's retaliatory affair with Tommy Barban, Dick's descent into alcoholic self-disgust, and the inevitable disintegration of the Diver marriage in 1930.

The effect of this unusual chronological arrangement is to keep the focus on Dick's rise and fall, but especially to engender sympathy for his struggles. Appearances, readers come to understand in Book One, are indeed deceiving, and Fitzgerald's charming hero lives anything but a charmed life. In fact, the trajectory of this bright star has already deteriorated, as Dick is all too fully aware, and it is that knowledge that gives the novel its poignant tension. Dick may earn readers' condemnation for his moral failings and personal excesses, but the sense of disaster that hangs over his life from the novel's beginning makes simplistic judgments impossible.

POINT OF VIEW

Fitzgerald manipulates the novel's point of view, or the perspective from which readers view the events, to enhance his structural effects. Book One begins from the perspective of Rosemary Hoyt, a naive young woman who is charmed by what she sees and seduced by her own romantic notions about the Divers' life. From her perspective, the world revolves around the Villa Diana and Dick. Seen through Rosemary's eyes, the Divers' world is self-contained and seemingly impregnable, but promises something memorable. The effect is to make both Dick and Nicole sympathetic characters. Dick especially is a figure to admire for his ability to orchestrate this life and for his resistance to Rosemary's obvious attempts at seduction, despite his own attraction to her young loveliness.

Fitzgerald, however, undercuts Rosemary's perceptions about the Divers by emphasizing her youth and naivete and her limited scope of reference, particularly her immersion in the illusory world of the movies. Rosemary, in other words, is not yet capable of seeing through surfaces. Rosemary's inability to understand fully the Divers' world helps to heighten the tension created by the novel's structure because, once again, readers find themselves distrusting appearances and their own reactions to characters and situations even as they are tempted to believe and to approve them by Rosemary's obvious affirmation of them. On balance, however, Fitzgerald's presentation of Dick Diver is primarily positive and sympathetic in Book One because Dick's own behavior supports Rosemary's perspective.

Fitzgerald adopts an objective, third-person point of view to control the material in Book Two, which begins with the flashback to Dick's youth. The effect, once again, is to keep the focus on Dick Diver and, at least initially, to engender sympathy for him. In Book Two readers see a man of promise destroyed by his own goodness. In marrying Nicole, who he genuinely loves, Dick sacrifices himself to another, never reckoning the consequences of his choice. Readers come to understand the complexity of the marriage and the corruptive nature of the Warren money. As they witness Nicole's madness and Dick's valiant efforts to contain it, they are willing to grant his flaws and weaknesses, to judge him perhaps less harshly than they might were circumstances different. The third-person point of view, in other words, guarantees a measure of objectivity that would be impossible if the events were filtered through the perceptions of a character involved in them. In fact, as Fitzgerald slips more and more into subjectivity midway through Book Two, the narrative, as literary critic Henry Dan Piper aptly observes, "at times becomes maudlin with self-pity" (209).

In the second half of Book Two, the narrative becomes increasingly subjective, conveying the self-disgust and self-pity of a rapidly degenerating Dick Diver. As he sinks into alcoholism, engages in a meaningless affair with Rosemary, becomes an embarrassment to his profession, and finally orchestrates his own emotional and physical breakdown during a drunken brawl in Rome, there is little to admire in Dick and even less to pity, at least in part because he pities himself so well. While Fitzgerald may have hoped, as Piper notes, "to show the extent of Dick's moral disintegration, and his growing sense of guilt, by adopting Dick's point of view" (209) in this section of the novel, the decision prevents him from maintaining necessary distance from *Tender is the Night*'s perhaps most personal and deeply felt material.

Fitzgerald regains control of his narrative in Book Three by presenting the events from Nicole's point of view. Like her, readers are thus aware that an inevitability is soon to happen, and they are equally uncertain of the extent to which Dick is orchestrating that inevitability. "It was as though an incalculable story was telling itself inside him," Nicole thinks, "about which she could only guess at in moments when it broke through the surface" (267). The effect of this narrative point of view is gradually to shift the novel's focus to Nicole. As she rises and takes flight, Dick seems little more than an obsolete launching pad battered by use. Yet it is also to rehabilitate Dick. With this shift in point of view, readers develop again a measure of sympathy for Fitzgerald's hero, who, even at the verge of defeat, will rush to the aid of Mary North, now the Contessa di Minghetti, and Lady Caroline Sibley Biers when they are arrested for impersonating men and attempting to seduce young women. He may be broken, but he no longer wallows in self-pity, and thus he regains a certain measure of dignity as he quietly accepts the inevitable.

THE ENDING

The deliberate shift in point of view in Book Three contributes to what Fitzgerald called the novel's "dying fall" or Dick's gradual fade into obscurity (*Life in Letters* 255). In relating the final episodes of Dick's life through Nicole's eyes, Fitzgerald subtly eases his protagonist from the stage of his greatest triumphs until he simply disappears from view, and this strategy was clearly intentional. When some of his friends and fellow writers complained about the novel's ending, Fitzgerald responded vehemently to their complaints. "Ernest Hemingway. . . developed [for] me . . . that the dying fall was preferable to the dramatic ending under certain conditions," he explained in a letter to the writer and critic John Peale Bishop (*Life in Letters* 255). The dying fall, Fitzgerald reminded Hemingway himself several months after the novel's publication, was one attempt "to appeal to the lingering after-effects in the readers' mind" (*Life in Letters* 264).

A man with so much promise might be expected to fail brilliantly, but Dick does not. In fact, it would be virtually impossible to isolate one event of his life and define it as the turning point. Instead, the steady accumulation of circumstance and the inexorable movement of time combine to create a life, as it does for most people. Readers, however, wanted more for Dick. They want him to succeed, and when he does not, his failure is forever there, even in his absence. The tragedy of Dick's life, then, is that it comes to nothing unspectacularly, and the dying fall makes this point most effectively.

Dick's dying fall is even more poignant because Fitzgerald never allows readers to lose sight of his hero's "whole personality" (*Life in Letters* 246). Consequently, when his editor Maxwell Perkins suggested during the novel's serialization that the scandalous episode, with its overtones of lesbianism, in which Dick rescues Mary North and Lady Caroline Sibley-Biers be eliminated, Fitzgerald insisted on its inclusion. Traces of the heroic Dick, Fitzgerald was convinced, must remain even in defeat so he will linger in the mind and heart, as everything about Fitzgerald's general plan and narrative strategies clearly intended.

CHARACTER DEVELOPMENT

Dick's dying fall depends as well for its effect on his inherent goodness and idealism, the key elements of his character. The twenty-six year-old psychiatrist who arrives in Zurich in the spring of 1917 has every reason to feel the aptness of his nickname, "Lucky Dick" (116). Dick Diver has a degree from Johns Hopkins, a Rhodes Scholarship to Oxford, an opportunity to study with Sigmund Freud in Vienna, and a career with so much promise that the government exempts him from military service in World War I (115). A man with the rigor and stamina to swim in the winter Danube and to burn his textbooks for fun, but only after he has committed to memory the essence of each (116), Dick will publish his first book before he reaches age thirty (116). This is, the narrator explains, Dick's "heroic period" (116). His self-control, self-discipline, and unprepossessing charm (116) make him seem utterly complete.

Dick's career choice reveals much about his essential self and his symbolic role in the novel. As a psychiatrist, Dick dives deep into the hearts and minds of those who suffer, unlocking the secrets of their inner lives in an effort to restore their psychic and emotional health. Dick, in other words, gives care, and he does so because he cares. His concern for others makes him the moral center of *Tender is the Night*. He assumes responsibility for the weak and the suffering; he attempts to unify chaos to create order from disorder. Dick is a sort of savior, the "spoiled priest" that Fitzgerald envisioned in his "General Plan" (Mizener, *Paradise* 307), capable of blessing the world he enters and fashioning from it bright moments of transcendence that link material and spiritual realities.

Nowhere are Dick's creative and restorative powers more in evidence than at the Villa Diana, the haven of order and harmony where Rosemary, like so many others before her, comes under the spell of the Divers. Rosemary's first glimpse of Dick, raking the beach of gravel as he gives a "quiet little perfor-mance" for the delight of his guests (6), offers an image of the psychiatrist that suggests method to his madness. Dick may seem to play the fool, but he does so at the service of others and, as his raking of the beach suggests, with the inten-tion of bringing order to and creating beauty from the world's natural disorder. As Rosemary observes the Divers' life, she realizes their lives held "a purpose, a working over something, a direction, an act of creation different from any she had known" (19). The Villa Diana, as Robert Sklar observes, represents "a world built in criticism of and competition with the 'true world' that was thun-dering by up north" (269). It is a world of civilized order, polite decencies, and comforting rituals. Evoking in its name the goddess of the moon and the hunt and, most significantly, the protectress of women, the Villa Diana provides so-lace to the world's wounded and weary, especially Nicole. Dick, the man with the megaphone (27), is the mastermind behind it. As the narrator observes about Dick: "people believed he made special reservations about them, recog-nizing the proud uniqueness of their destinies, buried under the compromises of how many years" (27). Such is the nature of Dick Diver's ability to heal the world, but not, rather ironically, to save himself.

The very quality—his desire to please—that makes Dick such a charismatic host and such an effective healer also makes him vulnerable to others. So in-grained is his habit of pleasing that even those who have abused Dick (although not without provocation), such as Mary North and Lady Caroline Sibley-Biers, know that they can seek his assistance in an emergency and he will respond to their pleas. Dick will undertake to fix anything, whether he cares about it or not, simply because it is part of his nature to please and to care to be loved.

Unlike another of Fitzgerald's idealized heroes, Jay Gatsby, with whom he shares much in common, Dick is utterly self-aware, so he recognizes this qual-ity in himself, just as he has recognized other aspects of his character. He knows, for instance, during his heroic period in Zurich, that he had not yet ex-perienced the hardships that test character. At thirty-eight, he knows that he only pretends to like helping everyone (84). He knows as well that his "power of arousing a fascinated and uncritical love" comes at a cost (27). Yet even self-knowledge cannot prevent his destruction, for the ideals by which Dick lives have fallen victim to a new world order, one that simultaneously repels and attracts him.

The son of a poor clergyman from Buffalo, New York, Dick had learned proper values and behavior from his father. Instilled with a belief in the value of "honor, courtesy, [and] courage" (204), Dick arrives in Europe untried and un-tested, his essential idealism still intact. That idealism, however, leaves him un-prepared for the world about to open to him. Dick's illusions, which are quintessentially American, make him a sort of innocent abroad, and the lessons he learns there challenge his sense of himself.

Those lessons have much to do with money, particularly its capacity to control and to corrupt, and Dick learns them chiefly through his association with the Warrens, one of America's "great feudal families" (127). When Dick marries Nicole, the troubled youngest daughter of the Warren clan, he enters a world of vast wealth that commands respect and demands service as its right. Although he remains financially self-sufficient to some degree throughout his marriage and pays for his own clothing and sundry expenses from a small income and the even smaller royalties from his publications (170), his independence is little more than pretense. Nicole's vast and ever increasing fortune inevitably changes the balance of their relationship. Money makes anything possible, and Dick is gradually seduced by its pleasures, eventually abandoning even the work (although it, too, has been purchased by the Warrens) that has been a source of self-definition. Too late, he comes to realize that "he had been swallowed up like a gigolo, and somehow permitted his arsenal to be locked up in the Warren safety-deposit vaults" (201). That knowledge sends him spiraling into self-disgust, self-degradation, and self-pity.

Dick Diver is certainly Fitzgerald's most complex hero. He is a man of internal contradictions that make possible both self-destruction and victimization, and both aspects of his fate are inextricably bound to his relationship with Nicole Warren. So deep is his love for his beautiful, half-destroyed wife and hers for her charming and courageous "Capitaine" (124) that they become one being, "Dicole" (103). This merging of selves is not healthy for either of them. As Dick's patient, Nicole gives herself over entirely to his care, depending on his strength of purpose and his self-discipline to keep her fragile psyche balanced. As Dick's wife, she requires of him those same qualities to shape and maintain their ordered and harmonious life. Nicole's need makes Dick forever her doctor as well as her husband, and he must be always vigilant in his treatment and care. Despite the strain of such responsibility, Dick struggles valiantly to restore Nicole to health, but the effort exacts a cost: "He could not watch her disintegrations without participating in them" (190–191). As is his nature, Dick will sacrifice himself. Nicole will accept his sacrifice because she is essentially selfish and self-centered, a product of the Warren world.

Just as Rosemary's first glimpse of Dick provides an image of his essential self, so, too, does her first glimpse of Nicole provide a similar picture. Lying under a beach umbrella, Nicole strikes Rosemary, who meets her eyes but is not seen, as "hard and lovely and pitiful" (6). She presents an image of perfect repose that in its deliberateness rings untrue. Subsequent glimpses of Nicole reinforce Rosemary's initial impression. Nicole, for instance, solemnly watches her child frolic in the sea (10). Several days later, Rosemary sees her sitting in her car, "her lovely face set, controlled, her eyes brave and watchful, looking straight ahead toward nothing" (14). As these descriptions suggest, Nicole's deliberate repose is a mask. "Hard" and "controlled," its "lovely" and "brave" exterior conceals only partly the "pitiful" emptiness that lies beneath.

Shattered by her father's incestuous possession of her body, Nicole keeps in check a jealous, irrational, manic self by utter self-absorption in a calm, methodical, mannered self that Dick has fashioned for her. By nature a creature of impulse, she is, following her psychiatric "cure," hungry for life and longs (or at least thinks she longs), as the brief, impressionistic summary of the Divers' years of early marriage in Book Two, Chapter Ten indicates, to find some meaningful work of her own (161). Yet she lacks the inner resources that would make possible such an existence. What she desires instead is the carefree life that her money can buy. As the brief summary of her marriage suggests, Nicole does indeed enjoy her life of "fun" with Dick (160). She likes the prospect of living near the beach, and her most worrisome bother involves translating recipes into French (162). Such an existence offers her at least a temporary stay against confusion.

Locked in their mutual love and unhappiness, Nicole leads a life of utter dependence on Dick. That life changes, however, in Book Three when, in an effort to save himself, Dick forces his wife to break free of her dependency on him and to redefine herself. Rather surprisingly, perhaps, Nicole has reached the point where she is ready to make such a break. Dick's self-degradation has become both a disappointment and an embarrassment to her, and she finds herself resenting his role in her life. Her feelings for him and about herself are particularly clarified for her on the day that Dick insists on performing his old feats of strength and daring on Gausse's Beach. Three times Dick attempts his "lifting trick" (283), and three times he fails, while Nicole watches with "smiling scorn" (283). At first she is irritated by his need to play again "the old game of flattery" (282) for Rosemary and then contemptuous of the sheer folly of his bravado. Upon her return to the Villa Diana, Nicole, no longer content to be a "huntress of corralled game" (300), determines to begin her affair with Tommy Barban.

The Nicole who emerges from Dick's protection is not, perhaps surprisingly, a new model, but rather the self she was becoming before her violation by her father. Nicole Diver becomes Nicole Warren, as cold and hard as the money that created her, proud of her "white crook's eyes" that connect her to her heritage (292), and determined to break free. By the time Dick blesses the beach in a gesture of absolution (314) before he fades into obscurity, Nicole feels little more than a vague regret for their shared past and a touch of pity for the man who saved her. She is a Warren again, sharing Gausse's Beach now with her lover and her sister Baby.

Nicole's pairing with Barban and Baby at the end of *Tender is the Night* emphasizes the nature of her transformation because each stands in stark contrast to Dick and the values he represents. Tommy Barban, for instance, as his name suggests, is a modern barbarian. Hard and cynical, Barban is a polyglot, half-French and half-American and educated in England. He is also a man utterly without loyalties, willing to fight for the sheer joy of fighting. In fact, he has worn the uniform of eight different countries (30). Like another Fitzgerald character with whom he shares a name, *The Great Gatsby's* Tom Buchanan, Barban believes in nothing but his own brute force (18). "Courage [is] his game" (196), not the courage demanded of self-sacrifice and self-discipline, but the brute force that instills fear in other, lesser man, as Barban's duel with the inept and pretentious Albert McKisco makes clear. Barban fights that duel not for a principle, not for honor, but because he is essentially a bully. In fact, contact with the Divers' world of civilized virtues and personal decencies makes him want to fight (30). Barban, in effect, is bent on destroying the world that Dick has created.

In her own way, Baby Warren is engaged in a similar dismantling of the Diver world, however much she may believe, in her pretentious love of all things English and her narrow-minded acceptance of conventionality that she is the guardian of civilized virtues. A woman of twenty-five when Dick meets her, shortly before his marriage to Nicole, she seems already pinched and inflexible, old beyond her years. Passionless and pruddish, she lacks the ability to enjoy life and seems repelled by her own nature, particularly her sexuality. Dick, for instance, notices immediately her habit of frequently crossing her legs "in the manner of tall restless virgins" (151). To Baby, Nicole's carefree manner is both an enigma and an embarrassment, and Dick is too much the intellectual. Cocooned in her money, Baby is utterly convinced of both her rightness and her ability to purchase whatever she wants, including a doctor-husband to manage her crazy sister, and Dick, despite himself, finds that he is attracted to her monied arrogance and self-assurance.

That monied arrogance, however, epitomized by Baby Warren, endangers the Diver world of civilized virtues and humane behavior. Baby, as her intention to purchase a doctor for Nicole clearly indicates, cares nothing about the needs or benefit of others. Her reason for purchasing the doctor, in fact, is primarily to relieve herself of the worry and bother of caring for Nicole. So accustomed is she to buying what she wants that she simply cannot fathom its impossibility (153), so when she takes on the Italian police and the American consul following Dick's drunken brawl in Rome, Baby is indeed a formidable force. Baby's willingness to come to Dick's rescue, however, an effort which could be construed as a kindness, has nothing to do with altruism and everything to do with avoiding scandal, preserving her family's reputation, and bullying others into service. Her actions, moreover, give her a certain welcome leverage over Dick. Whatever Baby does, then, and whatever she represents is motivated by self and stands in opposition to others. Others, after all, are intended only for use.

As both an observer of and a participant in the collapse of the Diver marriage, Rosemary Hoyt plays a pivotal role in *Tender is the Night*. Not yet eighteen when she meets the Divers on Gausse's Beach, Rosemary epitomizes the title of her debut film, *Daddy's Girl*. Her character has the ability to withstand the vulgar, and her unself-conscious naïveté exposes pretentious boredom. As her name suggests, Rosemary, the herb of remembrance, recalls Dick to his youth, to the best part of his ideal self, and he is drawn to her by his appreciation and need of the very qualities that he himself once possessed. In Rosemary, Dick senses "something blooming" (22). The question is into what will she flower.

While Rosemary may be "Daddy's Girl" on celluloid, in real life she is her mother's daughter, and Mrs. Elsie Speers has instilled in her a certain rigor and self-discipline. For example, Rosemary repeatedly dives into a Venetian canal in January for the sake of a perfect cinematic take and thereby develops pneumonia (17). A curious mixture of tough romanticism defines Rosemary's essential nature. She may stand ready to embrace life's possibilities, but she will do so on her own terms. Like Baby and Nicole Warren, Rosemary knows her own worth and possesses the capital to be her own person. She may have to work for her money, but as her mother tells her, "economically you're a boy, not a girl" (40).

Rosemary, with her "mature distrust of the trivial, the facile and the vulgar" (13), loves Dick for those qualities in him that are part of her best self, but she cannot win him because she is too much a product of her world of illusion. Rosemary draws everything about her frame of reference from motion pictures. A fantasy kiss, for instance, is "as blurred as a kiss in pictures" (39), and when she approaches a weeping Luis Campion in the early morning hours following the Divers' first dinner party, "a scene in a rôle she had played last year swept over her irresistibly" (44). Not quite certain of what to make of the unfamiliar world of the Riviera, Rosemary is relieved when director Earl Brady appears on the scene. Without a script, Rosemary, lacking any real experience of the world, must summon her imagination to effect passion for Dick, who recognizes that she does not yet understand that true feeling resides in the deep recesses of the heart (64). By the time she learns that truth (if indeed she learns it), her blooming self has gone, and she has perfected her role. By the time she and Dick engage in their affair, it seems little more than part of a script, a consummation of desire but not love because each is little more than a dream to the other.

Rosemary, as one of the characters that surrounds Dick Diver, exemplifies one of the weaknesses and temptations—infidelity—that leads to his destruction. Other secondary characters serve similar functions. Baby Warren, for instance, embodies Dick's desire for money, and Tommy Barban suggests something of his own anarchic impulses. Albert McKisco, the utterly conventional (and therefore highly successful) author (205), provides an image of Dick's own failure of ambition. Like McKisco, Dick has few original ideas, which his *Psychology for Psychiatrists*, published before he was thirty years old, represented (165). Even Abe North, the epitome of the self-destructive artist, foreshadows Dick's own nightmarish alcoholic existence. Extending himself into the lives of these secondary characters, Dick must eventually pay the cost in his own psychic deterioration. In their flaws and weaknesses ultimately lie Dick's own.

THEMATIC ISSUES

In this depiction of Dick Diver's self-destruction, Fitzgerald certainly develops one of *Tender is the Night*'s thematic strains and fulfills an element of his "General Plan." Despite his best intentions, Dick cannot overcome his need to be loved and his willingness to be of use. He cannot reconcile his conflicting desires for money, with its promise of ease and beauty, and for professional esteem and service, with their self-affirmative rewards. Dick's idealism does indeed fall victim to his own nature and to the seductions of the brilliant and glamorous world in which he must struggle to maintain his personal integrity. His is indeed a story of wasted promise, "a romance," according to Robert Sklar, "about the excesses and the failures of romanticism" (267). Dick believes in his ability to heal. He believes that goodness and love, decency and good faith can redeem human existence and give it meaning. Thus, the implications of his sad failure, accompanied only by the silent footfalls of his solitary departure from the stage of life, reverberate in the emptiness of his dying fall, just as Fitzgerald intended them to do.

By virtue of its contemporary setting, however, and its grounding in the processes of history, *Tender is the Night* is far more than a tale of romantic excess and failure. It is as well a critique of the brilliant and glamorous bourgeois world that contributes to that failure. In it, Fitzgerald examines a world gone mad. Chance, violence, and unexplained deaths are its norms; sexual confusion is rampant. Content to believe the beautiful illusions that are intended to conceal these awful truths, the people inhabiting this world lack the force of character to challenge and change them. Money makes possible their irresponsibility and callous selfishness. Fitzgerald had certainly covered such ground before, most convincingly in *The Great Gatsby*, but that novel's focus on the American scene makes its critique less comprehensive than *Tender is the Night*'s. Jay Gatsby embodies the dreams of a nation. Dick Diver, in contrast, represents the disintegration of Western civilization. In *Tender is the Night*, neither

Europe nor America is immune from the disease of modernity, which is the thrust of the novel's major theme.

Fitzgerald's critique of the modern world derives from his depiction of both its nature and its scope. Dick's life, for instance, plays itself out amid a background of random violence and unexplained death that evoke a sense of chaos and disorder. From a shooting in a Paris train station to the murder of an Afro-American whose body is deposited on Rosemary's bed, from Abe North's beating death in a New York speakeasy to Dick's own savage pummeling by the Italian police, the violence that lies just beneath the surface of strong emotion erupts in bursts of destructive force, even among those charged with upholding the law. Seemingly unencumbered by social and moral constraints, those who inhabit this world lack the self-control and concern for others that should keep such emotions in check within civilized society, so their world mirrors their selfish brutality.

Sexual confusion serves as yet another sign of the disintegration of Western civilization in *Tender is the Night*. Baby Warren's wooden sexlessness, for instance, suggests the dissipation of vital sexual energy. The unhappiness of the homosexual Luis Campion and the psychic torment of the Chilean homosexual whom Dick, knowing the futility of the charge, is asked to cure suggest that these same sex relationships are a perversion of the natural order. It is, in fact, the criminal nature of such relationships that so threatens Mary North and Lady Caroline Sibley-Biers when, dressed as French sailors, they attempt to seduce two young women late in the novel.

Fitzgerald pairs such obvious evidence of sexual confusion with a more subtle depiction of role reversal in the novel. Baby Warren and Rosemary Hoyt especially, but even to some extent Nicole and Mrs. Elsie Speers (as well as some of the other minor female characters), have become hard and uncaring. They are almost masculine in their approach to the world and therefore little different from the predatory males who control political and financial mechanisms. Dick, for instance, finds it most disconcerting that he must negotiate with Baby Warren when he proposes marriage to Nicole (158). She makes it clear, however, that she has the authority of any man and that she has, in fact, authority over him. Dick, of course, will eventually come to know this truth as the Warrens purchase more and more of his soul. Similarly, Rosemary has the power to exercise her own freedom. If she chooses Dick (19), she will have him, regardless of the consequences to him, to Nicole, or to his marriage, and her mother will encourage her pursuit of this married man (40). Rosemary, after all, has been raised to be self-sufficient and has thus earned the right to purchase (with whatever currency, including sex) whatever she desires.

Within the world of *Tender is the Night*, Dick is the character who assumes the traditional female role. He creates the haven of the Villa Diana, he nurtures

— 119 —

his children, and most important, he strives to preserve the values of order and decency that uphold civilization. For a time as she struggles to save her husband from alcoholic self-destruction, Mary North shares Dick's role in the novel, but eventually this "brave, hopeful woman" (62) abdicates her female responsibilities to the customs of a foreign culture (263) and flaunts convention without regard for the consequences. Similarly, Nicole, by virtue of her emotional fragility, may, for a time, be forgiven her disinterested mothering. When she endangers the health and welfare of her family, however, first by deliberately causing an automobile accident and then, in defiance of her husband's wishes, by callously tossing his special camphor rub to her lover (278), she forfeits her claim to such forgiveness. The women in *Tender is the Night* are "emergent Amazons" (177), a bold sort of conqueror exercising their power with the ruthlessness of any man and making Dick's efforts virtually futile. If, after all, the women who have traditionally sacrificed their desires to create and preserve an ideal are no longer willing to do so, how can the efforts of one man, who is himself struggling against a traditional role, do anything but fail?

Fitzgerald uses the motif of incest to make clear the destructive power of the violence and sexual disorder he depicts. Devereaux Warren's incestuous act of selfish possession of his daughter Nicole victimizes the vulnerable and innocent, mocking the very notion of parental love and protection, one of the most sacred trusts of virtually every civilization. Warren then compounds his crime first by refusing to accept responsibility for his actions, thereby hindering Nicole's treatment, and then by using his vast fortune to avoid punishment. Because Warren can afford the expense of Swiss sanitariums and brilliant psychiatrists who care only about their patient's recovery, he can even purchase a certain measure of self-absolution. He has, after all, provided Nicole with the best of care to heal her wounded psyche.

Another thematic concern, Devereaux Warren's ability to abrogate his responsibility and to purchase self-absolution, reveals money as a corrosive element of the modern world. While money certainly offers the potential for ease, grace, beauty, and all the benefits that have traditionally defined the good life, those who inhabit the world of *Tender is the Night* use their vast wealth to purchase little of such benefits. Instead, they buy power and influence and satisfy, at least temporarily, an insatiable longing for meaning and purpose by the acquisition of a vast array of material items that create the illusion of substance. Devereaux Warren certainly provides evidence of the first sort of purchasing power, and Baby Warren, having learned such lessons from the cradle, carries on the family tradition by bullying government officials into doing her bidding and even buying a doctor for her sister. Nicole's shopping trip is a revelation of the second sort of purchasing power.

Armed with a two-page list, Nicole buys an assortment of trinkets and luxurious yet frivolous items (54–55). Whatever she likes, she buys, for herself or others, it makes no difference. What matters is her ability to buy. Indiscriminate purchasing power drives the very engine of contemporary society, so it is certainly understandable that everyone wants to make a quick and easy fortune. From Franz Gregorovius to the "insistent American" (309) intent on selling the New York newspapers to the steady stream of tourists and expatriates arriving daily in Europe (93, 309) as he awaits his break in the movies, everyone is striving to the Warren state of being. They see only the tangible benefits and not the spiritual corruption of such a reality.

Money lies at the root of the social and psychic disintegration that Fitzgerald depicts in *Tender is the Night*, and nobody is unscathed by its influence. In fact, virtually everyone in the Diver world is willing to settle for the temporary antidotes to confusion and emptiness that money can provide. They are willing, in other words, to accept the illusion of reality, as Fitzgerald makes clear in his use of the novel's movie world to evoke unreal realities. Rosemary, for instance, as the analysis in the section on Character Development makes clear, is almost entirely a creation of her motion picture world and can barely respond to life without a script. Beyond the example of one individual, however, lies the pervasive cultural influence of Franco-American Films, the creator of illusions such as *Daddy's Girl* that move the emotions and shape the perceptions of a captivated audience. Now *The Grandeur that was Rome* exists on a studio lot, as a larger than life set that substitutes for the real thing and will thus become the real thing in the minds of an audience. Beautiful illusions now sustain a people grown weary of painful realities. In fact, within this context, Dick's affair with Rosemary, played out against the backdrop of motion picture reality, is itself a sustaining illusion. It allows him for a time to escape the demands of life with Nicole and to recover his sense of his best self (91).

Because *Tender is the Night* focuses on American expatriate life, America and Americans seem to bear primary responsibility for this disintegrating social order. As representatives of a new and emerging American aristocracy, the Warrens embody the ideals of a changing nation. They are rich and powerful. They are capable of running a submarine blockade on an American cruiser to bring Nicole to Europe for psychiatric treatment (128), and they want for nothing. This new generation of aristocrats—the Armours, Palmers, Swifts, Fields, McCormicks, and, of course, Warrens—epitomizes the American Dream as well, for these new "feudal families" (127) have earned their wealth, not inherited it. Sid Warren, Nicole's grandfather, had actually begun the family dynasty as a horse trader (143). Such a background makes them ruthless and pragmatic. They know what it is to claw their way to the top. They have had little opportunity to develop an understanding of and an appreciation for traditional values and virtues; such values and virtue may well have hindered their ascent if they had had them. Thus, Devereaux Warren may look like "a fine American type in every way" (125), but beneath the surface he is diseased and corrupt, every bit the "peasant" that Dr. Dohmler disgustedly names him (129).

In Europe, the American expatriates represent this new aristocracy. Liberated by money, they have the ability to do and to become whatever they wish, but they lack the imagination to reach beyond the mundane and the ordinary. People like the McKiscos, Mrs. Abrams, Collis Clay, and Baby Warren are little more than crass materialists who smugly believe in their own and their nation's superiority (except, of course, for the Anglophile Baby Warren). In Europe, they lead lives of restless dissatisfaction, as if hoping to find meaning in motion, but a nervous energy inevitably betrays their failure to attain it.

Other Americans, with fewer monetary advantages, make the journey to Europe as well. They are eager to share the experience and, with luck, profit by it. They, too, represent their changing nation. The newspaper vendor is one representative of this other class, but so, too, are the American women who barge into Nicole and Tommy's hotel room to wave farewell to their American sailors. The entire episode is a riot of sound and fury, including violence, raucous laughter, and bawdy behavior. It begins with a fight between two American sailors and ends when one of the two girls who enter Nicole's hotel room rips off a piece of her clothing and waves it like a flag. Presided over by two Englishwomen who sit in American rocking chairs studiously ignoring the whole ugly affair and punctuated by the strains of the "Star-Spangled Banner" being played aboard the battleship (296–297), the episode ridicules the very notion of American civilization by focusing upon its barbarians, including Nicole and Tommy (who is half-American). As counterpoint to Nicole's infidelity, in fact, the episode makes clear that the new breed of Americans, whether they command the cruiser or man it, whether they are Warrens or an anonymous parade of Bens and Charlies, is dismantling an old world order with its crass materialism, crude behavior, and selfish arrogance.

The foundations of that old world order, however, have also been crumbling in the Old World. The grandeur that was Rome now exists on a studio lot. Little different from the Warrens, the old Roman families are referred to as "bandits" by Dick (221). Baby considers the English the "best-balanced race in the world" (214), but Dick finds them unsympathetic and even distasteful in the aftermath of change (195). Paris is the new Babylon, a place of wild excess and debauchery. Europe and Europeans, as Fitzgerald depicts them, are hardly in a position to sustain civilization; they have exhausted their energy and resources and look now to America for both.

In the novel, Franz Gregorovius epitomizes the European state of affairs. Whereas Dick seriously aspires to become the greatest psychiatrist ever, Franz carries the weight of an oppressive past that limits his imagination and daring. When he looks out his window, he sees the monuments and memorials of past generations (132). Burdened by the past, Franz abandons a dream of establishing a clinic in New York, marries a stolid and practical woman, and settles for a drab existence as a competent clinician. He longs for a share in the postwar boom, evidence of which those American expatriates bring with them from a thriving homeland. Franz may disapprove of the amoral, monied culture of the victims he treats, but he comes to Dick, in the end, for the money he both envies and despises. He is as willing as any Warren to make use of an old friend and to reap his own financial rewards (174–176).

In both its nature and its scope, the world of *Tender is the Night* is a diminished thing, its glory transient, its loss bittersweet. Yet that diminished thing has the power to diminish the brave and the good who struggle against it, and herein lies the novel's major theme. Everybody, it seems, wants the new postwar realities epitomized by the Warrens, everybody, that is, except Dick, who has been largely isolated from his homeland and those postwar realities during his studies in Europe. Into his life, however, comes Nicole, and as Fitzgerald's language makes clear, she brings to him "the essence of a continent" (136). In the rhythm of American dance tunes and the unbridled excitement of youth, Dick, too, responds to the seductions of a new America, only to find himself as compromised as his compatriots. A world that does not value the talents of a Dick Diver, Fitzgerald seems to say, that selfishly uses and abuses such goodness and such potential, has certainly perverted its own potential for greatness.

FIGURATIVE LANGUAGE

Fitzgerald relies upon a pervasive military metaphor to convey the central theme of *Tender is the Night*, thereby suggesting that two opposing sets of values are in conflict in the postwar world, each mounting a campaign to topple the other. On one side lies the traditional values and human decencies embodied by Dick's father and the gold-star mothers. On the other side lies the vulgar materialism and crude pretensions of a new generation embodied by the Warrens. Dick is a contemporary General Ulysses S. Grant, as compromised as the historical military hero. Through his connection to Abe North, he is also a contemporary Abraham Lincoln. At stake in the conflict are issues every bit as important as those for which Grant and Lincoln fought.

Fitzgerald details the contending forces of modernity during the Divers' outing to the Western Front battlefield near Amiens where, Dick tells Rosemary, it once took "a whole empire" one month to walk to a stream that they could reach now in two minutes' time (56). Inspecting the trenches and surveying the landscape through his field glasses, Dick commands his own troops.

He wants Nicole, the Norths, and Rosemary to share his perception of the place and tries to communicate to them its significance.

To Dick, the world war had been fought to protect a way of life that was firmly rooted in the past, and the fact that so many were willing to die for its values was a measure of their idealism, a testament to their belief. Although a cynical Abe challenges this view, claiming that this kind of battle had been invented by General Grant during the American Civil War, Dick stands firm in his conviction, drawing a distinction between "mass butchering," a system of destruction, and "a century of middle-class love," a rationale for destruction (57). Dick mourns that the "beautiful lovely safe world" that they had fought to preserve was, rather ironically, a casualty of the conflict. He is aware as well that the young would no longer be willing to fight for such a cause, for such idealism, because such certainty had also been a victim of the fighting.

To reinforce Dick's argument, Fitzgerald draws Rosemary, a representative of that postwar generation, into the exchange. Dick looks to her for confirmation of his views, but she can offer nothing except "I don't know" (57), a response that clearly indicates her ignorance of the past. It suggests as well an absence of values that does indeed confirm his perspective, but not quite as he has expected. Rosemary, whose hair is "like an armorial shield" (1), cannot understand the old certainties and cannot appreciate the world they created. If she were asked to make the sacrifice of that previous generation, she would not have a reason (beyond her own self-interest) for doing so. She is as lost as the American girl, a second representative of that postwar generation, who cannot locate her brother's grave, and of the government that sends her to the wrong site (58).

In the Divers' encounter with the gold-star mothers and widows Fitzgerald again grounds the conflict between conflicting value systems in an evocation of the world war. In the middle of a luncheon made chaotic by a frantic and incoherent telephone call from Abe North (who should be aboard a ship sailing to America), the Divers and Rosemary find their attention drawn to a table of women who form a rather incongruous unit. They are gold-star mothers and widows, women who had sacrificed sons and husbands to the war. Their presence in the room, mourning "something they could not repair," makes it "beautiful" and recalls Dick to another time, a better era: "Momentarily, he sat again on his father's knee, riding with Moseby while the old loyalties and devotions fought on around him" (101).

As he did with his reference to General Grant on the occasion of the battlefield tour, Fitzgerald again evokes the American Civil War in his reference to Colonel John Moseby, the Confederate cavalry officer, deliberately yoking together two bloody conflicts separated by time and space but united in significance. In linking both as well to the gold-star mothers, Fitzgerald also invests them with honor and dignity, with ideals and values worth defending. In his reverence for these women, reflected through Dick's eyes, Fitzgerald conveys his appreciation of them.

Dick's response to these women, however, is little more than a brief interruption in a life increasingly punctuated by the violence and chaos embodied in Abe's telephone call. As the psychiatrist, "almost with an effort" (101), gives his attention once again to Nicole and Rosemary, Fitzgerald makes clear that Dick is less and less capable of aligning himself with all that these mothers represent. Dick, in other words, his allegiances shifted, now assumes the role in this episode that Rosemary played in the battlefield episode, representing "the whole new world in which he believed" (101). This tenuous shift in Dick's attitudes signifies the internal conflict that has resulted from external conflict between opposing value systems in the modern world.

Fitzgerald's allusions to the American Civil War make clear this dual conflict, the inner one of which plays itself out most fully in Dick Diver (although both Nicole and Rosemary struggle with it as well). Here, too, Fitzgerald uses a military metaphor, connecting his hero to General Ulysses S. Grant, to give resonance to the struggle. Twice Fitzgerald specifically compares Dick to Grant. In the first instance, at the end of the brief biography with which Book Two begins, the narrator summarizes Dick's career to that point and foreshadows its conclusion in a comparison to Grant's exile in Illinois following his disgraceful discharge from the army (118). In the second instance, at the end of the brief recitation of Dick's obscurity in the novel's final paragraph, the narrator rounds off Dick's life by observing that Nicole likened his career to "Grant's in Galena" (315). Fitzgerald's comparison is apt because Dick, like Grant, is both a commander leading the charge to preserve an ideal and a corrupted shadow of his former greatness.

Like Grant, who was tending his general store in obscurity until he was called to service during the American Civil War, Dick, too, Fitzgerald's comparison suggests, is biding his time in preparation for his "intricate destiny" (118), his meeting with Nicole. Then his charge is clear: He must, in the name of love, draw on all his ingenuity and skill to preserve "this scarcely saved waif of disaster" (136), just as Grant invented modern warfare to preserve the Union. Yet, as Dick's efforts to give meaning and order to their lives fall victim to his corruption by money, his own love battles assume a different cast. He tells Nicole he desires to throw a raucous party. Following such a riotous evening, however, he will be overwhelmed by "the waste and extravagance" required of his victory, and looks back on the evening as a "massacre" (27). However much Dick began his service with an idealistic purpose, he eventually derives nothing of meaning from it, and by the end of his campaign, his glory has faded. Thus, when Grant is evoked in the novel's closing paragraph, the allusion recalls not the great military hero but the dishonored president who profited by the rapacious capitalism of the Gilded Age and its robber barons. Dick is no longer capable of escaping his obscurity. His "intricate destiny," in fact, had never been quite like Grant's because the military hero had at least preserved the Union before his corruption. Dick, in contrast, had managed nothing more lasting than his *Psychology for Psychiatrists*, the projected second volume of which was to be merely an "amplification" of the first (165).

If Dick is *Tender is the Night*'s General Grant, then Abe North is its Abraham Lincoln, a comparison that underscores the tragic dimensions of the novel's conflict. Abe's sad face (9), his "brilliant and precocious start" (34), and "the solid dignity that flowed from him" (83) recall the person and career of a great man destroyed before he fulfilled his promise, too. Unlike Lincoln, however, Abe North self-destructs. Seduced by the gaudy spree of the postwar world, he ignores his talent and drowns his self-loathing in drink to catastrophic effect not only to himself but also to the people Lincoln made free. Abe's irresponsibility lands one Negro, Mr. Freeman, in jail, falsely accused of a crime, and leads to the death of another, the result of mistaken identity. The disjunction between the two Abes allows Fitzgerald to make clear the degree to which a modern generation, lacking a sense of purpose and responsibility, has perverted the ideals and achievements of a previous generation. In the modern world, Fitzgerald's comparison thus suggests, neither a Lincoln nor a Grant can withstand the forces of destruction.

However much Dick may romanticize the American Civil War and the world war, attributing to the people who fought them motives, beliefs, and emotions that may simply reflect his own hopes and needs, within the context of the novel, his perspectives do carry weight and seriousness because Fitzgerald renders them without irony. He does not, in other words, call them into question by verbal or situational contradictions. That fact, as well as the sheer pervasiveness of the military language and allusions, ultimately makes clear the importance of these literary devices to the development of the novel's theme. They provide a social and an historical context for all the private and personal battles in *Tender is the Night*.

A PSYCHOLOGICAL INTERPRETATION

Fitzgerald's exploration of the psychic disorder and disintegration that results from social disorder and disintegration certainly highlighted psychology as the new field of study coming to prominence in the twentieth century. His decision to make his hero a psychiatrist and to set much of the novel within psychiatric clinics makes it appropriate to analyze *Tender is the Night* from the perspective of the psychological critic. Such a critic applies the strategies of Freudian, Jungian, or some other theory of human psychology to fiction to explain characters' motivation and action in clinical terms. The focus of any

Freudian analysis of *Tender is the Night* must be the novel's motif of the fathers, which certainly evokes the Oedipus/Electra complex.

According to Sigmund Freud, the founder of psychoanalysis, every child experiences latent sexual feelings toward the parent of the opposite sex. He named these complex feelings after Oedipus, who in fulfillment of an oracle kills his father and marries his mother in the ancient Greek tragedy by Sophocles, *Oedipus Rex*. A daughter's sexual attraction to the father, which Freud labeled the Electra complex, also takes its name from a Greek play. Freud theorized that these feelings were initially positive, but if they were unresolved, they could be the source of adult personality disorder. In other words, the child must eventually suppress his or her sexual attraction to the parent of the opposite sex and identify with the parent of the same sex to become a fully integrated adult. Failure to achieve this transfer of affection and identity leads inevitably to psychological turmoil in adulthood.

The incestuous relationship between Nicole and her father is the most obvious example of the Oedipus/Electra complex. At her mother's death, Nicole becomes her "Daddy's girl." She shares his bed, sings him songs, holds his hand, and basks in reciprocal love and adulation until one day this father and daughter are no longer like lovers, but are in fact actual lovers (129). While the intensity of the father-daughter bond certainly includes, Freud would argue, a natural element of erotic love or sexual desire, Devereaux Warren's violation of his daughter is clearly an unnatural transgression, as the consequences show. Nicole suffers a psychic wound, a severing of herself, that makes clear the harm inherent in all the novel's various manifestations of sexual confusion. This obvious example of the Electra complex also provides the context for Dick's relationships with both Nicole and Rosemary, and for the conflicted emotions torturing his heart and mind.

When Dick marries "Daddy's girl," he betrays the doctor-patient relationship on which his profession is based. He does not intend to do harm, but does so nonetheless. He knows that he should not become personally involved with a patient, but he chooses not to stop himself, even when he can no longer justify his attachment to Nicole as treatment. When his colleagues remind him of his professional responsibility to sever the relationship, Dick half-heartedly concedes to duty. When he meets her again several months later, however, he cannot resist the force of her love and the seductive power of sex. On a train ride to Zurich, Dick realizes that "her problem was one they had together for good now" (157). As a man who needs to be loved, he simply cannot forsake this vibrant and beautiful waif who loves him, even if it dooms them forever to something pathological, distorting their relationship always into husband-wife, doctor-patient (and even father-daughter) and never, perhaps, giving Nicole the freedom to be well as herself.

In marrying Nicole, Dick also succumbs, however subconsciously, to the temptation of money. He knows that Baby Warren intends to purchase a doctor for Nicole. Although his pride and intellect make him scoff at such a plan, especially if Baby thinks he is such a commodity, he is also attracted to the life that money makes possible. Part of Nicole's attraction may be her wealth, so he may indeed have sold himself for love and money. Surely if they come together he cannot object. Dick's marriage to Nicole is thus a betrayal of both his professional self and his ideal self, and as such it is cause for guilt. In some ways, Dick is another powerful male figure, like Devereaux Warren, abusing his trust and taking advantage of "Daddy's girl."

Dick's guilt plays itself out in his affair with Rosemary Hoyt, who is yet another "Daddy's girl." Old enough to be the father of this fatherless daughter (whose father had, in fact, been a doctor), Dick is intelligent enough—and even trained—to know that Rosemary's love for him is merely "childish infatuation" (213). He is aware that Rosemary sees him "as something fixed and Godlike" (104) and knows the relationship can only bring difficulty. Yet despite this awareness, he is not immune to her charms, and he is flattered by her efforts at seduction. In Rosemary's love, Dick can recapture the illusion that he is his best self (91). Dick may hope to atone for his betrayal of self, but what he does instead is betray Nicole and their marriage and use another "Daddy's girl." When Dick, following his release from the Roman prison, wants "to explain to these people how I raped a five-year-old girl" (235), he reveals his perception of the criminal nature of his affair with Rosemary and even, perhaps, of his marriage to Nicole. It is as incestuous as Devereaux Warren's and thus makes him Warren's moral equivalent.

Sexual perversion and moral degeneracy, which take their most obvious form in incest, function in *Tender is the Night* as the measure by which to separate bad fathers from good fathers. In the first category are Devereaux and Señor Pardo y Ciudad Real, the father of the Chilean homosexual who Dick interviews for treatment. To a lesser extent, the hypocritical Australian who removes his son from Dick's clinic also falls in this category. These men have harmed their children in exercising power over them, and they use their wealth to coerce obedience to their will. They have, in effect, failed to father properly the next generation. In the second category is Mr. Diver, Dick's clergyman father, who teaches his son the value of decency and provides him with the moral foundation for right action. Dick pays tribute and bids farewell to such concepts when he visits the graves of his ancestors on the occasion of his father's death (204–205), for they have fallen victim to a new generation, in which he now includes himself.

As much as Dick might include himself within that new generation, as much as he might condemn himself immoral and degenerate, his fathering of his own children makes clear the complicated nature of his psyche. A conscientious parent, Dick devotes his time to his son, is prepared to answer his questions about life, and is intent upon serving as a proper model of conduct. Satisfied with the development of both his children, he tacitly conveys his approval and does not let bad conduct go unpunished. Dick also makes clear that he knows the proper boundaries of the father-daughter relationship (257). Dick intends and tries to be a good father. He is aware that nothing can take the place of dutiful, careful watchfulness that only a parent can provide his or her child (257). Hence, his abandonment of his children as he slips into obscurity is, on the one hand, a betrayal of his ideals and a denial of his responsibility and, on the other, an acknowledgment of his inability to be a proper father and a refusal to harm yet another generation of the young.

In many ways, Dick is *Tender is the Night*'s true neurotic, a Freudian term for the deeply troubled psyche. Granted, Nicole suffers from psychological wounds, but somebody else bears responsibility for her condition. She is not the agent of her own torment. She does, moreover, recover her essential self by the novel's end, and she does so with very little struggle (298). Dick, in contrast, is acutely aware of his good intentions and his moral failings and knows the torment of self-betrayal. He feels his emasculation, the loss of his male potency, by the Warren wealth and loathes his capitulation to it. He understands the trap of his need to be loved and his desire to please. He admits that his "politeness is a trick of the heart" (164) and is aware that his manners are essentially dishonest. Self-knowledge, however, does not give Dick the ability to resist his own conflicting desires. Moreover, it increases his sense of guilt, thus destroying his morale and his very will to resist. In the end, he can manage nothing more than retreat from the field of his greatest victories and bitterest defeats. It is simply impossible to balance between two competing conceptions of self.

To the extent that Dick's psychological struggle epitomizes an historical moment, it also evokes the Jungian concept of the collective unconscious, with its emphasis on the social rather than biological basis of human behavior. According to Carl Gustav Jung, the spirit of the whole human species manifests itself in what he calls the "collective unconscious" or cultural memory. We understand this deeper layer of the unconscious not through the techniques of analysis, but through our profound response to universal symbols. The manifestation of our collective identity is proved by the similarities between the myths and rituals of different peoples around the globe (see discussion in Chapter 5). For Jung, these similar mythologies were merely differing manifestations of deep structures within the human unconscious. Thus, each generation recapitulates in some ways the experience of previous generations.

Fitzgerald has developed Dick and Nicole as types, embodying the social, economic, and historical forces that have shaped them (21). Cut loose from the old certainties by a world war and given the freedom that money provides, the Divers epitomize a generation in flux. Their psychic disorder results from the flux.

Nicole brings Dick "the essence of a continent" (136), and he chooses it without fully understanding its power to corrupt and believing, in any case, in his ability to create the world he desires. But contact with all the modern world's tormented, broken souls does not make Dick strong; eventually, it even makes him one of them. And money does not bring Dick carefree happiness; it brings him instead a sense of his own corruptibility and an awareness of his own purposelessness. In the end, the Villa Diana is not a haven from the glittering, gaudy, amoral world, but a microcosm of it. At Dick's invitation, a whole brigade of callow and callous barbarians, the new world order, passes through its doors. From a Jungian perspective of the collective unconscious, the world of the fathers epitomized by Dick's father and the generations before him is dead and buried. It is a past no longer useable, a past that may itself have been misused. It has been displaced by a different generation of fathers, the dissipators and the exploiters (72), leaving people like Dick to wrestle with and to embody the consequences.

Both Freudian and Jungian psychology offer theoretical frameworks for the central themes of *Tender is the Night*. The novel does indeed explore the mind dis-eased by conflicting desires as it focuses on Dick Diver's struggle to resist the self-gratifications in gaudy wealth for the disciplined effort of goodness and courage. Dick's struggle, however, placed within an historical context, is representative as well as individual. It signifies the generational conflicts that had, from the beginning of his career, given focus to Fitzgerald's fiction.

Fitzgerald gives these conflicts his special imprint by locating their source in money. The quest for money has virtually destroyed the moral values of a civilization. The profit motive, for instance, lies behind the American Civil War and World War I as well as the pillaging of Rome by its own elite (221) and even the Swiss sale of worn-out cable, which they themselves will no longer use, to the Italians (147). Materialism is the focus of a modern generation's yearning and striving, yet great wealth does not fill the empty spaces in the hearts and minds of those who possess it. Instead, it corrupts even the best and the brightest, accounting not only for Dick's dying fall but also for Devereaux Warren's degeneracy, Nicole's insanity, and Baby's self-absorption. Fitzgerald knew the cost of living on the edge. He knew as well that the price had to be paid. In *Tender is the Night*, he shows what happens when the bill comes due.

7

The Last Tycoon
(1941)

The Last Tycoon, as Matthew J. Bruccoli correctly observes in his Preface to the authorized text of F. Scott Fitzgerald's final novel, is "properly read and judged as a work in progress" (xv). When Fitzgerald suffered his fatal heart attack on December 21, 1940, the forty-four-year-old writer had drafted seventeen episodes of a projected thirty. He left behind hundreds of pages of notes and drafts and a detailed prospectus of the novel's entire plot, enough to make clear his intentions and his potential achievement. Even as a work in progress, however, *The Last Tycoon* is a remarkable novel full of brilliant set pieces, intensely observed characters, and an uncompromising vision of the American Dream. In it, Fitzgerald dissects the Hollywood film industry, that purveyor of myths and dreams and that last western frontier, to expose the debased, materialistic power that ultimately destroys the icon of American success—the self-made man.

The Last Tycoon focuses on the life and death of fictional Hollywood producer Monroe Stahr, "the last of the princes" (27) of the film industry. "A Jay Gatsby with genius," as Bruccoli calls him (vii), Stahr has both the artistic integrity and the moral identity to inspire and to command the representation of his vision, but the industry that he benignly controls is in process of change. The profit margin is becoming the arbiter of taste, and everyone, it seems, now wants an increasing share of the take. They may not know how to use their money or their talent—that knowledge is Stahr's particular genius—but producers and writers alike now seek to wrest control from this captain of industry and thereby destroy his potential to create a meaningful artistic statement. Stahr will struggle valiantly to preserve the old order, but the system, like his heart, is damaged from within and beyond salvation. Indeed, his projected death in an airplane crash, the novel makes clear, signifies "The End" of the dream he embodies.

GENESIS AND CRITICAL RECEPTION

Fitzgerald based his Hollywood novel, which is generally regarded as one of the best depictions of the film industry, at least in part on his own experience of that illusory world. In 1927, Fitzgerald made his first foray into Hollywood when United Artists asked him to write the script for a flapper comedy starring Constance Talmadge. He and Zelda were a great success on the Hollywood social scene, lunching at Pickfair, the actress Mary Pickford's estate, and going to parties with Lillian Gish, John Barrymore, and Lois Moran, the young actress who was to become the model for *Tender is the Night*'s Rosemary Hoyt. Following the rejection of his script called "Lipstick," the Fitzgeralds made a hasty retreat to the East and then to Europe.

In 1931, Fitzgerald was again in Hollywood to write a screen adaption of a light sexual comedy for MGM. The producer Irving Thalberg, whose genius for developing stars and scripts and orchestrating hit films Fitzgerald much admired and later transferred to his own fictional producer, rejected the screenplay. No amount of admiration or effort, it seemed, could make Fitzgerald a Hollywood success.

In 1937, the financially strapped author returned to Hollywood determined to establish himself as a power in the film industry. Fitzgerald, according to biographer Arthur Mizener, "had always believed in the possibilities of the movies" (*Scott Fitzgerald* 98), and he was convinced that given absolute authority over his scripts, he, too, could dictate the terms of his success. The Hollywood system, however, which Thalberg had virtually created, was against him. As one of a team of writers working independently on the same idea to produce various screenplays from which the best elements of each would be culled and unified into a final product, Fitzgerald lacked the necessary autonomy to unleash his talents. He worked on several projects, even polishing the dialogue of *Gone With the Wind*, but he earned only one screen credit, for *Three Comrades*, during his two-year stint as a screenwriter for MGM. Following a drunken debauche at the Dartmouth carnival, where he had gone with writer Budd Schulberg to absorb local color in preparation for writing a screenplay for *Winter Carnival*, Fitzgerald found himself without a job when his contract expired. From that point, he worked as a freelance screenwriter but turned most of his efforts to fiction. His Hollywood experience had given him a subject equal to his talent. Fiction gave him the freedom and the autonomy that he had lacked as a screenwriter. Writing without a supervisor or collaborators, he could use that talent as he knew best.

By September 1939, less than three months after the studio had cut him loose, Fitzgerald had written the prospectus for *The Last Tycoon*, the novel with which he hoped to restore his reputation. He sent it to Kenneth Littauer, the editor of *Collier's* magazine, in hopes of selling its serial publication. Littauer agreed to pay $30,000 for the serial rights if he approved the first 15,000 words of the novel. The emotionally battered and physically ailing writer set to work on it, sometimes writing in bed because he was too weak to rise from it. Desperate for money, Fitzgerald frequently had to interrupt work on the novel to write short stories, chiefly for *Esquire* magazine, seventeen of which concern the Hollywood hack writer Pat Hobby, an impoverished alcoholic, part con man, part hanger-on, who sleeps at the studio but somehow manages to survive by his wits, rather like Fitzgerald himself.

Despite his best efforts, *The Last Tycoon* was incomplete at Fitzgerald's death, yet it still saw publication. Working from the draft manuscript, the detailed outline, and Fitzgerald's extensive notes, the writer and critic Edmund Wilson, Fitzgerald's friend since their days together at Princeton, edited and published the novel posthumously in 1941, even supplying the title, in a volume with *The Great Gatsby* and a number of short stories. Even in its draft form, *The Last Tycoon* earned praise from reviewers and led to a reassessment of Fitzgerald's talent. Reviewing Wilson's edition, Stephen Vincent Benét announced, "You can take your hats off now, gentlemen, and I think perhaps you had better. This is not a legend, this is a reputation—and, seen in perspective, it may well be one of the most secure reputations of our time" (Bryer, *Reputation* 375–376). Since that time, Fitzgerald's literary significance has seldom been challenged, nor has *The Last Tycoon*'s incomplete but potential greatness seldom been denied. In fact, a 1994 authorized text of the novel, edited by the scholar Matthew J. Bruccoli, restores much of Fitzgerald's original words, phrases, and images, including his intended title, *The Love of The Last Tycoon: A Western*, to make clear that the novel stands on its own as a work of art. It is certainly testament to Fitzgerald's achievement.

PLOT DEVELOPMENT

Although *The Last Tycoon* is fragmentary and incomplete, the prospectus that Fitzgerald submitted to *Collier's* as well as his extensive working notes and draft manuscript pages makes clear the outline of the novel's plot. Fitzgerald conceived it as a five-act structure delivered in a series of thirty episodes divided among nine chapters. In the first act, Monroe Stahr, the central character, is seen through Cecelia's eyes as they fly from New York to the West Coast (*Life in Letters* 409), thereby establishing Stahr's nature and Fitzgerald's intended narrative perspective. This act includes an impromptu visit to The Hermitage, President Andrew Jackson's mansion, by Cecelia, the daughter of Stahr's partner, and several others of the Hollywood crowd when a storm temporarily grounds their plane in Nashville, Tennessee. Essentially complete, the act constitutes Chapter One of the novel.

The novel's second act, which Fitzgerald intended to deliver in Chapters Two through Five, would feature a devastating earthquake that would reveal Stahr's ability to manage a crisis as well as lead to his encounter with Kathleen Moore on a studio lot as she and a friend float dramatically "down the current of an impromptu river" (26) on the dislodged head of a studio prop of the goddess Siva. Fitzgerald intended the focus of this act to be Kathleen and Stahr and their "love affair," which he conceived as "the meat of the book" (*Life in Letters* 410). Fitzgerald certainly delivers that love story in the draft chapters, but equally compelling is the set piece entitled "A Producer's Day" that once again reveals the dimensions of Stahr's talents and abilities. In the draft novel, this act ends with Kathleen's marriage to her American fiancé after Stahr hesitates to commit himself to her, thereby effectively ending the relationship. The prospectus and outline make clear that Fitzgerald eventually intended to resurrect the love story, but at this point, he clearly had written himself into a corner.

Fitzgerald in his outline had Chapters Six and Seven entitled "The Struggle" (*Tycoon* xviii). Here he intended to develop two secondary plots. The first and most important is "a definite plot on the part of Bradogue [Pat Brady], Cecelia's father, to get Stahr out of the company" (*Life in Letters* 410). That plot will include murder if necessary. The second plot element concerns Cecelia's desperate attempt to win Stahr's love and her bitter disappointment, which leads to a sexual affair with a man she does not love. Of this third act, only Stahr's confrontation with the union organizer Brimmer and Cecelia's effort to win the producer survive in the draft.

Act four, which Fitzgerald intended to dramatize as Chapter Eight, would focus on Stahr's defeat. The overworked Stahr has refused to heed his doctor's warnings about his precarious health, and now, when he is "plunged directly into the fight to keep control of the company" (*Life in Letters* 410–411), he nearly dies in New York. In his absence, Brady almost seizes control of the company, so Stahr must quickly return to Hollywood, where he plunges into the fray once again to salvage his life's work. During this act, according to Fitzgerald's prospectus, Stahr and Kathleen were going to rekindle their relationship, making plans to marry upon his return from the East, where he must go to settle company affairs. This act exists only conceptually because Fitzgerald drafted none of it before his death.

Fitzgerald intended the novel's final act to have both an ending and an epilogue. The ending would have been the plane crash in which the last tycoon meets his death and the pilfering of the wreckage. Fitzgerald thought this ending should give the novel its distinct quality. The epilogue would have had Kathleen standing outside the studio that she had never entered (another unresolved plot discrepancy), offering in her recognition of Stahr's achievement a fitting coda to his life and talent. It would have concluded with Stahr's funeral. None of Chapter Nine exists in draft form.

What is clear from Fitzgerald's prospectus, outline, and working drafts is that the novelist had not yet resolved some of *The Last Tycoon*'s major inconsistencies at his death. Nor had he quite managed to make the love affair "the meat of the book." The love of the last tycoon is certainly a touching and significant incident in Stahr's life, for he is a man who had learned young to control his emotions (97) and, especially after the death of his wife Minna, had focused all his energies on his work. His attraction to Kathleen thus suggests a reawakening from emotional numbness, a quickening of personal possibility. Fitzgerald, however, never fully renders Kathleen's appeal, and her disappearance from the novel has about it a sense of finality that undercuts her importance. Moreover, Stahr's character and struggle are far more compelling than the love story. Stahr simply dominates the narrative. He is the most fully rendered character in the novel, and that fact suggests that Fitzgerald was himself fascinated by and in awe of his hero's type. Clearly, the last tycoon and not the love of the last tycoon was his true subject.

CHARACTER DEVELOPMENT

The star of Fitzgerald's Hollywood novel is the last tycoon himself, the aptly named Monroe Stahr. He is closely modeled on the gifted producer Irving Thalberg, who, with Louis Mayer, had virtually created MGM when he was twenty-three years old. Stahr is a dynamic captain of industry, a dream merchant of the highest order. Part artistic visionary, part shrewd financier, Stahr brilliantly orchestrates success, including his own, and thereby commands the sometimes grudging respect of men nearly twice his age, men with the money but not the talent to match his. In a world of illusion, where virtually nothing and nobody are what they seem to be, Stahr is the real thing. His charm and good looks do not mask an ugly self. Rather, they express his kindness and genuine concern for others. Like Cecelia Brady, the narrator of the novel, he is a "nice" person who wraps his chewing gum in paper before discarding it, the mark of a civilized being (4, 57).

Fitzgerald dramatizes Stahr's personal and intellectual superiority in one of the novel's brilliant set pieces. Entitled "A Producer's Day," the narrative traces a typical day in the life of a man who is "able to keep the whole equation of pictures in [his head]" (3). On this day, Stahr learns of the attempted suicide of Pete Zavros, the best cameraman in the business, and, upon discovering the reason for such drastic action, puts to rest the rumors of poor eyesight that have undermined his credibility with the studios. He teaches the novelist George Boxley the art of screenwriting, counsels a leading actor suffering from impotence, and gets back on track the writers and director of a new film that is floundering in production. All this happens before lunch with Prince Agge of Denmark and the "money men" (44), a lunch at which Stahr insists upon producing a "quality picture" (48) that is certain to lose money. Between telephone calls and telegram messages in the afternoon, Stahr gently fires Red Ridingwood, a director who has lost control of the film's star, and reviews the dailies of several films, insisting upon minute—and expensive—but to his mind essential changes to each. By day's end, the exhausted producer, who at one point swallows Benzedrine tablets to stave off unconsciousness, has located and met the woman with the silver belt with stars cut out of it who he had encountered during the earthquake the previous evening. He has also read two potential new scripts. Stahr's genius, the narrative makes clear, is all-consuming and self-consuming, for he is "the unity" (58), as he unabashedly tells the writer Wylie White. He is the force that weaves together the industry's disparate elements, whether technical or human, into a coherent whole that expresses his vision.

To the extent that films express his vision, Stahr also functions as an artist figure in the novel. He possesses the ability to envision each line and every scene of a screenplay and to recognize the "trash" (54) that might satisfy others. Beyond this technical mastery is an intellectual conception that guides his judgments. A good deal of truth resides in Cecelia's conceit that Stahr was a sort of Icarus, the mythological maker who soared beyond the limits of man on wings of his own creation (21). Stahr refuses to accept "trash" because it violates his intellectual integrity and his artistic conception of his vision. In fact, he is so bothered on the night of the grunion run by the indifference to and criticism of the movies implied in a stranger's pronouncement that "There's no profit" (93) that the next day he cancels four films, including one that is about to go into production, and rescues another, a worthy but uncommercial project, to prove him wrong (96). The movies matter to Stahr. They give expression to desire and embody ideals, and in that alone is their profit.

As a business tycoon Stahr is, of course, aware of the other sort of profit that resides in the movies, but he strives not to be corrupted by it and to spend it wisely. He tells Wylie White, "I'm a merchant. I want to buy what's in your mind" (17). Consequently, he treats his workers with paternalistic concern, taking special care to soothe the fragile egos of writers and directors and paying well for the talents of all. He fights the writers' union not to deny his employees an adequate wage, but rather to maintain control of his product and to ensure the integrity of his vision. With his ingenuity and wisdom, he has the ability to inspire others to participate in his plans. He may be a despot, but he is an enlightened despot. Yet as the novel's title makes clear, he is the last of his breed.

None of the other male characters in the novel comes close to matching Stahr. Pat Brady, for instance, with whom Stahr will struggle for control of the studio, is a little man interested only in money. The scene in which his daughter interrupts his afternoon tryst with his secretary, who tumbles naked from a closet when Cecelia finally understands the reason for her father's breathlessness and profuse sweating, makes him little more than a laughingstock. Beneath the clownish exterior, however, is real moral corruption, the cliché of the casting couch embodied. Even his daughter, coming upon him unexpectedly, recognizes his self-disgust (22). The writer Wylie White is similarly flawed. Not nearly as clever as he thinks he is, White is doomed to failure "from lack of caring" (43). More concerned about the profit than the product, he can never be Stahr's equal as an artist.

The novel's female characters are more fully drawn, but similarly limited. Cecelia Brady, for instance, is a curious mixture of cynical romanticism, a veritable Hollywood product. Raised in Hollywood, she genuinely likes and understands the community (11–12). (This understanding, by the way, makes her a perfect narrator of the story.) A junior at Bennington College when the events of the novel take place, she is also in love with Stahr, whom she has known since childhood, and imagines that she can woo and win him. Five years later, however, when she is narrating Stahr's story, the wisdom of hindsight helps her to recognize her "reckless conceit" (18), which she credits to the movies (18). Nevertheless, the twenty-four-year-old Cecelia, a bit jaded and disillusioned by time and experience, still retains her essential romanticism, her belief in possibility. "I would rather think" (21), she prefaces her response to Stahr, thereby betraying the quality of hope that defines the romantic sensibility.

In contrast, Kathleen Moore, the object of Stahr's romantic pursuit, has no such illusions about life. A product of poverty, Kathleen is a realist and a survivor. In fact, she has twice saved herself by becoming the mistress of men who could take care of her. The first was a king, who educated her through travel and reading, and the second was an American whom she intends to marry. Attracted at first to Kathleen because she is the image of his dead wife, the actress Minna Davis, Stahr finds in her companionship temporary respite from his loneliness. Her "balance, delicacy and proportion" (80), indeed her very "niceness," bring him ease, and their sexual attraction rekindles his passion for life. Kathleen understands that Stahr, "like all Americans," has several personalities—none of which he conceals (116). She, in contrast, is "a European, accustomed to deferring to the powerful but with "a fierce self-respect that would only let her go so far" (117). When Stahr hesitates, his judgment restraining his emotions, Kathleen does what she must and marries her American fiancé

The sketchy nature of *The Last Tycoon's* secondary characters results at least in part from the novel's incompleteness. Fitzgerald was quite aware of this deficiency. He worried, for instance, that he had failed to convey Kathleen's attraction for Stahr. Yet the incompleteness of these secondary characters indicates Fitzgerald's primary focus. Monroe Stahr is the star of *The Last Tycoon*. His story and his fate carry the weight of Fitzgerald's own artistic statement.

POINT OF VIEW

Point of view, the perspective from which the reader sees the action, is another unresolved element of Fitzgerald's incomplete novel. Fitzgerald intended, as he had in *The Great Gatsby*, to use a partially involved character as the narrator of his tale. Cecelia, who is, as Fitzgerald noted in his *Collier's* prospectus, "*of* the movies but not *in* them" (*Life in Letters* 409) thus seemed aptly qualified to understand Stahr's story. Yet he recognized that the novel would dramatize events which Cecelia could not possibly have witnessed, so he decided to grant her the ability to imagine as well as to report the other character's actions.

The effect of this strategy is to create two narrative voices, Cecelia's and an omniscient, or all-knowing, narrator's, neither of which is clearly distinguishable from the other. Cecelia will occasionally attempt to explain her knowledge of certain events, thereby enhancing her credibility as a narrator. Of Stahr's luncheon with the money men, for instance, she states that Prince Agge told her the details (46), and she says that she learned the sorry ending of Stahr's love affair from Kathleen herself (121). At two points in the novel, Cecelia even announces that she is speaking as the narrator (77, 99). Clearly, Fitzgerald never quite resolved the inconsistencies of the novel's point of view. In fact, his working notes suggest that he may simply have determined to leave them unresolved, insisting that he only used Cecelia as the narrator when he could achieve "the effect of looking out" (*Tycoon* 139).

THEMATIC ISSUES

Despite the novel's problems, its central idea, or theme, is quite clear, even in the narrative's fragmentary state. Monroe Stahr, like Jay Gatsby, is an idealist destroyed by the corruption of his own dream. Like Gatsby, Stahr is a self-made man. He rises from the obscurity of a Jewish ghetto in the Bronx, New York, to become the ultimate purveyor of dreams. Indeed, he embodies the American Dream of Success, and he believes in the system that has enabled his self-creation. As Cecelia aptly observes, "he cherished the parvenu's passionate loyalty to an imaginary past" (119). In that loyalty, however, lies his tragedy and Fitzgerald's point because that system, if it ever really existed as Stahr thinks it did, exists no longer. Consequently, Stahr's struggle to retain control, to safeguard his fierce independence and his essential integrity, is doomed to fail. His failure, by virtue of his symbolic status, challenges the very notion of the dream that has sustained him, the American myth itself.

Fitzgerald makes clear Stahr's symbolic status as representative American hero both structurally, through elements of plot, and figuratively, through his connection to specific American myths and icons. At plot level, the trajectory of Stahr's rise to fortune and fame recapitulates the traditional rags-to-riches story that has become a foundational American myth. Like Jay Gatsby and his hero Dan Cody, Stahr has climbed from poverty and obscurity by a combination of hard work, shrewd instincts, and an utterly unflinching belief in his inevitable success. As Hollywood's "boy wonder of twenty-two," Stahr had been "a money man among money men" (45), and there he has remained. Though his education may have been second rate (18), Stahr has far surpassed his colleagues and competitors, and he has succeeded on his own. He is the ultimate entrepreneur, the quintessential tycoon, the epitome of the self-made man; he is the Andrew Carnegie, the Cornelius Vanderbilt, the John Jacob Astor of his day.

Having established the mythic nature of Stahr's success, Fitzgerald then connects his rags-to-riches story to two other equally evocative American symbols to intensify Stahr's own symbolic stature and thereby develop his larger theme about American culture. The novel's subtitle, "A Western," for example, connects Stahr's story to the epic tale of America itself. Like *The Great Gatsby*, it is a story of the West, of the frontier, of aspiration. Stahr embodies the last of the American pioneers. He is the immigrant son of people who risked all to attain their dream of success. When they found their passage blocked, they simply moved on, out into the vast American western frontier of perpetual promise. That frontier eventually became a state of mind—an expression of desire, a belief in possibility—and its promise beckons still, in the ultimate dream factory at the farthest reaches of the western frontier, Hollywood.

Hollywood, however, as Fitzgerald makes clear, can neither understand nor sustain such a vision. In fact, it is, as Wylie White observes, nothing more than "a mining town in lotus land" (11); its promise is as illusory as a stage set or the gypsies, citizens, and soldiers who lunch in the studio commissary (48). Fitzgerald renders this world in all of its seductive corruption. Here, rumor and innuendo, as Pete Zavros learns, may ruin a career. Here, the Jaques LaBorwits of the world note in their account books the lies that others tell in order to use them later for their own benefit (23). Here, the meretricious beauty of the film star counts for talent, and sexual favors may purchase a career. Yet for all its sham and insincerity, the attraction of this great "booming circus" (28) is undeniable. When, for instance, a group of visitors to the studio comes upon an actress filming a scene, they do not notice the eczema that covers her chest and back or her dyed-red hair; they are transfixed by the star herself. In fact, they do little more than glance at the real thing, Stahr himself. As the narrator observes, "They had seen the Host carried in procession but this [actress] was the dream made flesh" (50). It is Hollywood's ability to make the dream flesh that inspires an awe that gives it the power of religion.

Fitzgerald conveys the irony of this worship in the novel's opening sequence, where he establishes Hollywood's inability to understand the very ideals and traditions of American culture that it represents. During the episode, Cecelia Brady, Wylie White, and Mannie Schwartze, a producer temporarily fallen from power, find themselves grounded by a storm in Nashville, Tennessee, during a cross-country flight to the West Coast. To pass the time, Wylie, who had fled this city of his birth to follow his dream of success, proposes that they make a pilgrimage to The Hermitage, the stately home of President Andrew Jackson. The visit, which recalls the disillusioning scene in *The Beautiful and Damned* in which Anthony and Gloria Patch travel to Robert E. Lee's Arlington, Virginia, mansion on their honeymoon, is pathetic in both its execution and its effect. Arriving in the early morning hours before dawn, the trio finds The Hermitage locked and vacant; its meaning is contained within and thus escapes them. As they sit against the wide pillars of the mansion's steps, Wylie gives Schwartze a history lesson, citing Old Hickory's credentials. Jackson, Fitzgerald makes clear, had been the tycoon of his own era, and his house stands now as testament to his greatness. Despite Wylie's tutelage, none of these representatives of Hollywood seems enlightened by the visit, least of all Mannie, who commits suicide at this shrine to the American Dream.

Jackson is not the only historical figure that Fitzgerald evokes to develop his theme of an idealist destroyed by the corruption of his own dream. Another self-made man and political genius, Abraham Lincoln, carries thematic weight as well because Fitzgerald links him to Monroe Stahr. The first reference to this icon has the same effect as the trip to The Hermitage: It underscores the superficiality of Hollywood's representation of cultural myths. In this instance, Prince Agge, who has been touring the studio, understands for the first time the power and nobility of a hero whom he had hated because admiration had been forced upon him. But there, suddenly, in the studio commissary is Hollywood's Lincoln. So perfect is Hollywood's illusion that disbelief and cynicism are dispelled as they can only be in the face of the real thing. But in the next instant, as "Lincoln suddenly raised a triangle of pie and jammed it in his mouth" (49), Fitzgerald deflates the Hollywood image. Here is no hero, but merely a man enacting a part. Hollywood can do no more than create a facade. The substance inevitably eludes it.

Late in the novel, however, when Fitzgerald links Stahr to Lincoln, his use of the icon signifies something else entirely. In this instance, Stahr once again gives the writer George Boxley a lesson about the movies, explaining their mission of re-creating people's "favorite folklore" (106–107). Stahr's candid assessment of both the film industry's method and its limitation prompts Boxley to compare the producer to a commander in battle, specifically Lincoln (107). The analogy between Stahr and Lincoln enhances the producer's stature because Lincoln stands tall among the pantheon of American heroes. A backwoods boy who rose to prominence by virtue of hard work and his own innate intelligence, Lincoln, too, embodies the American Dream of Success. Yet Lincoln is more than a captain of industry or a representative of material success. As the leader who refused to acquiesce to a dis-United States and insisted on upholding (and even extending) the democratic principles of freedom and justice espoused by the founding fathers, Lincoln is also a representative of personal integrity and moral leadership. So, too, the analogy makes clear, is Stahr.

Fitzgerald extends (or intended to extend) the analogy as the novel reaches its climax and Stahr moves inexorably to his inevitable death. Like Lincoln, Stahr is engaged in a great civil war. All about him, the industry is changing. In fact, like the earthquake that wrecks such havoc in the studio early in the novel, its very foundation is in upheaval. Producers want more profit from their investment so they are less and less willing to finance the quality pictures that the visionary Stahr frequently champions. Because screenwriters want more consideration of their talent and more guarantees that their words will not be changed to suit another's vision, they are in process of forming a union to achieve their ends. In effect, the industry is undergoing a power struggle, and Stahr is fighting valiantly to maintain unity. His vision depends upon his control of all the various elements of the film industry; anything less is unacceptable compromise. Thus Stahr, like Lincoln, will eventually die for his principles.

At the moment of his triumph, Lincoln was assassinated by a Southern sympathizer. Stahr, in contrast, will die with no such victory. Following a beating by union organizer Brimmer, Stahr will have to battle his business partner, Pat Brady, who is involved in a plot to wrest control of the studio from him. He will die in a plane crash before he can achieve his ends. Like Lincoln, Stahr had driven himself mercilessly, sacrificing his health and denying his need to be loved, to create from the chaos of competing desires and motives a unified system, but he will die, in effect, because others can neither recognize that he is the "unity" (58) nor accept that his genius is their success.

Fitzgerald, however, did not intend Stahr's death to be a tragedy. In fact, he said as much in the novel's prospectus, writing, "Unlike *Tender is the Night* [*The Last Tycoon*] is not a story of deterioration—it is not depressing and not morbid in spite of the tragic ending" (*Life in Letters* 412). The prospectus also shows that the novel's *denouement*, or resolution, was to rest on a scene of moral triumph, thereby achieving its desired effect. In the aftermath of the plane crash, the prospectus details, three children scavenge among the ruins and pilfer the possessions of the dead. One boy rifles the possessions of a failed producer, a girl takes those of a motion picture actress, and one boy walks off with Stahr's briefcase. "The possessions which the children find," Fitzgerald explained to the *Collier's* editor, "symbolically determine their attitude toward the act of theft." The young girl would tend to a "selfish possessiveness" and one young boy to an "irresolute attitude." The boy who finds Stahr's briefcase, however, later confesses the theft to a judge, thereby redeeming everyone (*Life in Letters* 411). Even in death, this final scene suggests, Stahr inspires right action. Thus his legacy is not the illusory fictions of pictures, but rather the true moral authority and artistic integrity that defined his essential self.

In the end, then, *The Last Tycoon* is not an indictment of Stahr's individual failure, but rather the industry's. Stahr may be a man from another era. He may be playing the part of a brilliant capitalist from a previous decade. Yet in his desire to rise beyond his origins to become his vision of himself and then to give that vision—and its hope—to others, he expresses the longings of all men and women and the collective myth of a nation. His resistance to any devaluation of either lends him a noble authority that Fitzgerald clearly values and intends his readers to value as well. Thus, when people of lesser talents and vision, people who care only about personal gain and material success, challenge and eventually destroy this benevolent tycoon, Fitzgerald posits a wrong in both the system and those who control it. Some might be tempted to say that Stahr succeeded too well; in manufacturing perfect fantasies he made it impossible to apprehend and to appreciate the real thing in its human incarnation and thus he inadvertently engineered his own destruction. Such a view, however, is not Fitzgerald's. Rather, he suggests that the collective myth has been somehow perverted; the brilliant and bold, the industrious and true no longer command pride of place in American society. Stahr's displacement by the mediocre and the pretentious thus signals the end of an era. Stahr is, after all, the last tycoon.

A MARXIST READING

As one of the few American novels of business that celebrates the entrepreneur and, thus, by extension, capitalist economics, *The Last Tycoon* perhaps deserves a Marxist interpretation. Such a perspective, which is fully explained in

Chapter 4, develops from an antithetical political and economic theory. In a Marxist economy, a tycoon would be a symbol of an oppressive system that commodifies and devalues human beings, and his wealth would be an offense. A Marxist critic, who brings to bear on literature an understanding of class consciousness and class conflict, would certainly find evidence to support a belief in the injustice and perversions of a capitalist system in Fitzgerald's novel.

Fitzgerald's Hollywood, for instance, represents capitalism at its worst. It is a world of conspicuous consumption. Even in the midst of the Great Depression a privileged elite live in lavish comfort and entertain themselves like royalty. Money means so little to such people, because they have so much of it, that $5,000 donations to benefit those made homeless by the earthquake are "not charity." They do not give "as poor men give" (57), at great cost to themselves, but to purchase a pleasant self-satisfaction from excess. In this "perfectly zoned city" (69), everyone knows "exactly what kind of people economically live in each section from executives and directors, through technicians in their bungalows right down to extras" (69–70). Class is a tangible reality in Hollywood; one's value is easily distinguished by material possessions. In fact, it is Hollywood's tendency to reduce everything, including human beings, to a financial equation that is its most disturbing quality.

Everyone in Hollywood is buying or selling something, but chiefly himself or herself, thus making the individual a commodity under the capitalist system. Fitzgerald's language in the novel underscores this point. Of the writer Rose Meloney, for instance, the narrator wonders whether or not "she was 'worth it' or more than that or nothing at all. Her value lay in such ordinary assets as the bare fact that she was a woman and adaptable, quick and trustworthy, 'knew the game' and was without egotism" (36). Among the money men "there was a rating in the group" (45). Everyone in Hollywood carries an "account book" (23) on which to tote up the score in his or her favor. The language of commerce, as one might expect in a novel about business, permeates *The Last Tycoon*. Fitzgerald makes clear, however, that valuation has corroded even the human relationships. In the world of business, when a person like Martha Dodd is no longer worth enough to the larger enterprise, he or she is left to "slip away into misery eked out with extra work" (102).

Such a view perverts other areas of human relationships as well. Cecelia, for instance, a "veritable flower of the fine old cost-and-gross aristocracy" (103), recognizes her commercial value in the arena of love. She constantly focuses on and evaluates herself—her appearance, her intellect, her background and connections—to assure herself that she is good enough for purchase in a sexual marketplace (18, 68). Her intent, of course, is to use her assets to attract Stahr, but she is not adverse to entertaining a proposal from Wylie White. This proposal is itself a sort of business negotiation: "What have you got to offer,"

Cecelia asks her erstwhile suitor. While White insists that he loves her more than her money, in the same breath he suggests that her father could promote him. Convinced that she is worth far more than this man has to offer, Cecelia coolly dismisses him, pointing out that she could do better (68). As this exchange makes clear, a world that transforms every person into a commodity also reduces every human relationship, even love, to a business transaction.

Not surprisingly, given his own career and Hollywood experience, Fitzgerald focuses his most scathing critique of the studio system on its treatment of writers. Believing that "writers are children" (121) who lack "will" and must therefore be governed (122), Stahr has created a system whereby pairs of writers work independently on the same story idea, laboring under the knowledge that they can easily be replaced if they do not produce to their employer's satisfaction. The system, as Stahr tells the Marquands, a team of husband and wife playwrights from the East who have just learned its reality, is "a shame, . . . gross, commercial, to be deplored" (58), but, Stahr would say, necessary because it gives him control of the product. Moreover, he believes it is fair because he has purchased their talents. As he explains to Wylie White on being challenged about his failure to take advice from someone he pays, "That's a question of merchandise. . . . I'm a merchant. I want to buy what's in your mind" (17). Writers like White and George Boxley may resent the system and chafe under its control, but if they wish to reap the financial rewards, earning, in some cases, more than they could ever hope to earn in another marketplace (58), and receive the all-important screen credit upon which they can build a reputation and thereby increase their rate of exchange, they must acquiesce to it.

Stahr is not exactly running a sweatshop because he pays well for the talent he buys. However, he still creates and perpetuates an exploitive system that reduces the individual to a function and makes him or her a commodity, as Fitzgerald makes clear in the confrontation between the producer and union organizer Brimmer. The embodiments of two opposing ideologies, Brimmer and Stahr wage a verbal battle (that ultimately ends, rather pathetically for the producer, in physical violence) to defend their respective positions. Stahr's defense is convincing, Brimmer admits, and it is precisely because he is a "paternalistic employer" (125) that the union finds him most threatening to its efforts to help its members secure ownership of their own products. It is the system itself, however, Brimmer explains in an analogy that equates writers and farmers, that is the source of the corrosive problem. Writers, he argues, are "the farmers in this business. . . . They grow the grain but they're not in at the feast" (121). Stahr's solution is not to yield power, but to increase the writers' salaries. Money, after all, is cheap for a tycoon, and everyone, as he had learned during a previous dispute with directors (125), has a price.

Fitzgerald ends the scene with Stahr, who has initiated a physical confrontation, being knocked unconscious by Brimmer, a symbolic defeat that suggests the inevitable triumph of the Brimmer ideology and foreshadows the tempering of the tycoon's will. This outcome gives the Marxist critic cause for hope. For all his paternalistic benevolence after all, Stahr has been woefully mired in the past and has failed to keep pace with a changing world. He has rather pathetically, for instance, prepared for his meeting with Brimmer by watching Russian revolutionary films and *Doctor Caligari* and Salvador Dali's *Un Chien Andalou*, "possibly suspecting that they had a bearing in the matter" (119), but revealing, more importantly, his woeful lack of understanding of unionization and workers' movements. The "feudal system" (99) that is Hollywood can only be sustained by the perpetuation of inequality: the tycoon's will and the workers' labor. An enlightened despot is still a despot exploiting others for his or her own desires. Thus, the system deserves its demise, and the Marxist critic would argue that Stahr's defeat in this scene signifies Fitzgerald's understanding and perhaps even support of such change. Such a view would certainly be consistent for a writer who had himself experienced the system's victimization.

A Marxist reading of *The Last Tycoon* challenges Fitzgerald's compelling and sympathetic portrayal of his central character. It makes him in many ways a victim of his own success rather than a visionary leader. Yet despite the novel's fragmentary and incomplete form, Fitzgerald's admiration for his tycoon is clear, and the projected final scene suggests his intention to convey his point that something of value dies with Stahr. Hollywood may be a corruption of the American ideal, but so long as people such as Stahr exist to provide the "unity"—to make real a dream, to shine their light and illuminate the darkness—then belief in such an ideal is still possible.

8

Coda

A literary reputation springs from art, not life; it involves an evaluation of the work, and not the writer. Yet during his own lifetime, the literary reputation of F. Scott Fitzgerald was frequently conditioned by the art of his life–by the gaudy excess that epitomized a generation and the extravagant expenditure of effort and talent on so much of inconsequence–rather than the art of his fiction. Thus, at his death on December 21,1940, the forty-four-year-old writer had lived long enough to experience both the meteoric rise and the cataclysmic fall of his professional career. Nobody could have felt his failure more than he did himself.

In the more than half century since his death, however, Fitzgerald's literary reputation has again ascended the heights. The posthumous publication of the fragmentary *The Last Tycoon* in 1941 did much to rescue Fitzgerald's reputation among his peers and colleagues. With nothing but the work before them, they seemed capable of the critical distance that they had so often accused Fitzgerald of lacking. A decade later, following the publication of the first biography of Fitzgerald, Arthur Mizener's *The Far Side of Paradise* (1949); an edition of twenty-eight of his best stories in 1951; and a collection of appreciative reviews and essays by the leading critics of his time (Kazin), Fitzgerald's work was beginning to receive the critical notice that it rightly deserved. Today, all of his novels and stories are in print as well as his letters, ledger, and essays. This is testimony to the recognition of his achievement.

While there is no denying the extravagance of Fitzgerald's life and its intimate connection to his work, it is impossible to dismiss the achievement of even a flawed novel such as *Tender is the Night*, an incomplete tale such as *The Last Tycoon*, or his masterpiece, *The Great Gatsby*, which stands as a classic of American literature. Perhaps he could have achieved more and attained the greatness of his potential if he had lived life less on the edge, but Fitzgerald, like his characters, had to risk all to realize his dreams and aspirations—and he did. The result was a life lived amid disorder, but it was also the work, which captured the social, political, moral, and psychological upheaval and confusion of his own postwar generation and the sustaining illusions of a nation, in prose of exquisite delicacy and precision. In the end, he was indeed justified in granting his life and talent "some sort of epic grandeur" (*Life in Letters* 419).

Selected Bibliography

Page numbers in the text refer to the paperback editions of the authorized texts of F. Scott Fitzgerald's novels and stories.

LITERARY WORKS BY F. SCOTT FITZGERALD

This Side of Paradise. New York: Charles Scribner's Sons, 1920; Scribner Paperback Fiction, 1995.

Flappers and Philosophers. New York: Charles Scribner's Sons, 1920.

The Beautiful and Damned. New York: Charles Scribner's Sons, 1922; Scribner Paperback Fiction, 1995.

Tales of the Jazz Age. New York: Charles Scribner's Sons, 1922.

The Vegetable; Or, from President to Postman. New York: Charles Scribner's Sons, 1923.

The Great Gatsby. New York: Charles Scribner's Sons, 1925; Scribner Paperback Fiction, 1995.

All the Sad Young Men. New York: Charles Scribner's Sons, 1926.

Tender is the Night. New York: Charles Scribner's Sons, 1934; Scribner Paperback Fiction, 1995.

Taps at Reveille. New York: Charles Scribner's Sons, 1935.

POSTHUMOUS PUBLICATIONS

The Last Tycoon. Ed. Edmund Wilson. New York: Charles Scribner's Sons, 1941; *The Love of the Last Tycoon.* Ed. Matthew J. Bruccoli. New York: Scribner Paperback Fiction, 1994.

The Stories of F. Scott Fitzgerald. Ed. Malcolm Cowley. New York: Charles Scribner's Sons, 1951.

Afternoon of an Author. Ed. Arthur Mizener. New York: Charles Scribner's Sons, 1957.

Babylon Revisited and Other Stories. New York: Charles Scribner's Sons, 1960.

Six Tales of the Jazz Age and Other Stories. New York: Charles Scribner's Sons, 1960.

Pat Hobby Stories. New York: Charles Scribner's Sons, 1962.

The Apprentice Fiction of F. Scott Fitzgerald, 1909–1917. Ed. John Kuehl. New Brunswick, NJ: Rutgers University Press, 1965.

The Basil and Josephine Stories. Ed. Jackson R. Bryer and John Kuehl. New York: Charles Scribner's Sons, 1973.

Bits of Paradise: 21 Uncollected Stories by F. Scott Fitzgerald. Ed. Matthew J. Bruccoli. New York: Charles Scribner's Sons, 1973.

F. Scott Fitzgerald's St. Paul Plays, 1911–1914. Ed. Alan Margolies. Princeton, NJ: Princeton University Library, 1978.

The Price Was High: The Last Uncollected Stories of F. Scott Fitzgerald. Ed. Matthew J. Bruccoli. New York: Harcourt Brace Jovanovich, 1979.

The Short Stories of F. Scott Fitzgerald. A New Collection. Ed. Matthew J. Bruccoli. New York: Charles Scribner's Sons, 1989.

NONFICTION BY F. SCOTT FITZGERALD

As Ever, Scott Fitz-: Letters Between F. Scott Fitzgerald and His Literary Agent, Harold Ober, 1919–1940. Ed. Matthew J. Bruccoli. New York: J. B. Lippincott, 1972.

Correspondence of F. Scott Fitzgerald. Eds. Matthew J. Bruccoli and Margaret M. Duggan. New York: Random House, 1980.

The Crack-Up. Ed. Edmund Wilson. 1945; rpt. New York: New Directions, 1956.

Dear Scott/Dear Max: The Fitzgerald-Perkins Correspondence. Eds. John Kuehl and Jackson R. Bryer. New York: Charles Scribner's Sons, 1971.

F. Scott Fitzgerald: A Life in Letters. Ed. Matthew J. Bruccoli with Judith S. Baughman. New York: Simon and Schuster, 1994; Touchstone Edition, 1995.

F. Scott Fitzgerald: In His Own Time: A Miscellany. Eds. Matthew J. Bruccoli and Jackson R. Bryer. Kent, OH: Kent State University Press, 1971.

F. Scott Fitzgerald on Authorship. Ed. Matthew J. Bruccoli with Judith S. Baughman. Columbia: University of South Carolina Press, 1996.

F. Scott Fitzgerald's "Ledger." Ed. Matthew J. Bruccoli. Washington, DC: NCR Microcard Editions, 1973.

The Letters of F. Scott Fitzgerald. Ed. Andrew Turnbull. New York: Charles Scribner's Sons, 1963.

Letters to His Daughter. Ed. Andrew Turnbull. New York: Charles Scribner's Sons, 1963.

The Notebooks of F. Scott Fitzgerald. Ed. Matthew J. Bruccoli. New York: Harcourt Brace Jovanovich, 1978.

BIBLIOGRAPHIES AND CHECKLISTS

Bruccoli, Matthew J. *F. Scott Fitzgerald: A Descriptive Bibliography.* Pittsburgh: University of Pittsburgh Press, 1972.

Bryer, Jackson R. *The Critical Reputation of F. Scott Fitzgerald.* New Haven, CT: Archon, 1967.

BIOGRAPHICAL WORKS AND MEMOIRS

Bruccoli, Matthew J. *Fitzgerald and Hemingway: A Dangerous Friendship.* New York: Carroll and Graf, 1994.

———. *Some Sort of Epic Grandeur: A Life of Scott Fitzgerald.* New York: Harcourt Brace Jovanovich, 1979.

Buttitta, Tony. *After the Gay Good Times: Ashville — Summer of '35/A Season with F. Scott Fitzgerald.* New York: Viking, 1974.

Donaldson, Scott. *Fool for Love.* New York: Congdon & Weed, 1983.

Graham, Sheilah, and Gerald Frank. *Beloved Infidel.* New York: Holt, Rinehart & Winston, 1958.

LeVot, André. *F. Scott Fitzgerald: A Biography.* Trans. William Byron. Garden City, NJ: Doubleday, 1983.

Mayfield, Sara. *Exiles from Paradise: Scott and Zelda Fitzgerald.* New York: Delacorte Press, 1971.

Mellow, James R. *Invented Lives: F. Scott and Zelda Fitzgerald.* New York: Ballantine Books, 1984.

Meyers, Jeffrey. *Scott Fitzgerald: A Biography.* New York: HarperCollins, 1994.

Milford, Nancy. *Zelda.* New York: Avon, 1970.

Mizener, Arthur. *The Far Side of Paradise: A Biography of F. Scott Fitzgerald.* 1949. 2nd ed. Boston: Houghton Mifflin, 1965.

———. *Scott Fitzgerald.* 1972. London: Thames and Hudson, 1987.

Piper, Henry Dan. *F. Scott Fitzgerald: A Critical Portrait.* New York: Holt, 1965.

Sklar, Robert. *F. Scott Fitzgerald: The Last Laocoön.* New York: Oxford University Press, 1967.

Turnbull, Andrew. *Scott Fitzgerald.* New York: Charles Scribner's Sons, 1962.

CRITICAL STUDIES OF FITZGERALD'S WORKS

Aldrich, Elizabeth Kaspar. " 'The Most Poetical Topic in the World': Women in the Novels of F. Scott Fitzgerald." In *Scott Fitzgerald: The Promises of Life.* Ed. Robert A. Lee. New York: St. Martin's, 1989: 113–130.

Allen, Joan M. *Candles and Carnival Lights: The Catholic Sensibility of F. Scott Fitzgerald.* New York: New York University Press, 1978.

Arnold, Edwin T. "The Motion Picture as Metaphor in the Works of F. Scott Fitzgerald." *Fitzgerald/Hemingway Annual* 9(1977): 43–60.

Bewley, Marius. "Scott Fitzgerald and the Collapse of the American Dream." *The Eccentric Design: Form in the Classic American Novel.* New York: Columbia University Press, 1959.

Bloom, Harold, ed. *F. Scott Fitzgerald.* New York: Chelsea, 1985.

Bodeen, DeWitt. "F. Scott Fitzgerald and Films." *Films in Review* 28(1977): 285–294.

Callahan, John F. *The Illusions of a Nation: Myth and History in the Novels of F. Scott Fitzgerald.* Urbana: University of Illinois Press, 1972.

Cardwell, Guy A. "The Lyric World of Scott Fitzgerald." *Virginia Quarterly Review* 38(1962): 95–112.

Cowley, Malcolm, and Robert Cowley, eds. *Fitzgerald and the Jazz Age.* New York: Charles Scribner's Sons, 1966.

Dickstein, Morris. "Fitzgerald's Second Act." *South Atlantic Quarterly* 90(1991): 555–578.

Dixon, Wheeler Winston. *The Cinematic Vision of F. Scott Fitzgerald.* Ann Arbor and London: UMI Research Press, 1986.

Donaldson, Scott. "Scott Fitzgerald's Romance with the South." *Southern Literary Journal* 5(1973): 3–17.

Eble, Kenneth. *F. Scott Fitzgerald.* 1963. Rev. ed. Boston: Twayne, 1977.

———, ed. *F. Scott Fitzgerald: A Collection of Criticism.* New York: McGraw-Hill, 1973.

Fitzgerald, Zelda. *Save Me the Waltz.* New York: Charles Scribner's Sons, 1932.

Forrey, Robert. "Negroes in the Fiction of F. Scott Fitzgerald." *Phylon* 28(1967): 293–298.

Frohock, W. M. "Morals, Manners, and Scott Fitzgerald." *Southwest Review* 40(1955): 220–228.

Fryer, Sarah Beebe. *Fitzgerald's New Women. Harbingers of Change.* Ann Arbor and London: UMI Research Press, 1988.

Fussell, Edwin. "Fitzgerald's Brave New World." *English Literary History* 19(1952): 291–306.

Geismar, Maxwell. "F. Scott Fitzgerald: Orestes at the Ritz." *The Last of the Provincials: The American Novel, 1915–1925.* Boston: Houghton Mifflin, 1943.

Gindin, James. "Gods and Fathers in F. Scott Fitzgerald's Novels." *Modern Language Quarterly* 30(1969): 64–85.

Hindus, Milton. *F. Scott Fitzgerald: An Introduction and Interpretation.* New York: Holt, 1968.

Hunt, Jan, and John M. Suarez. "The Evasion of Adult Love in Fitzgerald's Fiction." *The Centennial Review* 19(1973): 152–169.

Kazin, Alfred, ed. *F. Scott Fitzgerald: The Man and His Work*. Cleveland: World, 1951.

Kolbenschlag, Madonna C. "Madness and Sexual Mythology in Scott Fitzgerald." *International Journal of Women's Studies* 1(1978): 263–271.

Latham, Aaron. *Crazy Sundays: F. Scott Fitzgerald in Hollywood*. New York: Viking, 1971.

Lee, Robert A., ed. *Scott Fitzgerald: The Promises of Life*. New York: St. Martin's, 1989.

Lehan, Richard D. *F. Scott Fitzgerald and the Craft of Fiction*. Carbondale: Southern Illinois University Press, 1966.

Leuders, Edward. "Revisiting Babylon: Fitzgerald and the 1920s." *Western Humanities Review* 29(1975): 285–291.

McCay, Mary A. "Fitzgerald's Women: Beyond Winter Dreams." In *American Novelists Revisited: Essays in Feminist Criticism*. Ed. Fritz Fleischmann. Boston: G. K. Hall, 1982: 311–324.

Miller, James E., Jr. *F. Scott Fitzgerald: His Art and His Technique*. New York: New York University Press, 1967.

Mizener, Arthur, ed. *F. Scott Fitzgerald: A Collection of Critical Essays*. Englewood Cliffs, NJ: Prentice-Hall, 1963.

Monk, Donald. "Fitzgerald: The Tissue of Style." *Journal of American Studies* 17(1983): 77–94.

Ornstein, Robert. "Scott Fitzgerald's Fable of East and West." *College English* 18(1956): 139–43.

Perosa, Sergio. *The Art of F. Scott Fitzgerald*. Trans. Charles Matz and Sergio Perosa. Ann Arbor: University of Michigan Press, 1965.

Petry, Alice Hall. *Fitzgerald's Craft of Short Fiction: The Collected Stories 1920–1935*. Ann Arbor: UMI Research Press, 1989.

Phillips, Larry W. *F. Scott Fitzgerald on Writing*. New York: Scribner's, 1985.

Riddell, Joseph N. "F. Scott Fitzgerald, the Jamesian Inheritance, and the Morality of Fiction." *Modern Fiction Studies* 11(1965–66): 331–350.

Shain, Charles E. *F. Scott Fitzgerald*. Minneapolis: University of Minnesota Press, 1961.

Spencer, Benjamin T. "Fitzgerald and the American Ambivalence." *South Atlantic Quarterly* 66(1967): 367–381.

Stavola, Thomas J. *Scott Fitzgerald: Crisis in an American Identity*. New York: Barnes & Noble, 1979.

Stern, Milton. *The Golden Moment: The Novels of F. Scott Fitzgerald*. Urbana: University of Illinois Press, 1970.

Way, Brian. *F. Scott Fitzgerald and the Art of Social Fiction*. London: Arnold, 1980.

Weston, Elizabeth A. *The International Theme in F. Scott Fitzgerald's Literature*. New York: Peter Lang, 1995.

Whitley, John S. " 'A Touch of Disaster': Fitzgerald, Spengler, and the Decline of the West." In *Scott Fitzgerald: The Promises of Life*. Ed. Robert A. Lee. New York: St. Martin's, 1989: 157–180.

Yates, Donald A. "The Road to 'Paradise': Fitzgerald's Literary Apprenticeship." *Modern Fiction Studies* 7(1961): 19–31.

THIS SIDE OF PARADISE (1920)

REVIEWS

Broun, Heywood. "Paradise and Princeton." *New York Tribune*, 11 April 1920: Sec. VII, 9.
Huse, William. "This First Book Has Real Merit." *Chicago Evening Post*, 30 April 1920: 7.
"Latest Works of Fiction—With College Men." *New York Times Review of Books*, 9 May 1920: 240.
Mencken, H. L. "Books More or Less Amusing." *Smart Set*, August 1920: 140.
Rascoe, Burton. "A Youth in the Saddle." *Chicago Daily Tribune*, 3 April 1920: 11.
"Reforms and Beginnings." *The Nation*, 24 April 1920: 557–558.
Review of *This Side of Paradise*. *New Republic*, 12 May 1920: 362.

CRITICISM

Hook, Andrew. "Cases for Reconsideration: Fitzgerald's *This Side of Paradise* and *The Beautiful and Damned*." In *Scott Fitzgerald: The Promises of Life*. Ed. Robert A. Lee. New York: St. Martin's, 1989: 17–36.
Kahn, Sy. "*This Side of Paradise*: The Pageantry of Disillusion." In *F. Scott Fitzgerald: A Collection of Criticism*. Ed. Kenneth E. Eble. New York: McGraw-Hill, 1973: 34–47.
Moreland, Kim. "The Education of F. Scott Fitzgerald: Lessons in the Theory of History." *Southern Humanities Review* 19(1985): 25–38.

THE BEAUTIFUL AND DAMNED (1922)

REVIEWS

Abbott, Samuel. "A Man and a Maid Tread the Maze of Modern Life." *New York Tribune*, 12 March 1922, Part V, 8.
Beston, Henry. Review of *The Beautiful and Damned*. *Atlantic Monthly*, June 1922: 897.
Bishop, John Peale. "Mr. Fitzgerald Sees the Flapper Through." *New York Herald*, 5 March 1922, Sec. VIII, 1.
Canby, Henry Seidel. "The Flapper's Tragedy." *Literary Review of the New York Evening Post*, 4 March 1922: 463.
Field, Louise Maunsell. Review of *The Beautiful and Damned*. *New York Times Book Review*, 5 March 1922: 16.
Littell, Robert. "*The Beautiful and Damned*." *New Republic*, 17 May 1922: 348.

Mencken, H. L. "The Niagara of Novels–II. Fitzgerald and Others." *Smart Set*, April 1922: 140–142.

Review of *The Beautiful and Damned*. *Life*, 6 April 1922: 33.

Sayre, Zelda [Mrs. F. Scott Fitzgerald]. "Friend Husband's Latest." *New York Tribune*, 2 April 1922, Sec. VII, 11.

Van Doren, Carl. "The Roving Critic." *The Nation*, 15 March 1922: 318.

CRITICISM

Astro, Richard. "Vandover and the Brute and *The Beautiful and Damned*: A Search for Thematic and Stylistic Reinterpretations." *Modern Fiction Studies* 14(1968–69): 397– 413.

Perosa, Sergio. "*The Beautiful and Damned*." In *F. Scott Fitzgerald: A Collection of Criticism*. Ed. Kenneth E. Eble. New York: McGraw-Hill, 1973: 48–59.

THE GREAT GATSBY (1925)

REVIEWS

Benét, William Rose. "An Admirable Novel." *Saturday Review of Literature*, 9 May 1925: 739– 740.

Butcher, Fanny. "New Fitzgerald Book Proves He's Really a Writer." *Chicago Daily Tribune*, 18 April 1925: 11.

Clark, Edwin. "Scott Fitzgerald Looks Into Middle Age." *New York Times Book Review*, 19 April 1925: 9.

Mencken, H. L. "New Fiction." *American Mercury*, July 1925: 382–383.

Overton, Grant. "Have You Read?" *Collier's*, 8 August 1925: 41.

Review of *The Great Gatsby*. *New Yorker*, 23 May 1925: 26.

CRITICISM

Bruccoli, Matthew J., ed. *New Essays on* The Great Gatsby. Cambridge: Cambridge University Press, 1985.

Carlisle, E. Fred. "The Triple Vision of Nick Carraway." *Modern Fiction Studies* 11(1965–66): 351–360.

Donaldson, Scott, ed. *Critical Essays on F. Scott Fitzgerald's* The Great Gatsby. Boston: G. K. Hall, 1984.

Doyno, Victor. "Patterns in *The Great Gatsby*." *Modern Fiction Studies* 12(1966): 415–426.

Gray, W. Russel. "Corinthian Crooks Are Not Like You and Me: Mystery, Detection and Crime in *The Great Gatsby*." *Clues* 16(1995): 35–45.

Hoffman, Frederick J., ed. The Great Gatsby: *A Study*. New York: Charles Scribner's Sons, 1962.

Korenman, Joan S. " 'Only Her Hairdresser . . .': Another Look at Daisy Buchanan." *American Literature* 40(1975): 574–578.

LaHurd, Ryan. " 'Absolution': *Gatsby*'s Forgotten Front Door." *College Literature* 3(1976): 113–123.

Lee, Robert A. " 'A Quality of Distortion': Imagining *The Great Gatsby*." In *Scott Fitzgerald: The Promises of Life*. Ed. Robert A. Lee. New York: St. Martin's, 1989: 37–60.

Lisca, Peter. "Nick Carraway and the Imagery of Disorder." *Twentieth Century Literature* 13(1967): 18–28.

Lockridge, Ernest. "F. Scott Fitzgerald's Trompe l'oeil and *The Great Gatsby*'s Buried Plot." *Journal of Narrative Technique* 17(1987): 163–183.

———. ed. *Twentieth Century Interpretations of* The Great Gatsby. Englewood Cliffs, NJ: Prentice-Hall, 1968.

Long, Robert Emmet. *The Achieving of "The Great Gatsby": F. Scott Fitzgerald, 1920–1925*. Lewisburg, PA: Bucknell University Press, 1979.

Magistrale, Tony, and Mary Jane Dickerson. "The Language of Time in *The Great Gatsby*." *Modern Fiction Studies* 34(1988): 541–558.

McCall, Dan E. " 'The Self-Same Song That Found a Path': Keats and *The Great Gatsby*." *American Literature* 42(1971): 421–430.

Morgan, Elizabeth. "Gatsby in the Garden: Courtly Love and Irony." *College Literature* 11(1984): 163–177.

Parker, David. "*The Great Gatsby*: Two Versions of the Hero." *English Studies* 54(1973): 37– 51.

Settle, Glenn. "Fitzgerald's Daisy: The Siren Voice." *American Literature* 57(1985): 115–124.

Sipiora, Phillip. "Vampires of the Heart: Gender Trouble in *The Great Gatsby*." In *The Aching Hearth: Family Violence in Life and Literature*. Eds. Sara Munson Deats and Lagretta Tallent Lenker. New York: Plenum, 1991: 199–220.

Stewart, Lawrence D. " 'Absolution' and *The Great Gatsby*." *Fitzgerald/Hemingway Annual* 5(1973): 181–187.

Way, Brian. "Fitzgerald and the Art of Social Fiction: *The Great Gatsby*." In *American Fiction: New Readings*. Ed. Richard J. Gray. Totowa, NJ: Barnes & Noble, 1983: 150–164.

Weinstein, Arnold. "Fiction as Greatness: The Case of Gatsby." *Novel* 19(1985): 22–38.

Westbrook, J. S. "Nature and Optics in *The Great Gatsby*." *American Literature* 32(1960): 78– 84.

TENDER IS THE NIGHT (1934)

REVIEWS

A[dams], J. D[onald]. "Scott Fitzgerald's Return to the Novel." *New York Times Book Review*, 15 April 1934: 7.

Butcher, Fanny. "New Fitzgerald Book Brilliant; Fails as Novel." Chicago *Tribune*, 14 April 1934: 7.

Canby, Henry Seidel. "In the Second Era of Demoralization." *Saturday Review of Literature*, 14 April 1934: 630–631.

Chamberlain, John. "Books of the Times." *New York Times*, 13 April 1934: 17.

Cowley, Malcolm. "Breakdown." *New Republic*, 6 June 1934: 105–106.

Gregory, Horace. "A Generation Riding to Romantic Death." *New York Herald Tribune Book Review*, 15 April 1934: 5.

Seldes, Gilbert. "True to Type—Scott Fitzgerald Writes Superb Tragic Novel." *New York Evening Journal*, 12 April 1934: 23.

Troy, William. "The Worm i' the Bud." *The Nation*, 9 May 1934: 539–540.

Weeks, Edward. Review of *Tender is the Night*. *Atlantic Monthly*, April 1934: 17.

CRITICISM

Bruccoli, Matthew J. *The Composition of* Tender is the Night. Pittsburgh: University of Pittsburgh Press, 1963.

Coleman, Thomas C. "Nicole Warren Diver and Scott Fitzgerald: The Girl and the Egotist." *Studies in the Novel* 3(1971): 34–43.

Doherty, William E. "*Tender is the Night* and the 'Ode to a Nightingale.'" In *Explorations of Literature*. Ed. Rima Drell Reck. Baton Rouge: Louisiana State University Press, 1966: 100–114.

Fetterley, Judith. "Who Killed Dick Diver? The Sexual Politics of *Tender is the Night*." *Mosaic* 17(1984): 111–128.

Fryer, Sarah Beck. "Nicole Warren Diver and Alabama Beggs Knight: Women on the Threshold of Freedom." *Modern Fiction Studies* 31(1985): 318–326

Haegert, John. "Repression and Counter-Memory in *Tender is the Night*." *Essays in Literature* 21(1994): 97–115.

Jackson, Timothy P. "Back to the Garden or into the Night: Hemingway and Fitzgerald on Fall and Redemption." *Christianity and Literature* 39(1990): 423–441.

LaHood, Marvin J., ed. Tender is the Night: *Essays in Criticism*. Bloomington: Indiana University Press, 1969.

Pitcher, E. W. "*Tender is the Night*: Ordered Disorder in the 'Broken Universe.'" *Modern Language Studies* 11(1981): 72–89.

Stern, Milton R. Tender is the Night: *The Broken Universe*. New York: Twayne, 1994.

———, ed. *Critical Essays on F. Scott Fitzgerald's* Tender is the Night. Boston: G. K. Hall, 1986.

THE LAST TYCOON (1941)

REVIEWS

Adams, J. Donald. "Scott Fitzgerald's Last Novel." *New York Times Book Review*, 9 November 1941: 1.

Benét, Stephen Vincent. "Fitzgerald's Unfinished Symphony." *Saturday Review of Literature*, 6 December 1941: 10.

Fadiman, Clifton. "Fitzgerald, McFee, and Others." *New Yorker*, 15 November, 1941: 107.

"The Last Romantic." *Time*, 3 November 1941: 95–96.

Marshall, Margaret. "Notes By the Way." *The Nation*, 8 November 1941: 457.

Rugoff, Milton. "*The Last Tycoon*: An Unfinished Novel." *New York Herald Tribune Books*, 26 October 1941: 18.

Thurber, James. "Taps at Assembly." *New Republic*, 9 February 1942: 211–212.

"Unfinished Life." *Newsweek*, 27 October 1941: 58–59.

Weeks, Edward. "*The Last Tycoon*." *Atlantic Monthly*, January 1942.

CRITICISM

Giddings, Robert. "*The Last Tycoon*: Fitzgerald as Projectionist." In *Scott Fitzgerald: The Promises of Life*. Ed. Robert A. Lee. New York: St. Martin's, 1989: 74–93.

Millgate, Michael. "*The Last Tycoon*." In *F. Scott Fitzgerald: A Collection of Criticism*. Ed. Kenneth E. Eble. New York: McGraw-Hill, 1973: 127–134.

Piacentino, Edward J. "The Illusory Effects of Cynthian Light: Monroe Stahr and the Moon in *The Last Tycoon*." *American Notes and Queries* 20(1981): 1–2, 12–16.

SHORT FICTION

Burhans, Clinton S., Jr. " 'Magnificently Attune to Life': The Value of 'Winter Dreams.' " *Studies in Short Fiction* 6(1969): 401–412.

Elstein, Rochelle S. "Fitzgerald's Josephine Stories: The End of the Romantic Illusion." *American Literature* 51(1979): 69–83.

Gervais, Ronald J. "The Snow of Twenty-Nine: 'Babylon Revisited' as *Ubi Sunt* Lament." *College Literature* 7(1980): 47–52.

Higgins, John A. *F. Scott Fitzgerald: A Study of the Stories*. Jamaica, NY: St. John's University Press, 1971.

Johnston, Kenneth G. "Fitzgerald's 'Crazy Sunday': Cinderella in Hollywood." *Literature/Film Quarterly* 6(1978): 214–221

Nettels, Elsa. "Howell's 'A Circle in the Water' and Fitzgerald's 'Babylon Revisited.' " *Studies in Short Fiction* 19(1982): 261–267.

Petry, Alice Hall. *Fitzgerald's Craft of Short Fiction: The Collected Stories 1920–1935*. Ann Arbor: UMI Research Press, 1989.

Podis, Leonard A. "Fitzgerald's 'The Diamond as Big as the Ritz' and Hawthorne's 'Rappaccini's Daughter.'" *Studies in Short Fiction* 21(1984): 243–250.

Rees, John O. "Fitzgerald's Pat Hobby Stories." *Colorado Quarterly* 23(1975): 553–562.

Toor, David. "Guilt and Retribution in 'Babylon Revisited.' " *Fitzgerald/Hemingway Annual* 5(1973): 155–164.

RELATED SECONDARY SOURCES

Ashe, Geoffrey. *The Discovery of King Arthur*. Garden City, NY: Anchor Press/Doubleday, 1985.

Berger, Arthur Asa. *Cultural Criticism: A Primer of Key Concepts*. Foundations of Popular Culture, 4. Thousand Oaks, CA: Sage Publications, 1995.

Bradbury, Malcolm. *The Modern American Novel*. 1983. Rev. ed. Oxford: Oxford University Press, 1992.

Bryer, Jackson R., ed. *The Short Stories of F. Scott Fitzgerald. New Approaches in Criticism*. Madison: University of Wisconsin Press, 1982.

Campbell, Joseph. *The Hero with a Thousand Faces*. 1949. Princeton, NJ: Princeton University Press, 1968.

Lewis, R.W.B. *The American Adam. Innocence, Tragedy, and Tradition in the Nineteenth-Century*. 1955. Chicago and London: University of Chicago Press, 1968.

Showalter, Elaine. "The Feminist Critical Revolution." In *The New Feminist Criticism: Essays on Women, Literature, and Theory*. Ed. Elaine Showalter. London: Virago Press, 1986: 3– 17.

———. "Toward a Feminist Poetics." In *The New Feminist Criticism: Essays on Women, Literature, and Theory*. Ed. Elaine Showalter. London: Virago Press, 1986: 125–143.

Swales, Martin. *The German Bildungsroman from Wieland to Hesse*. Princeton, NJ: Princeton University Press, 1978.

Wilson, Edmund. *The Shores of Light: A Literary Chronicle of the Twenties and Thirties*. New York: Farrar, Straus and Young, 1952.

ELECTRONIC SOURCES

F. Scott Fitzgerald links: http://www.netins.net/showcase/tdlarson/fslinks.html

Index

About the Author

LINDA C. PELZER is Professor of English at Wesley College in Dover, Delaware. A specialist in American Literature, and a former Fulbright scholar, her publications include *Mary Higgins Clark: A Critical Companion* (Greenwood 1995) and *Erich Segal: A Critical Companion* (Greenwood 1997). She is currently working on a biocritical study of Martha Gellhorn.